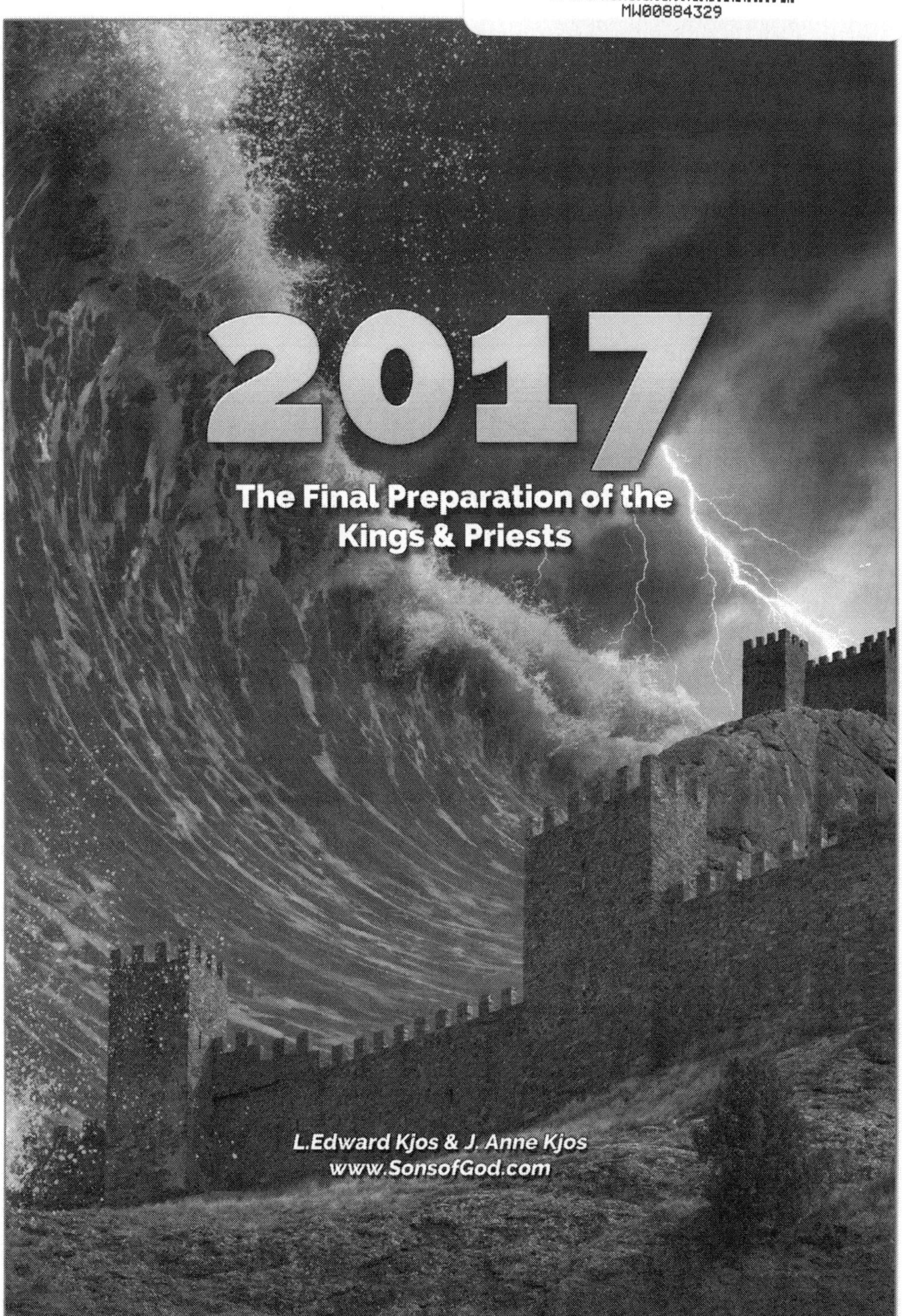
2017
The Final Preparation of the
Kings & Priests
L.Edward Kjos & J. Anne Kjos
www.SonsofGod.com

Many thanks to Tom & Bobbie Grayson
for their amazing help.

2017

The Preparation of the Kings & Priests

ISBN - 13 9778-1542446525

ISBN - 10 154244652X

Library of Congress Control #:

1-1787360239

Printed in the United States of America

Published by:

SonsOfGod.com

79 E. Daily Street, #169
Camarillo, CA. 93010

www.SonsOfGod.com
email: edward@sonsofgod.com

Other Books by Edward & Anne:

The Manifestation of the Sons of God

Unwrap The Sons

Spiritual Warfare

Table of Contents

Introduction

The title "2017" may give the feeling that this book is a prophetic declaration or prophecy, but actually, it is not. This book is about a state or plane of awareness, an awareness that is already here of what is happening in the realm of spirit and what is moving forward very quickly.

There is no question that we have entered the timeline of the judgments of God on the face of the earth. We have seen this approaching tidal wave of judgment coming for some time now. The Father has been patient in waiting for the precious fruit of the earth to come to maturity, *the harvest of His sons,* before He would release the judgments. The iniquity of this age has come to the full, and the tidal wave of His judgment has begun.

On a natural plane, before a tidal wave hits the shores, it will draw the waters back greatly, exposing the ocean floor. Then, it comes with a raging fury, as it hits land. In the last six to twelve months we have seen a progressive revealing and exposing of the darkness behind closed doors. There has been a great deal going on behind the scenes by the Nephilim and sons of Satan; and God is pulling back the curtain. That which has been done in darkness is being exposed by the light and coming under judgment. The exposing of wickedness in this age on every governmental and political level, is going to continue to unfold. The "waters" of this age, which have cloaked the working of darkness - like the tidal wave – have been drawn back. What happens next? The tidal wave of judgment - it quickly approaches.

This book is about the final preparation of God's kings and priests. This has been happening now for the past several years, but now we have entered a time that the work is hastening. It is being completed. What you have been raised up to do, that specific mantle destined just for you, is resting upon you. The ministry of the sons of God has not yet begun, for that ministry is on the other side of the transformation of sonship that awaits you. Everything in your life, until this point, has been preparation. You have been purged, purified and refined. You have been prepared for your destiny.

Some may think that they have been walking in their destiny by virtue of the outreach and spreading of the word throughout their lifetime. And that has been good, but it has been on the plane of the soul; in the day of the church age. But in the day of the kingdom, in the time of spirit, everything changes. The true spiritual fulfillment of kingdom evangelism is a spirit realm reality.

It is time for the sons to bring down the kingdoms of this age and subject them back to Christ. That will not be done by sons who are not prepared, who have not been unwrapped and brought into a level of abiding in the kingdom and the presence of the Father. This is what awaits you, and this is the transformation and change that you have been in the midst of - even if you have not understood it, until now. God is releasing the sons, His sons, to come forth in mighty battle array. The true ministry of the sons of God is only now just beginning.

The purpose for this book is to take another layer of grave clothes off of you. The spirit of God has been unwrapping the sons, one layer at a time, removing the grave clothes of death that they have been under, and bringing them into a newness of life that they have been destined for. The mystery of God is at work, and that mystery is the full revealing of who and what you have always been.

The sons are feeling the pull in the spirit as the command goes out: **"Come up higher. Come up higher".** The sons are being caught up into the presence of the Father and the Son, from which they will move and begin to subject the kingdoms of this age.

The prophecy in Daniel is being fulfilled, for the sons are the image cut out of the mountain, who have been sent into the earth during this time to bring down the last vestiges of the kingdoms of this age. You are being brought into a new life—a life that lives both in the realm of the spirit but still has a functional capacity within the natural plane. This is not a normal level of functioning for the average individual, but then God's sons are anything but normal. The sons have been destined to walk in both worlds, at the same time.

The sons are being birthed out of the last trappings of illusion that they have been under; the last elements of the darkness that has been upon this age, and which has tainted their ability to see the truth correctly.

It is crunch time; the sons are coming forth, and God is unwrapping the sons who have been sent into the earth, for such a time as this.

Your training is being completed. Your hands are being taught to war. And the true battle of the light verses the darkness is here. We already know the outcome, but it is your destiny to walk out that outcome and to be the administrators of the kingdom; to be the manifestation of God's grace and glory to a dead and dying age; to be His mouthpiece, His voice and His presence; to release the captives and set them free.

All creation has been travailing with the sons to see their release. You have been in travail for quite some time, a travail to be fully brought forth and manifested, and all of creation has been in travail with you, for their release and deliverance is tied into your release and deliverance. The same applies for the Cloud of Witnesses, those who died in the faith; who prepared the way for us to walk.

We are running with the baton on the last leg of this race, and we are breaking the tape so that those who have gone on before us, will also be released into their destiny and the fulfillment of the manifestation of the sons of God.

January 2017

Edward & Anne

Section 1

Breaking Through the Veil

Chapter 1

The Religious Spirit

As the preparation of the kings and priests comes to a point of completion during this time, there is one aspect of this preparation that has plumbed the depths of everyone who has been called to sonship. The deliverance from the religious spirit.

We have talked about being delivered from this age. We have talked about how the world exists under the canopy of darkness[1]. We know that God is in the process of delivering the sons out of Babylon. The words; "Come[2] out of her My people", or, "We are not a part of this age[3]" have taken on a much greater meaning. We have addressed this whole issue of being delivered out of this age, both in this book and other books we have written, and this deliverance is far more extensive than anyone has understood. Perhaps just now we understand how entangled and programmed we have been during our sojourn here in the earth.

This is a deliverance perhaps we knew that we were going to have to deal with, even before we left to come here in our present sojourn. The religious spirit, and the conditioning which has come from the exposure to this spirit, is one of the blocks in the road that needs to be fully removed now.

To be delivered from this age means that you are delivered from everything that has defiled you, that has programmed you and conditioned the way that you think. It is far more than just being raised in the flesh, having been exposed to peers and a society that has a certain modality of thinking. We have talked about the pervading influence of the principalities[4] and powers that govern this age, but we are only now realizing just how deep the darkness has become that is resting upon the earth. To be delivered from this age is more than just stepping away from organized religion, or stepping away from a way of thinking that we have known.

God has had to literally go in and extract out of the sons all the bonds and snares that have been placed there by the enemy to impede your progress as you began to come forth. In essence, a paradigm born out of the exposure to the religious spirit.

Satan and the hordes of evil know who you are. They know your calling. They know that you have been destined. But they don't really understand the whole picture. Never the less, the mindset of this age that has been created, fostered and propagated by the principalities and powers through illusion and through the paradigm that has been created in this age, has left areas within you that have needed to be removed.

Ever since we began this path God has said over and over, *"Let go. Let go. Let go of how you have seen reality. Let go of how you have interpreted My scriptures. Let go of the partial that I might bring the fullness to you."*

It may be hard to grasp, but every bit of teaching that has been given to you on your path has been riddled with the partial[5].... because those who have brought the teaching have themselves not been delivered out of this age, and out of programming that has gone on for centuries within mankind. The bonds and conditionings go very, very deep.

We are not talking about just this present incarnation. We are talking about a buildup of a mindset and a paradigm within mankind that has gone on for hundreds and hundreds of years. When you were born into this natural plane, you were born into a great deal of baggage that had been sown by the satanic hordes of evil since time began. And so the deliverance is great that has been needed.

We have said before that Satan is a religious spirit, therefore we must understand that the pervading spirit over this age is a religious spirit. Religion is not relegated to just a church. Just because it is called a religious spirit it is not limited to religion, as we have defined religion. Religion is a set of belief systems, and does not necessarily include a belief in "God". Business can be your religion. Hobbies and activities can be a religion to you. We have to understand that religion is far more expansive than just what we have understood it to be with church.

Now what I am going to say may be a challenge, but we need to realize that each and every one of us have, to some degree, a religious spirit, that God is still in the process of delivering us out of. Now I am not saying that you have the spirit of Satan. That is not what I am saying, but I am saying that you are still walking with the limitations that have been sown within your mind and spirit by the chief religious spirit, Satan himself. And that is a challenge, because as long as you have aspects of the religious spirit still within you, it makes it very difficult to hear and see the truth[6].

This is a very difficult topic to work through, and it is one that you will need to pray over, because I have seen it time and time again. People that are brought out of old order—even people that are brought out of movements that were on the cutting edge—even those movements, are still weighed down with the conditionings of religion.

What makes it interesting is that people do not know how deep the inroads have been sown within their thinking, not until you are able to see it for yourself. Typically the religious spirit brings with it a great deal of obligation[7] .... obligations born out of a way of thinking that is from the day of the partial. You might say, "Well, in the word it says thus and thus", so I have to be this way. I have to be that way."

Understand that the conditioning of this age and the exposure to the church mentality that you have been brought up under has created a way of viewing the truth, a filter if you will, that God wants to remove. This is the partial[5]. Am I saying that what you had is bad or wrong? No, I am saying it is from the day of the partial.

This is the day of the fullness[8]. This is the day that God is bringing the sons into a deep understanding; an ability to really grasp the truth of what He is saying ... without the filtering of the mind of the soul.

A classic man of God who did not have a religious bone in his body was Elijah. Elijah was a man of like passions[9] and he didn't care about what anyone thought. In fact when Elijah met Elisha, after the Lord had selected Elisha to be Elijah's man servant, Elisha said, "Well I need to go and feed my family, and slay the oxen[10]". To Elijah it did not really matter, "Go and do what you have to do, but I am on my way, I'm not going to wait for you." And Elisha went ahead and did what he needed to do, which in effect, was severing his bonds and his ties from everything that had defined him and everything that he had been.

It does not say that in the word, but that is what Elisha did. He went ahead and just began to let go of everything. Elijah did not get into his face and say, "Elisha you need to let go." Elisha just knew what he had to do. He let go of everything.

It can be very difficult to come out of the conditioning of the religious spirit, because the paradigm created by the religious spirit can have very far reaching tentacles within your mind. Your conditioning can say, for example: "God is love." And therefore we have to love everyone. We have to be a certain way ... very loving and very caring, and so the religious spirit has created a certain paradigm that says this is the interpretation of those scriptures, when it is just the soul trying to put God in a box.

We don't understand the Love of God. The only thing that we can see about the love of God is in Hebrews, and the book of John. He loved His son and He put Him on a cross. **John 3:16.** ***For God so loved the world He gave His only begotten Son.*** And the book of Hebrews; ***For every son He loves He scourges; those whom He receives to Himself.*** **(Hebrews 12:6)** That is love. The scourging of God is love ... not some soulish thing that just reaches out and wants to move in some obligation born out of your concept of what it means to be loving and godly and all of that.

The religious spirit is not limited to a church. This spirit has affected all of mankind, because this has been the prevailing canopy over mankind. In the business realm you have the same conditioning by the religious spirit. Everything has to be a certain way, every jot and tittle[11]. What God is doing is pulling you out of this age entirely. You are being delivered out of the religious spirit; out of a religious modality of thought and into the mind[12] of Christ.

You can't be driven and controlled by the mind that says, "Well, the Christian thing to do is to do this, and to do this. And you treat them this way and we go the extra mile," and so on and so forth. This Christian mentality is just a bunch of soul spun under the web of illusion and religion.

I would rather be as Christ. "I do only those things I see[13] the Father doing, and I speak only those things I hear[14] Him speaking." I am not going to be locked into some kind of obligation of how we feel we are supposed to be. No, the only way you are supposed to be is to be led[15] by the Spirit of God, not the soul. That is the demand that the Lord puts upon the sons as they are maturing. "You will hear my voice. You will see what I am doing. That is what you do. And you don't do anything else."

"Oh, but it crosses what I think the love of God is." Well then you didn't know what the love of God is. We have not realized that these strings and these little cords of thought are little land mines that have been put in place on your path by Satan and the hordes of evil - the religious spirit. Knowing that your calling was sonship, the enemy has attempted to put one land mine after another in your path to cause you to stumble.

How many people have walked with God and then walked away? Ninety Nine percent of them, because all of a sudden God began to cross them. They get confronted with a word or scripture which doesn't match up to their belief system and they say, "Well, God wouldn't do that." And they have no revelation. You look in the Old Testament and it talks about how God wanted to just kill[16] women and children and cows and animals - literally everything - to wipe out the Canaanites and the various civilizations that were at war with Israel. And you would say, "Well, how can that be God? God would never kill a child." Well then you don't know God.

God is pulling away another layer of religiosity, and it can be found even within the small elements within your thinking that will block you every step of the way from being able to hear the truth, because your mind is going to filter it. Or reject it. God is going to speak something and you won't even realize it. You will just reject it. You may not consciously say, "Well, I reject that". It just won't take root within you. It will just bypass you. You won't hear it. It just won't register. You will go on.

And the change that needed to happen won't happen, because you were not able[17] to hear. Why? The conditioning of the religious spirit. That is one of the biggest issues, this religious spirit, that I have seen over the last 15 years. This is one of the biggest impasses every son faces.

And this is primarily what causes them to stumble[18] and leave what God is doing. Because at some point, something in their thinking sown by the religious spirit says, "That's not God. I don't accept that". And they are not able to move forward. And so they end up rejecting and going on their own way to find something else that is more amenable to their belief system.

You can have those people that can be just as religious and say, "Well, I'm not religious". And they are out there drinking and carousing and doing whatever they feel is not religious and they are just as religious as everyone else. It is not about the acts[19]. It is about the spirit.

God is completing the deliverance in the sons. This is the time of the final preparation of the kings and priests, and they will not move into the mantle[20] and destiny that God has for them, as long as there remains any remnants of the religious spirit within them.

The extraction process can be very uncomfortable. The greatest concern is being able to see this, within yourself. I can't go and tell you, "So and so, you've got a religious spirit", because you would not receive it. You might think you would receive it and say, "Ok, I am receiving it and I'll go pray about it." But it is not going to happen. God has to reveal it to you, so that you are able to see the conditioning that has existed within your mindset, your belief system; how it has all been bred under a canopy of darkness[1] and religion with all of its do's and don'ts, all of its limitations and parameters.

This is a challenging word because no one really wants to hear this. Everyone has a concept of religion and religiosity, and if you were to go up to someone and say, "You are religious. You have a religious spirit", they would not be able to accept that. Even within the spiritual circles of those coming in to sonship ,it would be very hard to be open and receive that.

God is extracting this out of you. I would be bold enough to say, "If we could get this, then all the rest of the words in this book will come alive, and will make sense, and they won't trouble you, and you won't stumble[18]." But this is something that we need to get.

We do not understand how deeply it has been sown. We don't understand how much our exposure to this life, to our peers and to our culture; has been so focused against the sons manifesting. This sheds new light on the scripture about being new wineskins, and the need to be pliable. If we are not careful, it is easy to formulate a way of thinking that is partial and you find yourself become stiff necked[19], unable to really change. And that has always been the command in the New Testament; wineskins[21] being able to throw off the old conditioning. You don't sew a new patch[22] on an old garment, it will only split and tear with the new wine.

The new wine of the kingdom is not palatable to the soul. We may love it, but it is bitter - sweet[23] to the taste, but bitter in our stomach. But that is okay, that is what we want. We love that, even if it is difficult to accept. The Lord has always required that we let go of everything and keep letting go. How does the scripture go? "Except that you were a child[24] you would not enter the kingdom of God."

We need to understand what that scripture talks about, because we can have a tendency, as we have grown and matured in this path, to become a little stiff, not quite childlike, not quite moldable. And yet the Lord says: *"I am the potter[25] and you are the clay. And I require that you be moldable and flexible."* And we have had a tendency to say, "Well, Lord, I'm the potter. You're the clay." And sometimes we get it backwards.

A deliverance is happening. It has been happening to you progressively over the years, but now we are in the time where it is coming to a culmination. The last bit of extraction has to be done. There has to be a last minute surgery where the spirit of the Lord goes in and just surgically pulls out that last bit of religious conditioning sown by the spirits of darkness. **We must realize that the more you come into sonship, and the more you come into a spiritual walk with God; the less and less acceptable you will be to anyone.**

That might be difficult to swallow, because everyone likes to be liked. Everyone likes to be thought well of. "Oh what a great man of God." "Oh what a great word." But the more you walk in the spirit, the more you come forth; the less and less palatable and acceptable you will be. In fact the only ones who will be receptive to you will be those to whom the Father has revealed you to.

If the Lord reveals who you are to someone, then they will see past what they find unpalatable. You must face the fact that a man or woman that walks in the spirit, is not going to line up according to the thinking of the flesh and the soul. He or she is not going to match up to the concepts of what we have thought a son is. It will not be acceptable.

God is purposefully making the sons unpalatable. He is doing a good job in putting enough reproach on you, that unless someone has a revelation from the Father, they will not be able to accept you or open up to you.

Now a lot of people find that very difficult and this is where we lose a lot of people. They want to walk with God. They want the mysteries. They want the teaching. They really want to walk in these things, but they also want to be recognized. They want to be loved. They want to be accepted. It is that cozy feeling of the soul .... *be wary when all men speak well of you!*

How many people we have spoken to have consciously said, "You know, I understand the path you are on, but I can't walk that path because I need the social part of things. I need the feeling to be needed. I need that." And so they chose to walk away. We have seen that many, many times.

This is a choice that people make consciously, but it is also a choice that can be made subconsciously. Often times you don't even realize that you are making this choice, because the soul wants to be loved, wants to be accepted, wants to be thanked and patted on the back. It can be very subtle unless you have eyes to see within yourself.

When God says; "Come out of her my people. Come outside the camp," He means it! He will put a reproach[26] on you, however He does it - but He will put a reproach on you. The more you walk with God, the less acceptable you will be to the soulish Christian. God will put a reproach on you to guarantee that only those who have a revelation from Him will be able to see you. And that is a difficult cross to bear for many. If you don't have a reproach on you yet, just know that it is coming.

When the Father is ready, He will reveal[27] you, like He did with Christ to the disciples. He revealed to the disciples who the Lord Jesus was, and they gave themselves to Him. That scripture is no different for the sons. If someone comes to walk with you, to wash your feet, to receive your word, it will be because the Father has revealed you to them.

If you are still walking on the path of needing a little bit of recognition, or acceptance, then fine. But realize that you have not cut away the bonds or trappings of the conditioning of the religious spirit.

This is a difficult one. This is something that you need to pray about, because the Lord is positioning the sons as His mouthpiece. You will speak[28] the word to many people, nations and tongues. That's the prophecy in the book of Revelation. And I believe it applies to all of God's sons.

He has called you to evangelize the kingdom, but it is not what we think it is. It is not just saving souls. It is redeeming a kingdom unto Himself. It all has to do with spirit. We are talking about spirit here, not soul, and people aren't going to be able to receive you unless the Father has revealed you to them.

Most, if not all, people walk on the plane of the soul. All of them. This is why it gets very muggy out there with bonds and connections and cords and projections of thoughts. It's a mess out there in the world. Nobody knows who they are because there is so much transference. It is just like a spiritual matrix of mud. And programs like Facebook and Twitter and Instagram have only further muddied the waters. They are not a blessing, but a curse.

So it is very, very interesting. The majority of Christianity walks on the plane of the soul. They do not walk on the plane of spirit. That only comes through the very deep work of the cross[29]. And most people don't want that.

The kingdom is being taken by a remnant. And the Lord has said time and again, "It's a remnant of a remnant". If you are hearing this word, and this is coming alive to you, then it is because you are part of this remnant of a remnant. You are part of the "very few". **Many are called, but few are chosen.**

As much as you may want to reach out to someone and help them, you have to be careful. Be careful that you are not moving from obligation born of the soul and religious conditioning that might still be hanging on to you. Make sure that you don't leave a back door open for bonds and obligations, and cords of darkness and confusion, to minister back to you.

God wants the sons fully delivered from this age, and that would be from the time it began with the fallen angels - *everything*. There has been such a buildup of consciousness within the earth plane, and the sons must be fully delivered from this. When you hit the point where you are not acceptable, then know you have made some progress.

It is a fine line that we walk, because you come across people that love you, and they don't even know what you are about. They don't know that you are a man of God or a woman of God walking in the spirit. They just love you because their spirits are drawn to your spirit. And that is fine, and maybe that is all that it will ever be.

It is a fine line that we walk, because so much of what we do - and will do - is spirit; not soul. As much as you would like to go out and stand on the street corner and bring them in, or free them, or lay hands on them - you cannot. Most of that is from the plane of the soul. What is happening in the kingdom is a kingdom level reality, and the ministry and deliverances you bring will be a kingdom level reality.

That is how you get the job done. You move in the spirit. When it talks about evangelizing, what does the Lord say? "You first bind the strongman[30] and then you plunder his house." Whether we realize it or not, as we live day by day, we are binding the strongman and we are beginning to plunder his house. Both the strong man externally, *the principalities and powers, thrones and dominions of this darkness,* but also the strongman within the mind and heart of those to whom you want to reach.

You can't talk to anyone and expect that what you say is going to reach them, unless you first bind the strongman within them. Then you plunder his house. Then you speak the word. "Oh, but this one is such a spiritual person and they love God and they really have got a handle on things." That might be what it appears like, but it is only what it appears like. You bind the strongman, and then you plunder his house.

Within yourself you are binding the strongman, the remnants of a religious spirit and religious conditioning. And you are plundering where the enemy has laid land mines within your thinking and your life. God is uprooting them and delivering you. And I can say this - you are going to be the most spiritual men and women of God on the face of the earth. But on the flipside - the world will think they are doing God a favor[31] by trying to destroy you. Your Christian brothers and sisters will think they are doing God's will by crucifying you. That is what you have to look forward to. **You walk in the spirit and you become a son, and you will become completely unpalatable, except to those to whom the Lord has called. But that is just how it is.**

God is delivering His sons from the last vestiges and conditionings of the religious spirit. They will have nothing to do with Satan or the principalities or powers of this vast darkness. God is delivering each one of His sons, out of the realm of evil and darkness which has been a snare to them, and fully into the realm of His beloved Son.

Scriptures (NASB)

[1] 1 John 5:19
We know that we are of God, and that the whole world lies in the power of the evil one.

[2]Revelation 18:4
I heard another voice from heaven, saying, "Come out of her, my people, so that you will not participate in her sins and receive of her plagues;

[3] Romans 12:2
And do not be conformed to this world, but be transformed by the renewing of your mind, so that you may prove what the will of God is, that which is good and acceptable and perfect.

[4]Ephesians 6:12
For our struggle is not against flesh and blood, but against the rulers, against the powers, against the world forces of this darkness, against the spiritual forces of wickedness in the heavenly places.

[5] 1 Corinthians 13:10
but when the perfect comes, the partial will be done away

[6]John 8:32
and you will know the truth, and the truth will make you free."

[7]Colossians 2:14
It was for freedom that Christ set us free; therefore keep standing firm and do not be subject again to a yoke of slavery.

[8] Galatians 4:4
But when the fullness of the time came, God sent forth His Son, born of a woman, born under the Law,

[9] James 5:17
Elijah was a man with a nature like ours, and he prayed earnestly that it would not rain, and it did not rain on the earth for three years and six months.

[10]1 Kings 19:20
He left the oxen and ran after Elijah and said, "Please let me kiss my father and my mother, then I will follow you." And he said to him, "Go back again, for what have I done to you?"

[11] Matthew 5:18
"For truly I say to you, until heaven and earth pass away, not the smallest letter or stroke shall pass from the Law until all is accomplished.

[12] 1 Corinthians 2:16
For WHO HAS KNOWN THE MIND OF THE LORD, THAT HE WILL INSTRUCT HIM? But we have the mind of Christ.

[13]John 5:19
Therefore Jesus answered and was saying to them, "Truly, truly, I say to you, the Son can do nothing of Himself, unless it is something He sees the Father doing; for whatever the Father does, these things the Son also does in like manner.

[14]John 12:49
"For I did not speak on My own initiative, but the Father Himself who sent Me has given Me a commandment as to what to say and what to speak.

or [14]John 8:28
So Jesus said, "When you lift up the Son of Man, then you will know that I am He, and I do nothing on My own initiative, but I speak these things as the Father taught Me.

[15] Romans 8:14
For all who are being led by the Spirit of God, these are sons of God.

[16] 1 Samuel 15:3
'Now go and strike Amalek and utterly destroy all that he has, and do not spare him; but put to death both man and woman, child and infant, ox and sheep, camel and donkey.'"

[17]Hebrews 5:11
Concerning him we have much to say, and it is hard to explain, since you have become dull of hearing.

[18]Proverbs 4:19
The way of the wicked is like darkness; They do not know over what they stumble.

[19] Acts 7:51
"You men who are stiff-necked and uncircumcised in heart and ears are always resisting the Holy Spirit; you are doing just as your fathers did.

[20] 2 Kings 2:13
He also took up the mantle of Elijah that fell from him and returned and stood by the bank of the Jordan.

[21] Mark 2:22
"No one puts new wine into old wineskins; otherwise the wine will burst the skins, and the wine is lost and the skins as well; but one puts new wine into fresh wineskins."

[22] Matthew 9:16
"But no one puts a patch of unshrunk cloth on an old garment; for the patch pulls away from the garment, and a worse tear results.

[23] Revelation 10:9
So I went to the angel, telling him to give me the little book. And he said to me, "Take it and eat it; it will make your stomach bitter, but in your mouth it will be sweet as honey."

[24] Mark 10:15
"Truly I say to you, whoever does not receive the kingdom of God like a child will not enter it at all."

[25] Isaiah 64:8
But now, O LORD, You are our Father, We are the clay, and You our potter; And all of us are the work of Your hand.

[26] Psalm 44:13
You make us a reproach to our neighbors, A scoffing and a derision to those around us.

[27] Matthew 16:17
And Jesus said to him, "Blessed are you, Simon Barjona, because flesh and blood did not reveal this to you, but My Father who is in heaven.

[28] Revelation 10:11
And they said to me, "You must prophesy again concerning many peoples and nations and tongues and kings."

[29] Philippians 2:8
Being found in appearance as a man, He humbled Himself by becoming obedient to the point of death, even death on a cross.

[30] Mark 3:27
"But no one can enter the strong man's house and plunder his property unless he first binds the strong man, and then he will plunder his house.

[31] John 16:2
"They will make you outcasts from the synagogue, but an hour is coming for everyone who kills you to think that he is offering service to God.

Notes

Chapter 2

You Must Let Go

This word comes out of the book of Isaiah, and concerns the prophecy that the sons of God are to fulfill with respect to their ministry in the earth. However, it also addresses a level of deliverance and guidance that the Lord brings forth to the sons, prior to entering into the deep releases and changes that are slated to happen.

Let's read first from Isaiah 45:2. ***"I will go before you and make the rough places smooth; I will shatter the doors of bronze and cut through their iron bars. And I will give you the treasures of darkness and the hidden wealth of secret places, so that you may know that it is I, the LORD, the God of Israel, who calls you by your name."*****(Isaiah 45:2-3)**

Let's go over and read Isaiah 42:16 and then we'll talk a little bit about where we're going here. Verse 16. *"I will lead the blind by a way they do not know, in paths they do not know I will guide them. I will make darkness into light before them and rugged places into plains. These are the things I will do, and I will not leave them undone."*(Isaiah 42:16) Nor will He abandon His sons.

And Isaiah 58:12. ***"Those from among you will rebuild the ancient ruins; you will raise up the age-old foundations; you will be called the repairer of the breach, the restorer of the paths in which to dwell."***

What we are talking about is something that the Lord is doing very uniquely in the lives of each of those who are called at this time - both to become and to manifest - the reality of sonship.

We've spoken for years now about the effects of bonds and the blindness that can come with unequally yoked[1] relationships. We have talked about transference. We have spoken in all three of our books about these different aspects and how they can affect your spiritual walk and, how they have the potential to blind you.

In Isaiah 42 it says that ***I will lead the blind in a way they do not know***. (Isaiah 42:16) We may not think of ourselves as blind. Isaiah 45. ***I will go before you and make the rough places smooth[2].*** He's talking about removing the roadblocks in your path which come by virtue of the blindness that we're still coming out of, as we come into the Light.

We know that the path[3] of the righteous shines greater and greater unto the fullness of time. That is the word. How do these things happen? It starts with the removal of the spiritual blocks in your life.

I don't know that we have yet understood how deep the bondages and impasses have gone within each of our lives, but the promise is that the Lord will make your path straight[4]. He will straighten out the crooked path. He will remove the log jam. He will remove the boulder. He will make straight the path of the Lord. Easier said than done.

We have not realized how deeply entrenched we have been in this system, but God is extracting the sons out of the world. At every step, at every turn, there has been that challenge to let go and to trust the Lord - to allow Him to reveal to you the next step; the next level.

I know that we have made that commitment to lay down our lives. "Lord, whatever You say, that's how it's going to be." But we have not necessarily realized how stubborn and staunch the soul has been to resist what God is bringing to pass within each of us.

To this time, we have not realized how much of an antichrist[5] has yet existed within each of us. The promise is that He is going to make straight[4] your path. And the way He does that is to reveal to you, individually, where the log jams are. I will tell you this, we are close to the release, change and manifestation of sonship. Very close. In many ways it can seem far off, but that is more of an illusion than anything else.

We know that the Lord does not go against the will of the sons. He will lead you and bring you through places where you have to make decisions. Those choices or decisions determine how quickly you will mature and move in God. But He will not go against your will. It is necessary that we be new wineskins[6], pliable, to whom the Lord can reveal the mysteries, the secrets and the truths. If we do not stay pliable and maintain a level of abiding as a new wineskin, we will never enter into the kingdom fully.

The sons are coming to birth, and each of them, in their own unique way, have barriers or log jams that must be removed. What are the hidden rocks[7] in your love feast? There are boulders in the path that have to be removed, and unless the Lord does it, it will not be done.

In that respect we have been blind. As much as we see, there is still that part of us that does not see; that has not been able to discern the deep[8] things of Satan. We're not talking about casting out demons[9] or some odd heretical teaching. The deep things of Satan are those things that are hidden, hidden so well that without a revealing from the Lord, you will not be able to see it. And if you do not see it, you will not be able to move through it, and have dominion and understanding.

It is a precarious path that the sons are walking on right now, especially at this time of transition. You can come down to the wire and find that there are still major boulders that have to be removed, and we have to let the Lord remove the last blocks. If your path was completely clear; no log jams, no hidden rocks, nothing, then you would have arrived. But we're not quite there yet.

Paul strove that he might attain the out resurrection[10] from the dead. What are we doing? We are striving in God that we might also attain the out resurrection from the dead, even as Paul spoke of in Philippians. This is what is on the plate. This is what God has set before us. It is the out-resurrection from the dead, the transition from death into life. Resurrection life.

A lot of things will come with this release; not just a newness of life. The change coming will be so earth shattering, so universe demolishing, that there will not be one entity in the spirit that will not become immediately aware of the change that happens as the sons fully experience this metamorphosis into resurrection life.

Given the stakes, do you think that the enemy would not have gone to great lengths to conceal his workings, individually within the sons, to keep the hidden rocks[7] in your love feast positioned? You might say, "Well, I have such discernment, how is that possible? There are no hidden rocks in my love feast. There are no boulders in my path." But there are.

This word applies to everyone. And, it is the Lord who must do this. The Lord must bring this to pass. What is the promise? "I will go before you," says the Lord. The Lord will go before His sons and He will make the rough places smooth[1]. And He will shatter the doors of bronze[1].

We don't even realize the jeopardy of what we have been walking through.

We have talked about these revelations for years now. What about the whore[11] feeding off of the life of the sons? You can say, "Yes. I understand that one. And I have worked to get rid of all the bonds so that that whore is not feeding off of me." But I tell you, if the whore was not feeding off of you, even just a measure, you would have broken into resurrection life, because that is the bottleneck.

The promise has been ... that which has taken[12] your life, which has sucked your life, which has drained your energy, is going to be removed and brought under judgment. And with that judgment we will see a release; you will move into resurrection life. But the first step is that which has drained your life, that which has sucked off of you and taken your life in God, must be judged. This must be broken. Then, and only then, is resurrection life attainable.

The only reason the sons have not yet become is because they have not seen the Lord on a deep enough level. They have not really understood their blindness, nor what is truly at stake. As much as we have seen - we have still missed it, and this is why it is imperative to stay open and teachable ... new wineskins - if you will.

You might say, "Oh, Lord, I've already signed on the bottom line. I am absolutely given. This is my drive." Stay open, because there is another layer that is going to come off of you that will enable you to become even more given and more driven to finish this race.

Some of the log jams that exist could easily be narrowed down to family relationships, sons and daughters; people that you hold dear to your heart. We know that the sons will not get into the kingdom carrying baggage, nor will they make it through the eye of the needle. *A man's enemy will be those of his own household* - is a difficult word to embrace.

I hope you understand what I am saying, for there is a great deal at stake. You are not going to turn around and say, "Oh, let me grab all these lovely Christians, my family, my sister, my brother, my children and let me bring them along with me, because they love God and they hear the word of God."

Yes, maybe so, but they don't have the calling that is upon you. And you are not going to get through the eye of the needle[13] carrying the baggage of relationships that are unequally yoked[1].... unequally yoked because of the level of revelation and transformation that you have been brought into, which has separated you outside the camp of other Christians.

You have a choice to make. Are you going to go through and get the breakthrough? Or, are you going to stay encumbered and relinquish your heritage? A lot is at stake, but we haven't really understood how much. When we get the breakthrough, then we can turn and minister to those we have had to leave behind.

The promise has always been that if we hit a point where we cannot seem to deal with something in our life, then God will take care of it. He will get in there and He'll extract it out. But we have to be willing to let go.

It is all very interesting. In Isaiah 58 the word speaks about the sons who will be called the repairers[14] of the breach, the restorers of the path. The sons, themselves, will become the repairers of the breach. They will remove the barriers. They will remove the blockades and the hindrances for those that follow, that they also might become. But first the Lord must accomplish that within them. They will not become the restorers of the path, the repairers of the breach until that is first accomplished within them.

This is a deep probing word, because you have to be willing to let go of everything, again. You have to be willing to walk by yourself, alone if need be. You have to be able to let go of the good and the better, for the best, and that is something only the Lord can do - provided you have been able to let go and trust Him.

This is something that the Lord is doing right now, and this is why we're talking about this. He is beginning to remove the last roadblocks, the last hindrances, and the last barriers, in your path to becoming. And these are things you have not seen, and you have not grasped, until now.

The sons have been, as it says in Isaiah 42, "blind" to certain aspects within them. The Lord has needed to put His light deep within them and He has demanded that they do not look the other way, but that they embrace the fire of His appearing. We need to allow the Lord to deal with us, to expose the inner workings, and to extract that which has been a hindrance.

This is a heavy word, but this is a word of a deliverance. And the fruit of this will be open vision on a level that you have never experienced. That which has remained hidden is to be exposed and removed - now. It might seem a little painful, but God is going to take the scalpel and cut it out, and you must allow Him to do that. "Lord, cut this away from me, because if You do not, I know that I will not enter into my inheritance." We're speaking about Malachi 3; the Lord appears as a refiner's fire[15] and He purges the sons.

This has been your path. It is discipleship without reservation. This word is no different than the word from the very beginning, that you love[16] the Lord thy God with all thy heart, with all thy mind, with all thy soul, and with all thy spirit; everything within you. It cannot be anything less. We love the Lord, with everything within us, and we hold nothing dear.

Do not have any idols[17] in your saddlebags … if you remember the story of Rachel in the Old Testament. You have to be able to lay it all before Him, because if you do not, you will not make this last step.

Scriptures (NASB)

[1] 2 Corinthians 6:14
Do not be bound together with unbelievers; for what partnership have righteousness and lawlessness, or what fellowship has light with darkness?

[2] Isaiah 45:2
"I will go before you and make the rough places smooth; I will shatter the doors of bronze and cut through their iron bars.

[3] Proverbs 4:18
But the path of the righteous is like the light of dawn, That shines brighter and brighter until the full day.

[4] Proverbs 3:6
In all your ways acknowledge Him, And He will make your paths straight.

[5] 1 John2:22
Who is the liar but the one who denies that Jesus is the Christ? This is the antichrist, the one who denies the Father and the Son.

[6] Luke 5:38
"But new wine must be put into fresh wineskins.

[7] Jude 1:12
These are the men who are hidden reefs in your love feasts when they feast with you without fear, caring for themselves; clouds without water, carried along by winds; autumn trees without fruit, doubly dead, uprooted;

[8] Isaiah 45:3
"I will give you the treasures of darkness And hidden wealth of secret places, So that you may know that it is I, The LORD, the God of Israel, who calls you by your name.

[9] Mark 1:39
And He went into their synagogues throughout all Galilee, preaching and casting out the demons.

[10] Phil. 3:11
"that I may attain to the out-resurrection of the dead." (Greek Literal)

[11] Revelation 17:6
And I saw the woman drunk with the blood of the saints, and with the blood of the witnesses of Jesus. When I saw her, I wondered greatly.

[12] Joel 1:4
What the gnawing locust has left, the swarming locust has eaten; And what the swarming locust has left, the creeping locust has eaten; And what the creeping locust has left, the stripping locust has eaten.

[13] Mark 10:25
"It is easier for a camel to go through the eye of a needle than for a rich man to enter the kingdom of God."

[14] Isaiah 58:12
"Those from among you will rebuild the ancient ruins; You will raise up the age-old foundations; And you will be called the repairer of the breach, The restorer of the streets in which to dwell.

[15] Malachi 3:2
"But who can endure the day of His coming? And who can stand when He appears? For He is like a refiner's fire and like fullers' soap.

[16] Deuteronomy 6:5
"You shall love the LORD your God with all your heart and with all your soul and with all your might.

[17] Genesis 31:24
Now Rachel had taken the household idols and put them in the camel's saddle, and she sat on them. And Laban felt through all the tent but did not find them.

Chapter 3

A Walk in the Fire

We know that we are very close to the completion of this phase of our sojourn - training, purification and preparation. We are very close to the end of it. Even now we have been leaning into the next transition – from life into life[1], as we have said before.

At times you may find yourself leaning into a provision or promise before the time has fully come for its manifestation. You could compare this to the Lord as He spoke to Mary and said, "Woman, it is not My time[2]." It seemed like the transition for Christ was ahead of schedule, but we know it was right on time. It can seem that we are not yet prepared for a promise or provision, as the Lord begins to draw your spirit into it, but His timing is always perfect. What happens, inevitably, is that you get "stretched" beyond what you thought you were capable of. This time the change which is underway, is a type of change you have not experienced before, for He is bringing the sons into a new type of existence. He is doing something new, entirely new, within the sons.

> **"Many will be purged, purified and refined, but the wicked will act wickedly; and none of the wicked will understand, but those who have insight will understand." Daniel 12:10**

We are changing from one order into another order, and I know that is difficult for us to grasp. It may seem like we are talking about concepts, because we are not quite there, yet. We really don't know the experience that awaits us in this transformation that is happening, but we do know that we are in the midst of it. Until we are on the other side of this transformation[3], we will continue to go through the process of being purged, purified and refined. This is the on-going path.

Sometimes you can be right in the middle of the dealings of God, and the purifying work of the spirit, and not really understand, nor recognize it. The Lord is very good at getting right in your face, because this is about a walk with Him.

This is all about a walk with Him. He is our provision. He is our sustenance. He makes a way for His sons and daughters, a path in the wilderness[4]. He requires that we progressively lay more and more down and enter into a deeper trust and walk with Him, but it does not come easily. The soul is constantly bucking change - trying to stay on the throne and create a great deal of problems.

The word has always come: "Don't look for Me in the easy way out, but look for Me in the difficult path, because that is where you will find Me." When things get difficult and challenging, and you are up against a wall, that, in itself, is a strong sign that He is completing a change within you. Do not miss a season of His appearing[5] to you by getting caught up in all the issues and problems. It can be too easy to lose sight of the larger picture.

Anne's father, a ministry who has since passed over, had a humorous analogy he often shared. It goes like this: "When you are up to your ass in alligators, it can often times be difficult to remember that your original mission was to drain the swamp." I think we feel that way more often than we know.

Windows of opportunity are precious. The challenge, at times, is to recognize your window of opportunity. In those moments of deepest challenge, we need to recognize that His presence is even more available.

I know I am speaking to the choir here - we all know this, but it is good to rehearse. Are you a victim or are you a victor? How do you see the situation that you're in? We have the power to create. But that ability to create[6] goes both ways. You can create the positive or you can give ascent to the illusion, to the warfare - to what appears. You can create the positive, or you can give weight and credibility to the lie, and literally create that.

The word has come so many times; "You will praise your way into and out of everything I set before you." Our worship to the Lord is a state of heart, not just a moment of time at a church service. This is how we live. This is our life, and we have been around the horn too many times not to understand what is going on.

In these times of challenge, His presence is more available to us than ever. There is no doubt that His sons will continue to go through the fire until this transition is completed; it is our path.

"So let us know, let us press on to know the LORD. His going forth is as certain as the dawn; and He will come to us like the rain, like the spring rain watering the earth." Hosea 6:3

Just a little meditation. Something to think about. The promise in Hosea is one we live by: Hosea 6:3, "*So let us press on to know the Lord, for His coming is like the rain...*". He has broken the knees of the sons, but the promise is that the Lord appears as they press on. So you press on to know Him. Understand that in the midst of the greatest challenges; He is there, and with His appearing is an opportunity to break into a deeper relationship with Him.

Scriptures NASB

[1] Mark 9:3
Six days later, Jesus took with Him Peter and James and John, and brought them up on a high mountain by themselves. And He was transfigured before them;

Or [1] Matthew 17:2
And He was transfigured before them; and His face shone like the sun, and His garments became as white as light.

Or [1] Luke 9:32
Now Peter and his companions had been overcome with sleep; but when they were fully awake, they saw His glory and the two men standing with Him.

[2] John 2:4
And Jesus said to her, "Woman, what does that have to do with us? My hour has not yet come."

[3] Romans 12:2
And do not be conformed to this world, but be transformed by the renewing of your mind, so that you may prove what the will of God is, that which is good and acceptable and perfect.

[4] Isaiah 43:19
"Behold, I will do something new, Now it will spring forth; Will you not be aware of it? I will even make a roadway in the wilderness, Rivers in the desert.

[5] James 5:7
Therefore be patient, brethren, until the coming of the Lord. The farmer waits for the precious produce of the soil, being patient about it, until it gets the early and late rains.

[6] James 3:10
from the same mouth come both blessing and cursing. My brethren, these things ought not to be this way.

Chapter 4

Steadfast

Now it came to pass, when Sanballat, And Tobiah, and Geshem the Arabian, and the rest of our enemies, heard that I had built the wall, and that there was no breach left therein; (though at that time I had not set up the doors upon the gates;) [2]then Sanballat and Geshem sent a message to me, saying, "Come, let us meet together at Chephirim in the plain of Ono. But they thought to do me mischief. [3]And I sent messengers unto them, saying, I am doing a great work, so that I cannot come down; why should the work cease, whilst I leave it, and come down to you? Nehemiah 6:1-3

Keep this in your thinking for a moment.

Often it is good to reflect upon where we are, and the progress that we have been making in God. We understand that we are a living temple[1], made without hands, and that God has chosen to dwell within His people. We know that the Father's plan is to bring forth the manifestation of the fullness of His presence within you, as a living temple.

There are times when you wonder how much longer it will be until this temple is finished, and the walls of protection are completed around you. You recall the promise in Zechariah 2:5 that God will be a fire[2] around you and the glory in your midst? Now that is protection. What happened during the time of Ezra and Nehemiah? The temple was rebuilt and the walls were completed and fortified. But until the walls were completed, there were always those marauding armies that would come through the breaches in the wall and harass the Jewish people; trying to destroy what God was restoring. It was constant.

This is a type or shadow of what we are living in right now, in this day. God is establishing you as His living temple, yet, until the defenses are completed within you, the enemy has had access to come in and harass and try and undermine what God has been doing in your life.

This is one of the reasons the spirit of the Lord has been so adamant on this issue of bonds and contacts; relationships of the soul. Therein has been your breech in the wall - the breech in your defenses.

You could say God is building a wall around you, as He spoke in Zechariah, but those walls are still being finished and established. The Lord is the glory[3] in your midst. He is a wall of fire around you. But the full realization of this will not be experienced until God completes what He is doing within you. Until that is completed, we are still dealing with breeches in the wall, or more accurately, bonds and contacts of the soul.

> **"Awake, awake; put on thy strength, O Zion; put on thy beautiful garments, O Jerusalem, the holy city: for henceforth there shall no more come into thee the uncircumcised and the unclean. Shake thyself from the dust; arise, *and* sit down, O Jerusalem: loose thyself from the bands of thy neck, O captive daughter of Zion." Isaiah 52:1-2**
>
> **"Then you will know that I am the LORD your God, Dwelling in Zion, My holy mountain. So Jerusalem will be holy, and strangers will pass through it no more." Joel 3:17**

This is what is happening. Until your awareness comes up to a level of clarity and understanding, and your remembrance of who you are plumbs deep enough within you, you will still be dealing with the access of the unclean to you. Can you see this? Bonds of the flesh have continued to exist because you have not really known who you are. The sons are still waking up and arising. They are still in the process of shaking[4] off the dust. And as this happens, the satanic access to you will come to a screeching halt.

The doors of access into you are closing; the wall is being completed. We are leaning into this as quickly as we are able to "see". The key word here is: <u>see</u>.

We may think that we are in control of ourselves, and that we really have a handle on things, but only now are we realizing how subtly the enemy has had access into us. This is why the teaching on bonds, contacts, and cords - the whole principle of how the spirit world works - has been unending and important to really experience and understand.

You might say; "Well, I don't understand. This all sounds very intrusive and defiling." And you are right, this is very intrusive, and until the work is finished within you, that vulnerability will still exist. You must understand that the enemy works through concealment. He works behind closed doors. What is the prophecy about the end times that we are in?

> **"For there shall arise false Christs, and false prophets, and shall shew great signs and wonders; insomuch that, if *it were* possible, they shall deceive the very elect." Matthew 24:24**

More and more, we are beginning to understand that it is not what you can see that you should be concerned about, but; what you cannot see that you should be concerned about. Satan is the master of illusion, and he can create illusion after illusion that will suck you in, unless you are able to rightly discern. That is why the promise and prophecy of Isaiah 52 is so important.

What is the command to the sons? Arise. Wake up. Shake off the dust. Then, and only then, will you find that the unclean will no longer have access into you.

> **3And I sent messengers unto them, saying, I am doing a great work, so that I cannot come down; why should the work cease, whilst I leave it, and come down to you? Nehemiah 6:3**

So often the enemy prods you to stop what you are doing and come down off the wall. "Come on. Just go ahead. Take me on." The principalities are constantly warring against the saints of the most high, until it seems like it is a daily life style, and you are constantly prodded to stop and just go and deal with it. "I am going to tune into the spirit. I am going to deal with this thing. I am going to take dominion. You know, I'm going to go after it." There are times when the Lord may direct you, but often, it is only a distraction to keep you off focus, and off the mark of what you are truly to be doing.

We choose to stay in the presence[5] of the Lord. We will not come down out of His presence. Often times we don't realize how this goading of the spirit realm pulls you out of the vibration and energy of His presence, to go and deal with the witchcraft and all of that which is so prevalent in the realm of spirit. Without realizing it, you can go from warring in the spirit, to warring from your soul, and that is a problem.

The effective way to war in the spirit is really very simple; stay in His presence. We call that "aerial supremacy". You don't come down off the wall. Although the enemy might goad you, "Come down. Come down. Let's talk. Come down. You need to really discern this. You really need to get involved here." But that is all a distraction, for your presence is His presence, and you are the Light that judges - even more than the words you speak. The words we speak are very important, creative and powerful, but even more important than that is the presence of the Father and the Son within us.

> **"This is the judgment, that the Light has come into the world, and men loved the darkness rather than the Light, for their deeds were evil." John 3:19**

What you are judges the enemy. I am not saying that we take a passive stance. It takes a great deal of intensity and focus and push to live in His presence, and to stay in His presence. But we are not going to be pulled into a lot of small little skirmishes and battles, and issues that say, "Come over here and deal with this. Well, come over here and deal with this. Well, come over here and deal with this." We are going to stay in the presence of the Lord, and our presence will emit judgment and will bring the presence of the Father into every situation.

This is not new teaching. These are things we know, but it is always good to rehearse it as we see what Nehemiah and Ezra experienced with the warfare that came against them in the building of the temple. And, once it was built, to protect it from the ravages of the inhabitants of the land that came to destroy what God was doing.

God is completing the building of the wall around us, fulfilling Zechariah's promise, that Christ will be the glory within us, and the fire[2] around us. Immunity comes with maturity, and maturity comes as God finishes putting the fire to His sons, that they might stand dressed in robes of righteousness.

Scriptures (NASB)

[1] 2 Corinthians 6:16
Or what agreement has the temple of God with idols? For we are the temple of the living God; just as God said, "I WILL DWELL IN THEM AND WALK AMONG THEM; AND I WILL BE THEIR GOD, AND THEY SHALL BE MY PEOPLE.

[2] Zechariah 2:5
'For I,' declares the LORD, 'will be a wall of fire around her, and I will be the glory in her midst.'"

[3] Ezekiel 28:22
and say, 'Thus says the Lord GOD, "Behold, I am against you, O Sidon, And I will be glorified in your midst. Then they will know that I am the LORD when I execute judgments in her, And I will manifest My holiness in her.

[4] Isaiah 52:2
Shake yourself from the dust, rise up, O captive Jerusalem; Loose yourself from the chains around your neck, O captive daughter of Zion.

[5] Psalm 37:7
Rest in the LORD and wait patiently for Him; Do not fret because of him who prospers in his way, Because of the man who carries out wicked schemes.

Notes

Chapter 5

Breaking the Veil

In our first book, *The Manifestation of the Sons of God,* we spoke about the signs that come to your body as you experience progressive levels of renewal. Let me explain this further.

As you continue to come alive to God, you begin to hear His voice, you begin to comprehend what He is speaking ... you begin to know His presence. That happens at the same time that your entire being comes alive. It's more than just hearing and seeing and sensing, but your whole being is coming alive. And that was the promise in the book of Hebrews, that He would save you to the uttermost[1]; spirit, soul and body.

So what happens as the sons enter into this experience of ascension, or as they are caught up[2] to the throne of God? What exactly is happening to them? Well, we have spoken about the fact that their vibration is changing. Their frequency, their energy, all of it is changing and coming up higher and higher, as they enter in, more and more, to the realm of light; the realm of the Father. The realms of darkness are realms of low vibration, and low energy. But as you come higher up in the spirit, everything is at a higher frequency, higher vibration, and higher energy level. This is the realm of light.

As your body begins to respond to the input of the spirit, you will find that even though you exist in the body, your spirit is becoming more actively engaged in the conflict, as it carries out the directives of the Lord. Please bear in mind that the spirit realm is really the realm of reality, the realm of God's presence. This is the realm of reality.

The realm that we walk on, in the natural, is really more a realm of illusion. As you continue to ascend into His presence, your body will begin to reflect, more and more, that which your spirit is experiencing, whether it's warfare, or the presence of God. We explained many of the signs in the first book. And, as we have said, the signs which come in the body have been like a seeing-eye dog, giving the sons insight into what was (and is) happening in the realm of the kingdom.

In essence, the sons are coming alive to the whole realm of the Father's kingdom, and they are are beginning to understand that we are first and foremost, a spiritual being. We've had things out of order. We have seen ourself as this physical manifestation of the soul, the mind, the intellect, the emotions, and the physical body with its various issues. And we have identified with ourselves as being that - when this is not who or what we truly are.

We are first a spiritual being. God has placed within us a spirit that He earnestly desires to commune with. Your spirit is more in line with the truth of who you are than your soul, which is passing away and being renewed[3]. God has been redefining our paradigm, as we have said. And we are beginning to see and understand the whole world around us much differently.

We are beginning to understand that we truly are living in two worlds, at the same time. And as such, that which our spirit is doing and entering into, is beginning to be reflected, more and more, in our physical body. What is happening is translating down from the realm of spirit and manifesting within your body. We are in a hastening time of the restoration of the kingdom of God in the earth, and that restoration has to do with the manifesting of the Father's sons and daughters. Progressively more and more, you are coming alive to God.

This is what we seek. We do not want to meet the Lord, on the other side of the veil, after we pass through and have been buried six feet under. The promise is that on this side of the veil we will experience the transformation and the change. We need to get out of our thinking anything of a future tense. We still tend to think too much in a future tense, so we must catch ourself and be aware that we don not project something into the future, when God says it is here now.

What does it mean to come alive? It means that there is an integration happening within your soul, your physical body, and your spirit. You are becoming one. You are becoming one before the Lord, within yourself. **You are beginning to discover that you are more of a spiritual being than you have understood.**

With this transition the spirit moves, more and more, into the dominant position over the soul. It has not yet arrived, but as the soul dies out, the spirit takes over. I know it's difficult to understand, because we still walk to a great degree by faith and our awareness is still in the process of opening up - but we are beginning to experience, more and more, what we have become in Christ.

The sons of God are quickly becoming God's plumb line[4] in the earth.

> **Thus he shewed me: and, behold, the Lord stood upon a wall made by a plumbline, with a plumbline in his hand. And the LORD said unto me, Amos, what seest thou? And I said, A plumbline. Then said the Lord, Behold, I will set a plumbline in the midst of my people Israel: I will not again pass by them any more. Amos 7:7-8**

That is a huge statement, because when you build a house, the foundation is measured to a plumb line. The plumb line is the gauge. God's sons are literally a plumb line in the earth, from which everything will now be measured, for they are the embodiment of His righteousness. And that is why the work of the cross[5] and the preparation of spirit, has had to be thorough in the sons. The preparation has to be complete, so that God can then use the sons as a plumb line from which everything else will be judged. You might still be in the process of being completed, but God has raised the sons up as a plumb line in the earth. God's sons, His plumb line, will be the basis for many of the judgments that are to come forth.

The more the spirit of the Father and the spirit of the Son come alive within you, the more your physical body will go through change after change.

This is the time of the fulfillment of the Feast of Tabernacles, the third feast that was given to be followed. The Feast of Tabernacles deals with the full indwelling of the godhead[6] within the sons. This has been happening, and the more this takeover of the Father within you goes forward, the more your body will go through changes; coming alive to the world of spirit.

There is a quickening happening within you, and it is happening in correlation to the deep indwelling of the godhead within you. One doesn't happen without the other. You don't come alive without which the indwelling of the Lord and the Father first happens to you. And as that happens to you, your body comes alive and begins to conform to the reality of the spirit. The end result of this indwelling of the godhead will be resurrection life.

It may seem like your life is somewhat limited, because you have been boxed into this physical manifestation that you presently have, but it really is an illusion. You are much more free, and much more in a state of functioning, than you have understood. God has pulled you into a whole different world and you're coming alive to it, progressively more and more. As this continues to unfold, the sons will more fully understand that they are first and foremost - a spiritual being.

This reality has not been a present truth for the sons, but it is becoming that. As we have said - as you begin to come alive, your eyes will begin to open, and you will begin to see what your spirit is seeing. You will begin to hear what your spirit is hearing. How did the Lord move? The scripture says that He only did those things that He saw the Father doing, and spoke only those things that He heard the Father saying[7]. It is no different. The oneness and the connection that is happening within you, is bringing you into that same state of awareness and functioning.

You are living in both worlds at the same time. It can seem like you are more anchored in the natural plane right now, but that's only because your consciousness has not caught up to the depth of what your spirit is doing. The more you come alive, the more you will become aware of the world of spirit, and the more quickly the transition will happen.

A vision came many years ago. The teaching had to do with the transition that the sons of God are in. The word was simply that the sons are pushing up against a wall. And, that they have been living in a state of always pushing, pushing against the realm of illusion ... an illusion that has been so masterfully created to appear as though it is reality, when indeed it is not.

The sons are pushing against this wall of illusion, right now, and it will give way. What happens next? All that we are, will manifest. The illusion wants to say that we are separate, that we do not have that which we have sought, and that we are not whom God says we are. This is all an illusion. **And when this illusion gives way all that we are will manifest.**

There's a great deal being said here, because as the sons break through the veil; as they break through the veneer of the illusion, all that they are will not only be manifested to the world, but it will be manifested to them. And they will know[8], even as they have been known. But it's all contingent upon breaking through the veil of illusion that has resisted this breakthrough.

There are times when it can be very difficult to correlate the fruit of what you are doing, with the manifested reality of it. In other words; the Lord leads you to move in judgment or speak a word over a given situation, and you do so in obedience. Yet you may not see what it is you anticipated to happen, even though every bit of it happened. That is because it was manifested on a different plane or in a different region.

Let me see if I can break this down a little bit. Many times in the past we have prayed over a situation or moved with authority and seemingly nothing changed as far as what we saw visually. Yet as the Lord began to reveal, we saw the fulfillment of that word or prophecy on the other side of the globe happening. But, without revelation, you would not be able to connect the two events.

So what I am saying is that what the sons are doing, as they forge ahead in the spirit, is happening. But it will take revelation to understand or "see" what you've done, and put together the connection or correlation of those events.

It's like having the Lord come to you in a vision and speak to you, cryptically. This happened to Daniel many times. Without subsequent interpretation by the Spirit of the Lord, you would have no idea what was just conveyed. When you read through the book of Daniel and you look at the visions that he had received, you realize that the spirit of the Lord had to interpret to Daniel what was being said. Without that, Daniel wouldn't know.

So often God will bring dreams, visions, or experiences, to His sons in the night and if they look at it - at face value - they would not be able to understand exactly what it was He was saying. Because it takes that input of Spirit. It will be similar as the sons begin to move with dominion in the earth. You need revelation to see what you are creating, and to see how it is manifesting, because so often it will not be as you expect, or as you anticipated.

You're tracking more in the realm of spirit than perhaps you know. The signs that are coming to you - in your body - can be hard to recognize. You may think they are a physical symptom, but the fact remains that you are moving more and more in the realm of spirit. God is changing how you look at everything, even how you look at your body, and how it is responding to the energy of what your spirit is being pulled into and engaged in.

A lot of times we talk about warfare. And it may be difficult to understand, because often it is difficult to discern the source. We know and understand that there is a whole spirit realm that is at war against the sons of God; resisting what God is pulling them into. That really is the battle. And the spirit realm seeks any channel, any open door, to come against the sons and try to abort the process.

The more that your spirit is pulled into the administration of the kingdom, the more you will experience the resistance and the conflict. More and more you are becoming aware of this, and a shift of consciousness, within the sons, is happening . This shift is bringing about a conjunction of the spirit realm and the natural realm.

This conjunction has been going on for a great deal of time, and we understand that it is not happening not outside of you; rather this conjunction of worlds is happening within you. This conjunction is very internalized. It is one that the sons are experiencing, because they have been pulled into living a life in both realms. They have been pulled into living a life that tracks in the realm of spirit. And they are learning what it means to understand the signs that come to them in their body. More and more, the sons are understanding that their entire being is coming alive.

Expect a lot, because change is happening - and it is accelerating. More and more your eyes and ears are opening up. Be expecting.

Scriptures (NASB)

[1] Hebrews 7:25
Therefore He is able also to save forever those who draw near to God through Him, since He always lives to make intercession for them.

[2] Revelation 12:5
And she gave birth to a son, a male child, who is to rule all the nations with a rod of iron; and her child was caught up to God and to His throne.

[3] Ephesians 4:22-24
You were taught to put off your former way of life, your old self, which is being corrupted by its deceitful desires; to be renewed in the spirit of your minds; 24and to put on the new self, created to be like God in true righteousness and holiness

[4] Zechariah 4:10
"For who has despised the day of small things? But these seven will be glad when they see the plumb line in the hand of Zerubbabel-- these are the eyes of the LORD which range to and fro throughout the earth."

[5] Philippians 2:8
Being found in appearance as a man, He humbled Himself by becoming obedient to the point of death, even death on a cross.

[6] Colossians 1:19
For it was the Father's good pleasure for all the fullness to dwell in Him,

[7] John 5:19
Therefore Jesus answered and was saying to them, "Truly, truly, I say to you, the Son can do nothing of Himself, unless it is something He sees the Father doing; for whatever the Father does, these things the Son also does in like manner.

[8] 1 Corinthians 13:12
For now we see in a mirror dimly, but then face to face; now I know in part, but then I will know fully just as I also have been fully known.

Notes

Section 2

The Approaching Storm

Chapter 6

This Window of Time

There are a number of changes happening right now, and we are becoming more and more aware that this window of time that we are in, is closing down. We should be expecting much.

We are in a meeting with the Lord right now, and it is unfolding. I don't know how aware we are of this, but what is happening, is something entirely different.

"In my Father's house are many mansions: if *it were* not *so*, I would have told you. I go to prepare a place for you." John 14:2

We have read this scripture many times, and we know and understand that this is not talking about rooms, or "mansions", the word is speaking about levels of dwelling. In our Father's "house" are many levels; many dimensions. As you go up to a new floor in the house, the word becomes new to you, all over again. You can hear and understand levels of truth that you were not able to before, because you did not have the ears to hear[1] at that time. This is what a walk with God is. We continue to move up in the Father's house, and with each new floor that you come to, one of the benefits is having a new set eyes and new set of ears to hear the word on a level that you were not able to previously.

Understand - there is a change happening within God's people. I'm not isolating it to one or two, but I believe it is a provision that is opening up to the sons as God begins to usher them into a deeper level in His presence. With this, comes a greater awareness of His inner working within you. At times you can feel like you are half here, and half not here, because something of God's spirit is taking hold within you. You are becoming aware of His presence, you are becoming aware of the "dunamis" of His spirit within you .... and yet you still have a consciousness that is on this level. It can sound weird, but this transition into sonship is nothing like anyone can possibly imagine.

We are walking with one foot[2] in the spirit, and one foot in the natural, and this transition is continuing to deepen. We are taking a big leap forward in what God is bringing forth; be expecting a lot. I know that over the next period of time there is a great possibility of some tremendous changes, and we are holding everything before the Lord to see what is going to unfold.

A word came a few months ago: "Keep speaking the word." The admonition continues to come; keep speaking the word, keep framing the judgment, keep creating. The directive for many years has been: "You will prevail by the word." And in the book of Revelation the Word is; "they prevailed[3] by the word of their testimony and the blood of the Lamb." We are saying pretty much the same thing.

The direction for the last six or seven years has been that there is no answer for the sons on this level. God will continue to throw monkey wrenches into their system, and they will not find an answer on this level. **But**, *the answer will come as they continue to speak the word and create it.*

We all know that God has a unique way of driving the sons into His presence on a deeper level. He will put you in a corner, and there is no way out, but up. He has a way of squeezing the sons, stretching them, to grow and mature quickly. It has a great deal to do with speaking the word, because the word is already resident within the sons.

> **"Whose voice then shook the earth: but now he hath promised, saying, Yet once more I shake not the earth only, but also heaven." Hebrews 12:26**

I know that we have entered the timeline of the judgments of God, and I know that at this point, we really do not understand it. We are experiencing this timeline; we sense it, but we have not really grasped yet what is coming. What is coming, *and it is here now,* is a shaking of both the heavens and the earth. We are living in the book of Hebrews, as God commences to ramp up the violent shaking in the earth.

I know that God's sons have gone through the deep dealings and preparation over the last several years. What is unique about this window of time that we are in, is that this is the time of His deep appearing in His sons. And with this appearing comes a deep, and violent release of judgment. I know that the judgments have been released; they are already in motion, but they are first happening in the plane of spirit.

We have come to another plane of consciousness, and you are hearing on another level. You may not be able to put all the pieces together yet, but you clearly know that your spirit is hearing the word and the word is: the judgments are done. They are completed and they are released, and with this comes a deep sense of finality.

Imagine standing on the shore of the ocean. You know a tsunami is coming, a 100 foot tsunami, and that nothing is going to stop it. It is coming like a freight train. What will happen? Devastation on an unparalleled level, yet for God's sons, that Tsunami will just pass over them. I have seen this, a number of times. The tidal wave represents judgment, but it does not come nigh[4] the sons. But, when it hits landfall, the earth will be decimated.

There is something about this window of time that has taken on a little different complexion. The difference is that a finality of judgment has been released.

> **"and they cried out with a loud voice, saying, How long, O Lord, holy and true, will You refrain from judging and avenging our blood on those who dwell on the earth?" Revelation 6:10**

We read in the book of Revelation about the prayers of the saints; "How long, O Lord, before You avenge Your servants?" God has heard, and the prophecies and the word spoken have released the flow of judgment. It is coming now. We have not seen it yet, but it is like that tsunami; it is barreling down upon the face of the earth and it is coming very quickly.

This is the sense that we feel during this window of time, as we have just left the elections in the United States, which seem to line up with a lot of other issues in the earth right now; whether they are global economics, or the governments of this world. The dominoes are in play right now; all we need to see is the first domino fall. The sons of Satan and the Nephilim are doing everything in their power to maintain control. What they do not know is that they no longer have any control. The Father's plan is in full motion.

They do not realize that at this point that they have utterly lost control. I believe they sense it, and some of the signs of it can be seen even now. They definitely have lost control. The more the satanic world becomes aware of this, the more they are going to turn loose a violence in the earth that we have not seen before. Violence is filling the earth on an unprecedented scale, and on every level.

> **"Now the earth was corrupt in the sight of God, and the earth was filled with violence." Genesis 6:11**

The scripture speaks about the earth experiencing the judgments. What happens? The people learn righteousness. I know there have been prophecies and aspects in the word which speak about a violence filling up the whole earth. Do not misread the signs, it is happening, full blown, on every level now, and you have not seen anything yet!

We do not know how wicked the earth had become in the times of Sodom and Gomorrah, prior to the judgments of God. But that is the analogy, and we are here. There is no question that what is filling the earth right now is an energy, a vibration, if you will, of hate and violence on a scale we have never seen. This was the word which came one year ago ..... ***"you will see released in the earth plane of consciousness - a negative and very dark energy - that will pervade the entire earth. No one is immune, unless they are walking with God".***

You can call this a canopy of spirit that has begun to affect everyone that walks the face of the earth. We see the violence rising; it is increasing every day. I know, without question, that we are headed into a conclusion or wrap up in this age.

Anne and I were talking about the number nine recently as God began to speak to Anne about the timeline that we are in. We are in a countdown and if you have studied numerology, nine is the number of judgment, and it is also the number of finality.

There is something that is happening right now, concerning the finality of God's dealings with man. Delay has come to an end. There is no longer going to be a delay.

> **"Therefore be patient, brethren, until the coming of the Lord. The farmer waits for the precious produce of the soil, being patient about it, until it gets the early and late rains." James 5:7**

We have seen what we would call the longsuffering of the Father, waiting for the precious fruit of the earth *to come to maturity.* What has appeared as a "delay", has been more about the longsuffering of the Father, and His patience. But that window of time is over. It is closed.

The judgments that are coming will affect both the just and the unjust alike. The only insurance is that you have submitted deeply to the work of the cross in your life. Judgment is not a respecter of persons, as we have said recently. What is coming now is going to judge the just[5] and the unjust alike. I believe that the positioning of the sons is completed; therefore that which is coming will not come nigh[4] the sons, because the preparation has been done deep enough.

There is a tremendous potential of many things that can happen in this window of time, and I know that we are in an appearing, in the midst of all of this, which is happening within the sons. I also know that we are not that aware of it, but I believe that is going to change soon. We are going to become more aware of what is happening within us, because there is a deep stirring that is happening ... *deep changes are coming.* It has been released; the changes are in motion.

Do not be surprised at the experiences that will come to you over the next period of time—days and weeks—whatever, because it is something that is going to change us on a level that we have never experienced.

We are travailing to get into the depth of what God is releasing right now, within the spirits of His sons. A deep birthing of the sons is happening.

We acknowledge, Father, the deep working and the deep appearing that is happening. A deep transformation is happening within your sons, while the steamroller of judgment is coming upon this age. Nothing will side step this steamroller, it will take everything out in its wake.

Scriptures NASB

[1] Mark 4:22-23
[22]For everything hidden is meant to be revealed, and everything concealed is meant to be brought to light. [23]If anyone has ears to hear, let him hear."

Or [1] John 16:12
"I have many more things to say to you, but you cannot bear them now.

[2] Revelation 10:5
Then the angel whom I saw standing on the sea and on the land lifted up his right hand to heaven,

[3] Revelation 12:11
"And they overcame him because of the blood of the Lamb and because of the word of their testimony, and they did not love their life even when faced with death.

[4] Psalm 91;7
A thousand may fall at your side, ten thousand at your right hand, but it will not come near you.

5 Matthew 5:45
so that you may be sons of your Father who is in heaven; for He causes His sun to rise on the evil and the good, and sends rain on the righteous and the unrighteous.

Chapter 7

The Approaching Storm

It would be good to take a look at what is happening right now in the earth, and what appears to be lining up. I will present to you a few things to pray about and look to the Lord about concerning this timeline.

Over the years we have been shown a number of events that will come to pass during this period of time that we have entered into. What we have not known is exactly at what point all of these "end-time" events will unfold. We do know, however, that they are going to unfold in conjunction with the manifesting[1] of the sons of God. In many ways they go hand-in-hand and they are tied into the judgments that are coming forth, and will come forth, concerning the realm of spirit that has been so set against the Father's plan. And that plan concerns the release of the manifested sons of God.

I know that some of the events that we see unfolding have a timeline anywhere from the next 60 days upwards to the next ten or twelve months. Like a puzzle, the Father's plan will seamlessly fit together, even if the details are still vague.

We have seen America going to war, and with the present rhetoric, that is not too hard to imagine. We have seen naval ships, as they leave anchor in the Hawaiian Islands, going out to battle. We have seen this coming for some time.

We have seen the deployment of massive amounts of troops in California, itself. Whether a defense mechanism or whether that has to do with civil unrest, I am not exactly sure.

For some time now we have seen, and have known, that America, as well as the world, is on a headlong collision course with an economic upheaval on a scale that we have never witnessed in our lifetime.

A number of times the Lord has cautioned us concerning what was coming for the U.S. dollar. We are going to hit a point where the dollar will not be worth the paper that it is printed on. The dollar, and specifically our banking system, as you may know, is part of what is called a "fiat system". When banks were first created, they were a part of a monetary system based on gold and silver. There was a commonality of financial exchange within countries that was based on the exchange of gold. Later, gold was held in vaults, and certificates were issued representing the gold held in storage. This was the method of currency exchange, hundreds of years ago.

However, what has evolved in the last hundred years, since World War I, has been a banking system and a federal reserve built upon a policy of just printing money with no gold or no silver backing behind it. All of the governments of this world are based upon this system of fiat money, where no real gold or value is behind the currency issued.

There are no currencies in this world presently that are backed by anything except the law that was passed stating that these printed dollars must be acknowledged and utilized in merchant trade. In short; *our financial system is based on nothing.* There is nothing behind it except the law that requires the holder of the note to acknowledge it as legal tender.

We are quickly facing a point where all of this is going to implode, without question. I have seen where the time is coming that people will wallpaper the walls with money, because it will be absolutely worthless. It is quickly coming, and if you follow current events, you can see the writing on the wall. The governments and financial institutions of this age have been putting band-aides on the system for so long, barely holding it up, and it is only going to hold so long before it completely unravels. We are at that point. We are at the point where the system, as we have known it, is going to unravel.

> **"And the fourth kingdom shall be strong as iron: forasmuch as iron breaketh in pieces and subdueth all *things*: and as iron that breaketh all these, shall it break in pieces and bruise.**
>
> **And whereas thou sawest the feet and toes, part of potters' clay, and part of iron, the kingdom shall be divided; but there shall be in it of the strength of the iron, forasmuch as thou sawest the iron mixed with miry clay.**

And *as* the toes of the feet *were* part of iron, and part of clay, *so* the kingdom shall be partly strong, and partly broken.

And whereas thou sawest iron mixed with miry clay, they shall mingle themselves with the seed of men: but they shall not cleave one to another, even as iron is not mixed with clay.

And in the days of these kings shall the God of heaven set up a kingdom, which shall never be destroyed: and the kingdom shall not be left to other people, *but* it shall break in pieces and consume all these kingdoms, and it shall stand for ever.

Forasmuch as thou sawest that the stone was cut out of the mountain without hands, and that it brake in pieces the iron, the brass, the clay, the silver, and the gold; the great God hath made known to the king what shall come to pass hereafter: and the dream *is* certain, and the interpretation thereof sure." Daniel 2:40-45 KJV

What is coming has been foretold in the book of Daniel. The last image, described in Daniel 2, will be destroyed by the stone cut out of the mountain. We will cover this further, in just a minute.

We are in a very precarious timeline for the earth. We have seen major geophysical events on the horizon. In recent appearings, over the last couple of months, it was conveyed that the earthquakes that are going to be hitting the West Coast and the Midwest, are coming fairly soon. You can say, "What timeline does that mean?" My best guess is sometime in the next 12 months.

All of this is on the horizon. We are in this window of accelerated judgment, if you will, and upheaval, and the imploding literally of a culture and way of life that we have known.

It will be interesting to see how the global Nephilim overlords, you might say, will continue to try to maintain some sort of order that does not allow things to descend beyond what they can control. All of this is just what we see on one level; the level of the natural plane.

It is easy to get caught up in the signs of the times and what is happening, or the satanic order of the global elite, that is gaining more and more presence in the earth. However, to those who have eyes to see, the real action is happening on another level, the level just beyond sight: the realm of the spirit.

We would be missing it, big time, if we stop at this level of discernment and say, "Okay, this is what is happening. We have got to pray against this battle, we have got to pray against this warfare; you know, pray for America and what not." That is probably what the religious community is going to be doing, if they have not already been in this mode. But their intercession will fall short, because they really have no understanding on what is truly happening.

We are walking out the last part of the vision of Daniel concerning the image that he was shown.

> **"You continued looking until a stone was cut out without hands, and it struck the statue on its feet of iron and clay and crushed them." Daniel 2:34**

The stone cut out of the mountain hits the image at its feet and it implodes. That last kingdom represents the governments and kingdoms of this present age, and they are comprised of clay and iron. The clay and iron, as we know, represents the attempt of the satanic seed to completely infiltrate and merge within the seed of man. However, as the prophecy goes, the clay and iron do not mix. And the stone cut out of the mountain? *The sons.*

We have been in this for a good long season, and some may say, "Oh, well you're missing it, Edward. That was fulfilled hundreds of years ago. We have had the Medes, the Persians, the Romans and you can always say, 'Well it was this one, or that one.'" Maybe there was a partial fulfillment at one time of this vision, but it would have only been the partial[2], for this vision speaks of the days to which we have come. So much of what Daniel was shown, throughout his life, pertained to days far in the future, culminating in the timeline where he is once again raised up to enter into his inheritance. We are here, now.

The stone, cut out of the mountain, are the sons that God is raising up. They have hit the image, and are hitting the image, even now. I know the prayers and prophesies are continuing to expose the darkness behind closed doors. The whole satanic system, that has controlled, manipulated, and driven this world, is being up-ended.

The kingdom, which is coming forth, will not be built upon that which is passing away. God is bringing this age down, and the kingdom of God is being established on an entirely new level. It is a whole new thing that God is doing.

We are in the time of judgment. It is happening, and it is moving very quickly. For those who do not have understanding it will all seem to be about what is happening in the earth; the politics and the nations in a furor. There is a great deal to be concerned about, if you do not have an eye to see. The prevalent energy in the world, more and more, will be focused on the illusion of what is being propagated.

All of this chaos is happening simultaneously with the releasing of the sons of God. And it is for this time that you have been brought forth. The difficulty has been that we have had to pave this road for the first time. Kingdom pioneers, if you will, carving out a map for many to follow.

As we have said, there is no signpost in the road that tells you what to expect, or what to do, as you reach various intervals in the path. We just know that we are in the time of God releasing the sons. Sometimes it may feel like everything goes the opposite way before the reality really happens and breaks forth. But the Lord is faithful, and He is leading His army, one step at a time.

The travail of all creation will become progressively more and more evident. Earthquakes and geo-physical changes are coming, but they are all part of the travail that is happening right now. Look around you. What do you see? Chaos, war, economic upheaval? No, you see a world in travail[3], a travail that will bring to birth the sons, and a new kingdom upon this earth. That is the truth.

As this timeline intensifies and deepens, the flip side of these developments are like a yin/yang act of balancing, for with the judgments come the release of the sons.

So, we are in the midst of a release, a deep transformational release, and it can be very difficult at first to discern. It is almost like you don't quite have your footing, you don't quite know what is coming through. Bear in mind the accuser[4] of the brethren is always there to accuse you, to put you down, to come in the back door and restrain your manifestation. It's just what he does.

God has to do this. God has to finish it. He began this and He is working in us both to will and to do of His good pleasure[5], but He has to complete it. We cannot complete this. We can't even finish the race, holding the baton on this last leg of the race, without His grace and enabling.

Be so careful not to draw any conclusion[6] on the events going on around you, whether they are events that we do not have direct involvement with, or the events that we are intrinsically involved with and face every day.

We have to be so careful not to draw a conclusion by what our emotions or senses feel, because it is all part of the illusion. We stand upon the word that, "Faithful[7] is He who has begun a good work, that He shall complete it - ***within you*** - unto the day of Christ." That is a promise.

You may fall on your face seventy times seven, a hundred and seventy times seven, but the only demand that He has made of us is to just stay open. "We are open, Lord." We are reaching in, the best we can, while we finish going through the work of the cross[8].

A word came several years ago concerning this transition into resurrection life: **"You will barely remember what it was like to have lived in the battle, the oppression, and the restraint, that you have lived under all those years."** I am looking for that. This is one of the promises He spoke as we move into this change.

No one is going to pat anyone else on the back and say; "You did a good job; you did it." We didn't do it. The only way this process completes is that He has done it. He has done it through us and within us. In spite of us!

Our hearts are open; we lay ourselves down, we tie ourselves to the horns of the altar. We say, "Lord, our hearts cry is to finish the race, and to please you."

This is His program. It is His deal. It is His calling upon us. We say, "Lord, be it done unto me according to Your word[9]." That was Mary's cry. "Lord, just be it done unto me according to Your word." That's all we have to say.

Not by might[10] nor by power but by Your spirit within us. Complete, Lord, the great thing that You are doing within Your sons.

Complete it now. Finish it, Lord. None of us are worthy. None of us are capable. None of us have the strength in ourselves to do this." But it was never about any of that. It was always about Your faithfulness to Your word.

And when the man that had the line in his hand went forth eastward, he measured a thousand cubits, and he brought me through the waters; the waters *were* to the ankles.

Again he measured a thousand, and brought me through the waters; the waters *were* to the knees. Again he measured a thousand, and brought me through; the waters *were* to the loins.

Afterward he measured a thousand; *and it was* a river that I could not pass over: for the waters were risen, waters to swim in, a river that could not be passed over. Ezekiel 47:3-5

We are in this window of time that I have seen coming for ten or fifteen years. Many of you, as well, have seen this coming. We are smack dab in it. We are into the changes up to our ankles, up to our knees, and it is going to get real interesting. The more interesting it gets, the greater the release will be that is coming to us, because they are tied together: judgment and release.

We thank You, Lord, that even though in many ways the mantle[11] rests upon our shoulders, it's really resting upon You, Lord, it's resting upon You to see this completed. We stay the course, Lord. We keep the focus. We keep pushing and pursuing, because it is time now for the changes; the physical changes, to accelerate.

Imagine what it must have been like for the disciples, as they waited in the upper room[12]. So many were gathered together after Christ's ascension, and they waited. They had no idea what was going to happen. They didn't know what to expect. There was nothing they could read which said, "Okay, this is what is going to happen." They just waited before the Lord, in intercession and prayer, and God brought the baptism[13] of the Holy Spirit and a change that began a whole new dispensation of His dealings with man.

We are looking at something that is going to change everything. It is going to change the playing field of everything that we have ever known. It is going to bring in a level of the kingdom that has never been here before. This is where we are.

As this transition completes, we will walk as Christ, who had access to both realms; the spirit realm and the natural plane. We must realize that resurrection life will be a life in the spirit, but also a life in the natural plane. You will be able to move and maneuver in both worlds, simultaneously, but without any vulnerability. A new level of life, or life change, is coming to the sons, and we are right on track.

Scriptures (NASB)

[1] Romans 8:19
For the anxious longing of the creation waits eagerly for the revealing of the sons of God.

[2] 1 Corinthians 13:10
but when the perfect comes, the partial will be done away.

[3] Galatians 4:19
My children, with whom I am again in labor until Christ is formed in you—

[4] Revelation 12:10
Then I heard a loud voice in heaven, saying, "Now the salvation, and the power, and the kingdom of our God and the authority of His Christ have come, for the accuser of our brethren has been thrown down, he who accuses them before our God day and night.

[5] Philippians 2:13
for it is God who is at work in you, both to will and to work for His good pleasure.

[6] Isaiah 11:3
And He will delight in the fear of the LORD, And He will not judge by what His eyes see, Nor make a decision by what His ears hear;

[7] 1 Thessalonians 5:24
Faithful is He who calls you, and He also will bring it to pass.

[8] Philippians 2:8
Being found in appearance as a man, He humbled Himself by becoming obedient to the point of death, even death on a cross.

[9] Luke 1:38
And Mary said, "Behold, the bondslave of the Lord; may it be done to me according to your word." And the angel departed from her.

[10] Zechariah 4:6
Then he said to me, "This is the word of the LORD to Zerubbabel saying, 'Not by might nor by power, but by My Spirit,' says the LORD of hosts.

[11] 2 Kings 2:14
He took the mantle of Elijah that fell from him and struck the waters and said, "Where is the LORD, the God of Elijah?" And when he also had struck the waters, they were divided here and there; and Elisha crossed over.

[12] Acts 1:4
Gathering them together, He commanded them not to leave Jerusalem, but to wait for what the Father had promised, "Which," He said, "you heard of from Me;

[13] Acts 2:2-4
2Suddenly a sound like a mighty rushing wind came from heaven and filled the whole house where they were sitting. 3They saw tongues like flames of a fire that separated and came to rest on each of them. 4And they were all filled with the Holy Spirit and began to speak in other tongues as the Spirit enabled them....

Notes

Chapter 8

Countdown

It is an interesting position where God has the sons at this time. As much as we look around, we do not see much awareness of what is really transpiring.

A lot of people are getting dreams and visions about catastrophes and geo-physical events that are coming for the West Coast and the Midwest. And I do believe that the Lord does bring revelation; visions, and dreams, to warn His people, based on the level of their spiritual growth at the time. In spite of this, however, there has been really no awareness[1] of what is happening in the earth.

You can get caught up in this "end-time disaster scenario" where you are out there preparing and praying, "Oh God, save America." But that, which is apparent, which can be seen with the eye, is not at all what is truly transpiring.

You can read the scriptures all day long, and you can see what is prophesied concerning the coming judgments, and find it very interesting. But the reality is that we are walking in these days right now. We have hit timeline after timeline, within the book of Revelation, that we are walking out.

What is really happening?

It is all about Christ ruling and reigning.

Take a look at the following scriptures; they paint a very vivid picture.

> **"For He must reign until He has put all His enemies under His feet." 1 Corinthians 15:25**

> **"Who has heard such a thing? Who has seen such things? Can a land be born in one day? Can a nation be**

brought forth all at once? As soon as Zion travailed, she also brought forth her sons." Isaiah 66:8

"You have made them to be a kingdom and priests to our God; and they will reign upon the earth." Revelation 5:10

"But you are A CHOSEN RACE, A royal PRIESTHOOD, A HOLY NATION, A PEOPLE FOR God's OWN POSSESSION, so that you may proclaim the excellencies of Him who has called you out of darkness into His marvelous light;" 1st Peter 2:9

It is about the sons coming to birth. It is about the ruling and reigning of the kings and priests. It is about the chosen royal priesthood that God is raising up. It is about the manifestation of the sons of God, and Romans 8. **This is what is happening.**

People have no clue. And this includes the "prophets" and ministries in most of the churches. I am not saying that there are not a few who see, but by and large, what is out there is "blind, leaders of the blind[2]."

Look at the book of Revelation, chapter 8, or Daniel, chapter 2: "This is happening now". It can sound like such an arrogant statement. Who are you to make such a profound statement; just a voice[3] in the wilderness, making straight the path of the Lord.

I am not here to judge anyone, but the problem is that people don't see the whole picture. It is like looking at an elephant. The elephant is a large animal, and based upon where you view him, could give you a different description of what the elephant is. Similar to how you see the moving of God during this time. You see one part of the elephant and you say, "This is what God is doing." Someone else sees another part of the elephant and says, "No, this is what God is doing." God's people are not seeing the time of their visitation.

"to whom God willed to make known what is the riches of the glory of this mystery among the Gentiles, which is Christ in you, the hope of glory." Colossians 1:27

God's sons are beginning to experience the reality of *Christ[4] in you* on a whole different level. The reality of the indwelling of the godhead, is happening. How does the scripture go? "And I will be their God and they will be My people, ... My sons and My daughters[5]." That has always been the promise.

> **"Wherefore come out from among them, and be ye separate, saith the Lord, and touch not the unclean *thing*; and I will receive you, and will be a Father unto you, and ye shall be my sons and daughters, saith the Lord Almighty." 2 Corinthians 6:17-18**

What is the seal of sonship?

Is it the fact that you have a revelation of it? No, the seal of sonship is the transformation of your body. Call it immortality, resurrection life, from a worm to a butterfly; in any event it is a whole new thing. Isaiah prophesied it well:

> **"Behold I will do something new ... *a whole new thing, a whole new creation* ... will you be aware?" Isaiah 43:19**

God's plan is written all throughout the word, yet people do not see it. They have not recognized that the plan of God has been to redeem a people unto Himself; a people that will become *(and we are at the end of this phase)* the essence and presence of God in the earth.

We are at the end of this process. The change is imminent. Whether our carnal minds can grasp this or not, it does not matter. You have been sent and prepared, to experience this metamorphosis.

It is time to cash in on your inheritance.

The inter-penetration of God in man, (within you), is happening. You have been in a protracted state of being "taken over" for a long time now. This is not a new thing, but you are coming to a point of completion now. This is why the work of the cross has always been with you.

> **"But who can endure the day of His coming? And who can stand when He appears? For He is like a refiner's fire and like fullers' soap." Malachi 3:2**

How does Malachi go? "Who can stand when He appears[6]? He is like a refiner's fire..." What has been happening to you in your walk with God over these last many years? It could be one year or it could be twenty, or it could be forty. **His appearing**. He has been appearing to you consistently, and His appearing has been the fire.

You have been embracing and living a life in the fire. There has not been a day—if you are truly chosen as a son, that you have not been living in the fire. Something deep is happening, and we are just beginning to awaken and realize that something has changed within the makeup of our being.

We have talked about the judgments that God is bringing in the earth. First, however, He has been baptizing the sons in the judgments that are to come. Who experiences the judgments[7] of God first? The sons. Before it happens to the world, it happens within the sons. But we are at the end of this process, and the judgments are now coming forth in the earth, on a unprecedented scale.

What has the fire burned off? The dross; that you might be able to stand in His presence, dressed in white robes.

God is not a respecter[8] of persons, for He judges the just and the unjust alike. Just make sure the work has been done within you.

It has been about five years since the Lord brought a word that He was standing in intercession before the Father. The precious fruit of the earth was not yet ready. Had the Father moved in the judgments for this age back then, it would have taken a lot of the sons. It is the word which judges, and if you are in the path of the judgment, it will catch you too. This is why the dealings of God and the fire of God in your life have had to be so thorough.

The judgments, which are coming right now, are already established. They are already done. They are already in motion.

We need to understand the dynamics of the judgments, for God's sons are His mouthpiece in the earth. The sons have already begun to move into the authority of the kings and priests, and as such, the word they speak continues to frame the last chapters for the earth.

Reading from Daniel, chapter 2:

> **"There will be a fourth kingdom as strong as iron; inasmuch as iron crushes and shatters all things, so, like iron it breaks in pieces, it will crush and break all these. In that you saw the feet and toes, partly of potter's clay and partly of iron, there will be a divided kingdom; but it will have in it the toughness of iron, inasmuch as you saw the iron mixed with common clay.**

As the toes of the feet were partly of iron and partly of pottery, so the kingdom will be strong and part of it brittle. And in that you saw the iron mixed with common clay, they will combine with one another in the seed of men; but they will not adhere to one another, even as iron does not combine with pottery.

In the days of those kings the God of heaven will set up a kingdom which will never be destroyed, and that kingdom will not be left for another; it will crush and put an end to all these kingdoms, but it itself will endure forever. Inasmuch as you saw that a stone was cut out of the mountain without hands and crushed the iron, the bronze, clay, silver and gold." Daniel 2:40-45

We have spoken about this last kingdom in Daniel's vision, and one thing that we need to understand is that we are walking this out presently. This last kingdom is in the throws and upheaval of coming down. Perhaps you have felt the energy in the spirit shifting constantly; it is because this last kingdom is being brought down. It is being brought down right now as we speak.

The unfolding judgments are predicated upon the word of authority that must continue to be spoken right now. God has put upon the sons a mantle[9]. It is a mantle of authority. It is a mantle of the word.

It is no coincidence that the nations of the world are being turned upside[10] down at this time. The world is in chaos. We have never seen this level of chaos. The ability, in the satanic camp to communicate, literally doesn't exist. The bankers are having a heck of a time communicating amongst themselves. The global elitists, as some would call them, (*the Nephilim, the seed of Satan*) in the earth, are in a state of dis-array.

We must get out of any conditioning that puts fulfillment in the future. We are in the time of fulfillment and we continue to stay open. We cannot make the mistake in judging by what our eyes see, for God is doing something entirely new. What we are seeing unfold, right before our eyes, is the culmination of God creating a whole new creation; the sons of God.

There is no roadmap; you are blazing the trail. The ministry of the kings and priests, the true rulers of this age, is unfolding right now.

Not when the ascension, so to speak is complete, but right now – in real time. If you haven't yet begun to wield the authority, then do so. Change how you have seen yourself. The authority of this age will not be found in the rulers who are passing away, the authority is found in the sons who are taking their place.

We are not waiting for that time when we appear before Him and He puts a crown on our head, to begin to function as the kings and priests[11] of this age. We are still coming into an awareness of who we are, and that is okay.

The kings and priests are here now. **<u>You</u>**. Those that God has sent into the earth for the time of final change and transformation are here now. The stage is set and being set, and we must realize the unique part that each one brings to the table. The sons of God, the body of Christ, are not complete without each member functioning as he or she have been sent to do. He has been waiting for us to believe what He has spoken over us, and to just do it.

That which is happening in the earth right now is happening because a word has been spoken - and is being spoken. It is a word of judgment and a word of dominion, and discernment has been coming more and more to reveal the enemy behind closed doors. The sons of God are the major players in this. We are the anchor in this race. We are the mojo ministry, if you want to call it that.

As long as Satan can keep you doubting, or believing that your entrance into sonship will yet come at some point in the future, then he will have succeeded in keeping you "on-hold". In spite of what you see, in spite of what you feel, in spite of what your emotions are saying, you are a king and a priest before God.

Upon your spirit He has put a mantle, a mantle[9] to bring in the kingdom. It is a mantle of authority to speak the word. You are a chosen vessel through which the power, authority and dominion of Christ does flow. This is how it works.

Has there been a carefulness on the part of the sons to move carefully and not miss His leading? Absolutely! But at some point, hesitation to move, becomes unbelief. Waiting for confirmation after confirmation can easily become unbelief when the Spirit within is bearing witness.

I recall a vision which came about four or five years ago. It had to do with the abject arrogance that was on the satanic seed; the Nephilim, the principalities, and the fallen angels. I saw a whole group of these ancient spirits, gathered in mid-heaven. I could see the Earth below as these spirits were discussing something of importance. Then, a voice came from behind me and I heard the Father as He addressed them. He looked at them and said, "You thought that I would never bring judgment." They were shocked, these ancient evil angelic entities of old, for they truly believed that the Father would never bring judgment upon them.

This is the time that we are in. A wrap up, a finality of judgment, and it is coming now. We are in a countdown. This countdown is short, very short. I am not even going to put months or days or weeks upon this timeline. This countdown is tied into the word of authority that is being spoken through the mouths of the sons, as they speak the judgments of God into the earth.

We are declaring an absolute end to the control and manipulation of the satanic seed in the earth; to that which has been going on behind closed doors, and to the manipulation of mankind that has been going on. The satanic seed is looking for the extinction of the human race. What they do not realize is that we will see an "extinction", oh yes, but it will be an extinction of the satanic presence in the earth.

Every day the satanic seed start with marching orders, only it has become progressively more and more difficult for them to communicate amongst themselves with understanding. Even the ability to grasp, is breaking down in the rank and file of those evil entities that dwell in the spirit. Needless to say, this has had a long-range effect on the human channels that exist: the bankers, the globalists, the elitists, the Nephilim, the seed of Satan, and the sons of Satan - and all of them.

Understand, it all shakes down from the realm of spirit. You deal with the spirit realm first, and that will deal with the natural plane. Those that dwell on the plane of the natural get their "mojo" from the spirit realm. Everything first[12] comes from the realm of spirit. Even the sons, themselves, do not find their solutions on this plane. The answers all come from the realm of spirit. This is why the authority is being committed to the sons; because what must be done, will not be done by power, it will be done by Christ's authority. This is what is shaking[13] the heavens.

"And His voice shook the earth then, but now He has promised, saying, "YET ONCE MORE I WILL SHAKE NOT ONLY THE EARTH, BUT ALSO THE HEAVEN." Hebrews 12:26

We are in this window. Now, more than ever, it is expedient that we stay on our face and keep speaking the word. Keep speaking the word. This word is part of that stone[14] cut out of the mountain. The Word is hitting the feet of that image, over and over.

It is like the story in 2 Kings 13. Elisha told the king to take the arrows[15] and beat them not once. And the king didn't have enough faith and only beat the arrows a couple of times. Elisha said, "Boy, you missed it, because you are only going to have victory a couple of times."

It is the same thing for the sons. In our hands we hold the arrows. What does it mean to beat the arrows? Well it doesn't mean going before God and placating Him; "Oh God, hear my prayer," and pray, pray, pray. No. To beat the arrows means you stand as a son and you keep speaking the word. And you keep speaking the word.

God is going to bring the kingdoms of this world down. If America is part of that, then fine. People get so caught up in praying over their concepts, without really understanding what the Father is doing.

The word is hitting the image at the feet[14] ... and it is beginning to break. The image has not been fully pulverized yet, but we are seeing cracks in the image. Things are shaking up a lot, but we are not quite there yet.

When you look at the kingdoms of this world, you realize they are running around with Band-Aids and gauze trying to hold things together. The rulers of this present age are frantically trying to cover their backside as God begins to bring them down. The decisiveness of what is happening is going to be very complete. When God finishes judging the media, you will know it.

God is not going to let anything stand of the evil and iniquity that dwell in the earth. All of it is coming down. It is going to be the most horrific thing this earth has ever seen, and we are not even talking about the geo-physical events that are coming. We have seen what is coming over the next period of time, and it does not look good; not for those who are not walking with God.

> **"...that the creation itself will be set free from its bondage to decay and brought into the glorious freedom of the children of God. We know that the whole creation has been groaning together in the pains of childbirth until the present time." Romans 8:21-22**

What we are talking about is another layer of God's judgments in the earth. But it is more than that, for it is the travail of all creation[16]. It can be difficult to fathom how alive and viable creation is, and what creation is. All of creation is in travail right now with the sons. There is a consciousness to everything that God has created. We are speaking of Romans 8; all of creation, both seen and unseen, are in travail. For what? - the full birthing and manifestation of the Sons of God, through whom their release and deliverance will come.

Sometimes the signs of this are so strong - you can get up in the morning and feel like you are pregnant. Woman who have been through the birthing process know what it is like when you start having these aches and pains in your back, or in your sciatica. And you're just like, "Oh my gosh. What's going on?" Simple, you are pregnant. You are giving birth.

We are pregnant. We are giving birth to the kingdom. Like everything, our "reality" is constantly being re-defined. And that was always the promise from the Lord; as we let go of our paradigms of limitation, He would re-define to us what is real and what is not.

> **"When the Lamb broke the seventh seal there was silence in heaven. 2And I saw the seven angels who stood before God and seven trumpets were given to them. 3Another angel came and stood at the altar holding a golden sensor and much incense was given to him so that he might add to it the prayers of the saints on the golden altar which is before the throne."**

This is so much happening; so much happening.

> **"And the smoke of the incense with the prayers of the saints went up before God out of the angel's hand. And the angel took the censor and filled it with the fire of the altar and threw it to the earth. And there followed**

peals of thunder and sounds and flashes of lightening and earthquake." Revelation 8:1-5

Revelation goes on to talk about the things that happen with this as far as the levels of judgment that began to unfold. It says ***The first sounded and there came hail and fire mixed with blood and they were thrown to the earth and a third of the earth was burned up*** (Revelation 8:7). And a lot of people can go back and say, "Revelation 8 already happened. I can give you a year and a date," and so on and so forth. That could very well be true, on one level, but what we are looking at is the fulfillment on a spiritual level of something that has not yet happened.

And the second angel sounded something like a great mountain burning with fire was thrown into the sea and a third of the sea became blood. Revelation 8:8

And a third of the creatures which were in the sea and had life died. And a third of the ships were destroyed. And then you know the third angel sounded and a great star fell from heaven burning like a torch. And it fell on a third of the rivers and the springs of waters. And the name of the stars called wormwood and a third of the waters became wormwood and many men died from the waters because they were made bitter. Revelation 8:9-11

There are so many areas of symbolism in these scriptures. If you are looking for a third of the waters of the world, literally, to become wormwood, I think you would be missing it. This has to do with something that is unfolding in the spirit.

Further back in the book of Revelation, it talks about how the devil goes after the woman who gave birth to the child and out of his mouth spewed forth a torrent, a flood, of deception, lies, and illusion[17].

What is happening in the earth is complex and layered over several realities, if you will. You have a layer of illusion and deception that is constantly being propagated by the news media and TV, sending into the Earth a constant stream of consciousness, based on the lie. This is one reason it is vitally important that you speak the word, and we are not talking about prayer. That is not what God is asking for.

He is asking for the sons to be to speak[18] the word, because the word spoken in the spirit is what counteracts the flood of deception and lies that is spewing out of the mouth of the dragon through millions and millions of people. The end goal of this flood of darkness ... to bring a conditioning and a dullness to the people of the earth, and specifically, to the sons He is bringing forth. People seem to walk about in a stupor, because they do not have an ear to hear. This is just one level of reality flowing into the earth. On a higher vibration or frequency, can be found the word of God, emanating, like pure energy. The word keeps resounding ***..... "come out of her My people[19]".***

Revelation, chapter ten, hits a point where it says,

> **"the angel whom I saw standing on the sea and on the land lifted up his right hand to heaven, 6and swore by Him who lives forever and ever who created heaven and the things within it and the earth and the sea and things within it that there will be delay no longer, 7but in the days of the voice of the seventh angel, when he is about to sound, then the mystery of God is finished, as He preached to His servants the prophets." Revelation 10:5-7**

We are in the days of seventh angel. But you know that. And this is why we are being driven and pushed to speak the word, because we are in a crucial time. God is tearing down the evil and every kingdom that has withstood His kingdom. They are coming down.

Look at Revelations 10:7, it says: ***"the mystery of God is finished". "The mystery of God is finished[20]."*** To me that is more than Christ in you, the hope of glory. This speaks of the resurrected Christ, in you, and with that the corresponding completion of the work of redemption; the glorification of your body.

You are the mystery[4] of God. The angels look on, and it is hard for them to fathom. The satanic world looks on, and they cannot fathom, nor understand, how, or why, God would take these humble earthen creatures - in some ways the lowest order of creation - and bring forth a whole new creation; the sons of God.

> **"to whom God willed to make known what is the riches of the glory of this mystery among the Gentiles, which is Christ in you, the hope of glory." Colossians 1:27**

Understand, these principalities and powers, these angels who have existed for eons of time and stood in great places in the presence of the Father, cannot fathom how the Father would take something so loathsome (to them) and put them above everything. So great are they, in their own eyes, and they look down at this lowly creation, and they can't fathom it. It's like, "What?" But you are the mystery of God and this is the time that you are being finished. And finished means resurrection. It means your body will be fully resurrected.

The Lord has been speaking for some time now about resurrection life. He has said that resurrection life is literally right below your skin. Your new body is a hairs breath away. If you can just peel off one layer of skin, the resurrected body would be right beneath it. We are that close to the reality of the promise, the provision, and the completion of the mystery of God.

Another word came; "Visualize yourself on the other side of this transformation." The interpenetration of God in man - what a mystery. A mystery to the sons, themselves, because they must come to grips with the enormity of what is happening within them, right at this very moment. There has been nothing like this ever before, nor will there be again.

Give yourself to speaking the word, bringing in the judgments, and declaring authority over the principalities[21] and the powers, thrones and dominions. We go after the spirit realm, and as we change it, (and mark my words it is happening right now moment by moment), then everything on the natural plane is going to change.

This is where we are and life, as we know it, is going to change. I know out there in the unreal world that people are saying; "Well, life is going to change as you know it." They are referencing the catastrophic economic collapse that is coming, along with other scenarios that are on the horizon, any or all of which could set off a huge domino effect in this age. When that happens, to those who live on planet earth, there is no doubt that life will change for them, forever. But this does not concern the sons, for they have a different destiny. To those who are being raised up in this time of final completion, life will never be the same, because you are becoming and being completed[20] as a whole new creation.

In the midst of all of this, continue to break bonds with yourself, because you are in a state of becoming. How you see yourself is in flux. Do not lock yourself into any prior conditionings.

Every morning you have to get up and say, "This is not who I am - you know; the aches, the pains, the problems." Just break your connections, break your ties with yourself and any other latent bonds, and reach into your true identity. Who are you? Who are you? "I am the Christ." That is who you are. And ... "I am the Father." That's kind of scary, isn't it? "If you have seen me, you have seen the Father." At some point you will wake up and realize those shoes fit you now.

The voice of the sons is loosed to bring in the kingdom. They are destined to bring in the judgments of the Father, and the earth is going to bear witness to the travail of the sons. All of creation is going to bear witness. I know that they, (creation), are more aware of it than we are. We have been shown bits and pieces along the way, and so much more is coming. So much more is coming.

I bless this word to the true kings and priests of God. To the kings and priests[11] of God that reign right now..... not later, not in the future, but now. From His presence, the kings and priests are ruling. They have the scepter in their hand, and judgment is being administered.

It has been a wild and crazy last several months, but I tell you this, it is nothing to what we are going to see in the next period of time.

We refuse to allow the mind enter in and judge and say, "Well not yet. You're not there. I haven't been walking with God long enough so it must apply to someone else." No. If you are hearing this word, and if it is bearing witness in your heart, and your heart is burning, then this is your word. This is your truth, and this is your time.

Scriptures NASB

[1] Isaiah 43:19
"Behold, I will do something new, Now it will spring forth; Will you not be aware of it? I will even make a roadway in the wilderness, Rivers in the desert.

[2] Matthew 15:14
"Let them alone; they are blind guides of the blind. And if a blind man guides a blind man, both will fall into a pit."

[3] Matthew 3:3
For this is the one referred to by Isaiah the prophet when he said, "THE VOICE OF ONE CRYING IN THE WILDERNESS, 'MAKE READY THE WAY OF THE LORD, MAKE HIS PATHS STRAIGHT!'"

[4] Colossians 1:27
to whom God willed to make known what is the riches of the glory of this mystery among the Gentiles, which is Christ in you, the hope of glory.

[5] 2 Corinthians 6:17-18
17"Therefore come out from among them and be separate, says the Lord. Touch no unclean thing, and I will receive you." 18And: "I will be a father to you, and you will be My sons and daughters, says the Lord Almighty."...

[6] Malachi 3:2
"But who can endure the day of His coming? And who can stand when He appears? For He is like a refiner's fire and like fullers' soap.

[7] 1 Peter 4:17
For it is time for judgment to begin with the household of God; and if it begins with us first, what will be the outcome for those who do not obey the gospel of God?

[8] Acts 10:34
Opening his mouth, Peter said: "I most certainly understand now that God is not one to show partiality,

[9] 2 Kings 2:14
He took the mantle of Elijah that fell from him and struck the waters and said, "Where is the LORD, the God of Elijah?" And when he also had struck the waters, they were divided here and there; and Elisha crossed over.

[10] Acts 17:6
When they did not find them, they began dragging Jason and some brethren before the city authorities, shouting, "These men who have upset the world have come here also;

[11] Revelation 5:10
"You have made them to be a kingdom and priests to our God; and they will reign upon the earth."

[12] Colossians 1:16
For by Him all things were created, both in the heavens and on earth, visible and invisible, whether thrones or dominions or rulers or authorities-- all things have been created through Him and for Him.

[13] Hebrews 12:6
And His voice shook the earth then, but now He has promised, saying, "YET ONCE MORE I WILL SHAKE NOT ONLY THE EARTH, BUT ALSO THE HEAVEN."

[14] Daniel 2:34
"You continued looking until a stone was cut out without hands, and it struck the statue on its feet of iron and clay and crushed them.

[15] 2 Kings 13:18-19
18Then he said, "Take the arrows," and he took them. And he said to the
king of Israel, "Strike the ground," and he struck it three times and
stopped. 19So the man of God was angry with him and said, "You should have struck five or six times, then you would have struck Aram until you would have destroyed it. But now you shall strike Aram only three times."...

[16] Romans 8:21-22
21that the creation itself will be set free from its bondage to decay and
brought into the glorious freedom of the children of God. 22We know that the whole creation has been groaning together in the pains of childbirth until the present time.

[17] Revelation 2:13-16
13And when the dragon saw that he had been thrown to the earth, he
pursued the woman who had given birth to the male child. 14But the
woman was given two wings of a great eagle to fly from the presence of the serpent to her place in the wilderness, where she was nourished for a
time, and times, and half a time. 15Then from the mouth of the serpent
spewed water like a river to overtake the woman and sweep her away in
the torrent. 16But the earth helped the woman and opened its mouth to swallow up the river that had poured from the dragon's mouth.

[18] Jeremiah 5:15
Therefore, thus says the LORD, the God of hosts, "Because you have spoken this word, Behold, I am making My words in your mouth fire And this people wood, and it will consume them.

[19] Revelation 18:4
I heard another voice from heaven, saying, "Come out of her, my people, so that you will not participate in her sins and receive of her plagues;

[20] Revelation 10:7
but in the days of the voice of the seventh angel, when he is about to sound, then the mystery of God is finished, as He preached to His servants the prophets.

[21] Ephesians 6:12
For our struggle is not against flesh and blood, but against the rulers, against the powers, against the world forces of this darkness, against the spiritual forces of wickedness in the heavenly places.

Chapter 9

It is Crunch Time

The word which has come over and over, during the last several years, has been that we will not prevail by might nor by power, *nor ingenuity, or charisma ...* but we will prevail[1] by the word. And not just any generic word, but the word that has been quickened within you, for it is the word that you speak.

A lot of people believe that you war by the word by pulling out of the scriptures random verses and quote them and assume that in this way that they are warring by the word. But the truth is that the only way you war by the word, is that the word must first be indelibly written upon your heart. Then, you are able to war by that word.

However, let's take this to the next level. It's not just a word that is real to you, and that you ponder on like Joshua did; but it must be the word that you speak, which comes out of your mouth. **We prevail by the word which comes out of our mouth, but only after that word has been written on our hearts.**

What makes the word so powerful? Your level of abiding[2] in God. You can speak the word from various levels, as we know. You can conversationally speak to one another, and there are times that word can be on a very high level. The level of the word goes hand in hand with your level of abiding, which is in relationship to the work of the cross in your life.

It is the level in God that you speak from, that is the activating force behind the Word. We overcome by the word, but it is a word that comes out of your mouth by virtue of the level that you are speaking from.

Everything that we do is predicated on hearing His voice, and that has been an ongoing challenge that every son faces, as they mature in God. We know that the Lord only spoke those things He heard the Father saying and did only those things He saw the Father doing[3]. That is an example of how the sons are to move. We have moved in and out of that level, but as the culmination of God's dealings and purifying of the sons are finished, this will be the only level from which you will speak.

You might say the sons are coming into a synchronicity with the Lord, and the drive must continue to be that we hear Him clearly. His voice will not be a sound like distant thunder[4] or like a confusing gong or symbol. That sound, His voice to us, will be very clear. This determines, to a great deal, the level of effectiveness that we have. I wish that there was an easy way to find an answer to moving on this level, but the only answer is the work of the cross, and the dying out of the soul flesh. The removal of the veil and of those things which have hindered our ability to hear and see clearly, is of paramount importance.

We love the word, and we love the challenges that the word presents to us. We are always admonished to reach in and believe for more. Christ and the Father live within the sons, even though we may not be as aware at this point as we will be.

The fact remains that this indwelling is a reality and we are being challenged more and more to accept it, and to let it really take deep root within. It must stop being a truth that we acquiesce to, it must become a truth realized within us. No matter how strong the winds of hell may be that would come against you, you will not be moved from the knowledge of what you are, and who you are, and who the Father and the Son are, within you.

What does it mean to have the indwelling[5] of the spirit? What does it mean to come to the place of sonship with the measure and fullness of Christ dwelling in us that far exceeds our ability to understand it? It may seem like a hidden mystery, but to the sons, that mystery is becoming a reality.

God is always going to stretch you to believe and to reach out beyond your comfort zone. He will always challenge you to reach in and believe for more. That is the path to sonship.

What are the sons experiencing during this time? A great illumination. The sons are being quickened and made alive on a whole new level. This has been unfolding at a quickening pace, over the past six months to a year, as the work of the cross comes to a completion.

Malachi prophesied about those who would stand in the presence of the Lord. Read Malachi 3:3. It says of the Lord that He appears as a smelter and purifier[6] of the sons of Levi. A word recently came in the midst of the conflict, and it was not about the enemy, the witchcraft, the transference, or all of the battle that was going on. It was really a very simple word. The word was: purged, purified, and refined[7]. That was the word.

The focus has been about finishing the preparation of the sons, not are about the cords of evil that have amassed against the saints of the Most High. Have they amassed against the saints? Yes they have. However, they are just unwitting tools being used in the process of maturing and bringing forth the sons of God.

So what happens when you are purged, purified and refined[7]? Well the first step is God purges you, purging out the iniquity and the defilement - even the small little things that seem inconsequential at this point. Then He purifies you. Purged and purified. The net result? Sons that are refined as fine silver.

As the fire in your life has been turned up, so has the refining process within you, as the smelter refines silver ... ladling off the impurities. What remains is pure silver. The sons are being purged. They are being purified as the heat is turned up, and they are being refined as pure silver, as the defilements are ladled off.

There are times when this deep work of the cross can feel like you have been alienated from His presence. We can look at Christ and the experience He had as he was hanging on the cross, carrying the sins of mankind. What did He say? "My Father, My Father why hast Thou forsaken[8] Me?" The iniquity and sins He carried, for a moment, gave an illusion of separation, because for a moment, the Father could not look upon Him.

As you go through a similar process, you can feel like you have been alienated from the Lord, and alienated from the Father. But you have not been. It is the process of being purged, purified and refined, and the subsequent removal of that dross, that creates an illusion of separateness. There may be those moments when you might have a tendency to question, "Where Lord hath Thou gone?" Yet as the dross is removed, you will find that you have come up higher in the Father's house, and that your awareness has opened up on a much greater level.

We must realize that sonship comes with a great responsibility. Sonship comes with great authority and many demands. The more Christ comes forth within you, the more responsibility you have. It is the king and priest ministry. The sons of God have a great responsibility - *for they are the progenitors of a new age.* They are those who are ushering in the new age of the Kingdom of God.

The sons are responsible for bringing in the kingdom and for bringing down that which has withstood the kingdom. That is a great deal of responsibility, and this is happening now.

I don't know how many of you remember Martin Luther. But he made a statement which I'll paraphrase and I think is appropriate. He said: If he didn't pray for the country for one day he would know it. If he didn't pray for two days his family would know it. And if he didn't pray for three days all of the country would know it. The bottom line is if he didn't pray for three days the whole kingdom recognized it because of the importance of who and what he was in that generation.

And Martin Luther knew who he was. He knew the responsibility that he had to that age. He knew if that if he didn't move in the authority and as a conduit of prayer, that things were not going to happen and things were not going to change, that needed to happen. The buck stopped with him.

It is definitely crunch time. And crunch time means that there is another requirement coming in the spirit and that requirement is that we begin to stand as the oracle of the living God and speak the word on a whole new level. Not pray, but speak. That level is here, but we must give ourselves to it.

I have said before that if we only realized who we were in God, that we would be so driven to speak the word and move accordingly, because you would be aware of the great deal of effectiveness and authority that flows through you. To a degree we are still coming into the realization of what God has accomplished within us. It seems to still be a bit of a mystery, but this will change.

"Christ in you the hope of Glory[9]" (Colossians 1:27). "The mystery of ages[10]..."

The mystery of what God is doing in the earth right now is still hidden to a great deal from the sons, themselves, and that is a hard one to digest. *But we are just having a little table talk here.* We are just laying it out the way it is. We don't realize, yet, the magnitude of what God has done and accomplished within the sons.

We are coming to see it, more and more, but in my book it needs to be quicker. The illuminating or "quickening" within the sons has to happen more quickly. There may still be too much dross separating our ability from seeing the truth of who we are; but that is God's problem, as the Word says: "Faithful[11] is He who has begun a good work for He will complete it within you." We give ourselves to Him, and it is His responsibility to complete what He has begun.

Over the next six months to a year we are facing a window where it will be very important that we begin to move in the king and priest ministry. That has to do with speaking the word, moving in authority, moving in judgement, and interceding for those that are caught in the way.

The king ministry is a little bit different than the priest ministry, for the king ministry is one of authority, and the priest ministry is one that goes before God in behalf of others. The sons of God are both, and it is important that we move more and more in this ministry.

I'll repeat what I said a moment ago. We've already become, we just haven't quite realized it yet. This has a jeopardy to it, because we are in a time in the earth where everything is moving much more rapidly now, and we must move as the sons of God that we are. Otherwise, there may be a delay in what is set to unfold, because everything is contingent upon the sons of God moving into the reality and knowledge of who they are.

There is no question that there is a great deal of chaos, disinformation, illusion, deception, and darkness flowing into the earth right now. This is not hype. This is not sensationalism. This is truth.

The dragon[12] is spewing forth, as it mentions in the book of Revelation, a flood of deception and lies into the earth, and the darkness is getting more and more pervasive. The people who dwell upon the earth, who live in this vast darkness, are some of the greatest conduits of the lies and the deception, because they in turn speak or echo this darkness as they ingest it. You literally have millions, upon millions, of people broadcasting the darkness, whether audibly, or through their consciousness. And that is what is prophesied for this time, for it has become a day of great darkness[13]... darker than we have ever seen on the face of the earth before this time.

You might say, "How can these things be?" We are now in the greatest period of darkness, since time began, that is upon the face of the earth. Greater than the days of Sodom and Gomorrah[14]. Greater than the times of Noah[15]. Greater than the times when the fallen angels came down and dwelled among men.

We are living at the culmination of time and the iniquity has come to the full[16]. The iniquity coming to the full covers a lot of ground. When the Father says the iniquity has come to the full, it is a lot greater than what we can imagine. There is so much yet that is hidden, but it will be exposed. We are living and experiencing this timeline, the only difference is that we have eyes to see what is happening, while the world remains in darkness.

There is only one counter to the flood of darkness that is pervading the earth. And I know that you know the answer. The answer is the word out of your mouth. The answer is the arising and manifesting of the saints of light[17]. And that is why it is so important that the word is spoken. Not the word of prophecy, which can put things in the future, but a word that is for the present.

We are not prophesying about what is going to come. We are speaking a word about what is here. And we are speaking a word that is changing an age. So prophecy means something different in the days of the kingdom than it meant in the days of the church age. But this is the force that counteracts the evil. It is the word out of your mouth. It is the consciousness within you that emanates the light.

This could seem like a daunting scenario. One can look at all the evil and perhaps be overcome by how enormous it is, or it seems to be. But it's all a lie and an illusion.

What happened when the children of Israel went to spy out the land of Canaan? Joshua and Caleb saw the giants[18], which according to some accounts, were men of twenty and thirty feet high. These were the children of the Nephilim[18]. But Joshua and Caleb saw that their aura, or protection, had been removed. The other spies did not see that, and so they were very fearful. Yet Joshua and Caleb knew it was just going to be a mop-up operation. Well, we all know what happened. They didn't go in until that generation passed away[19].

In many ways it is similar, now, in this time line. The evil is becoming more and more dominant and yet the protection of the satanic hosts has been removed. The principalities, the powers, the families of great wealth — through which the spirits of darkness control this world — have had their satanic protection[20] or covering removed. And so it could seem like a daunting enterprise which the sons are faced with, but it is not. It really is a mop-up operation that God has set before the sons, and it is critical that we continue to speak the word.

How many times have you hit roadblocks? How many times have you come up to situations with no answers? Probably more than we know. We understand that there will be no amount of wisdom that will prevail; the only way that we will prevail, will be by the word. And that is the crunch time that we are facing. God has positioned the sons in a battle that they can win, because they will prevail by the word[21] that they speak, and continue to speak. And every time a roadblock arises, a lie or a deception, it will be taken down by the word that you speak.

If you were to see the word on a spiritual plane flowing out of your mouth, you would realize that the word is not just theory and concept, it is living. This is nothing new. You read it in the scriptures. It's a living word[22]. But often times the experience of understanding that escapes us. But imagine, as you speak the word, that the essence of the Father and the Son flow out of your mouth. Where the darkness flows out of the mouth of the dragon - and it's very tangible and substantive - so the spirit that flows out of the mouth of the sons is not a concept or theory or wind. It is spirit, and it is substance, and it is God[23]. We have seen this, in conversation, over the years. As one of us would speak, a beautiful green mist would flow from our mouth, into the one receiving the word. It was a beautiful experience, and you realize; although the word out of the dragon is black as ink, the Living Word out of the mouths of the sons, is living and substantive, and life giving.

That is why you prevail by the word. It's not just wind that you're speaking. The word is spirit. The word is God. As it comes out of your mouth, out of your being, it is God. You are God, because you are His sons, and as you speak, God speaks.

I know that in the New Testament we are admonished: "If any man speak, let him speak as an oracle[24] of God," as if that was a decision, a point, "Okay this is how I'm going to walk." That was an admonition given to the early church, but the reality, in these days of the kingdom, is that the sons are the living oracles of the living God. As they speak, it is a living word that flows out of their being.

We have the indwelling of Christ, the Father and the Holy Spirit. We have that. We just need to take another little step. Whatever has been pushing you back, we need to just let go. We need to see. We need to know the truth. Because what we are, in God, is not predicated as to whether you had a good day or a bad day; whether things happen that line up to what you think or not. And that is why we have to be very careful not to judge ourselves, nor to judge our circumstances, because we are still coming out of seeing in the partial.

You are Christ. You are the living word made flesh[25]. You are the sons of light[26] and your Father is the Father of lights[27]. And the word you speak is light, and it shall bring judgment upon all of the darkness. And not only that; your very presence brings forth judgment.

In this day the sons of God do not move in the ministry of judgment; they are judgment - because they are the light[26,28]. This cannot be dissected from you. More and more you will see that as you walk through your day that you are a confrontation to this age, because what you are is a living judgment[28].

Let me rephrase that again. You are a living judgment[26,28]. You are the light[26]. You are the word[25]. You are judgment[28]. You don't have a choice in the matter. Whether you open your mouth or not, your presence is going to bring judgment.

And that is an interesting way to look at many of the things that you go through during the day. Whether you are aware of it yet or not, the darkness that is so present is being constantly confronted by the truth and the light of who you are. At first it may put up a little battle, but they can only succumb to the authority of the light.

Lord, you're exposing the darkness. You're exposing that which has been done behind closed doors. You're exposing the working of the satanic seed in the earth and all of it is coming down. We're in the time that the image of stone[29], or the last image in Daniel, is coming down completely.

It's crunch time, because now we are to see an accelerated time of judgment and the exposing of darkness in high places over the next several months. This is a word for right now. Not a word of concept or theory, but a very present reality.

Scriptures (NASB)

[1] Psalm 12:4
Who have said, "With our tongue we will prevail; our lips are our own; who is lord over us?"

[2] John 15:7 level of abiding
"If you abide in Me, and My words abide in you, ask whatever you wish, and it will be done for you.

[3] John 5:19
Therefore Jesus answered and was saying to them, "Truly, truly, I say to you, the Son can do nothing of Himself, unless it is something He sees the Father doing; for whatever the Father does, these things the Son also does in like manner.

[4]John 12:29
So the crowd of people who stood by and heard it were saying that it had thundered; others were saying, "An angel has spoken to Him."

[5] Romans 8:11
But if the Spirit of Him who raised Jesus from the dead dwells in you, He who raised Christ Jesus from the dead will also give life to your mortal bodies through His Spirit who dwells in you.

[6] Malachi 3:3
"He will sit as a smelter and purifier of silver, and He will purify the sons of Levi and refine them like gold and silver, so that they may present to the LORD offerings in righteousness.

[7] Daniel 12:10
"Many will be purged, purified and refined, but the wicked will act wickedly; and none of the wicked will understand, but those who have insight will understand.

[8] Mathew 27:46
About the ninth hour Jesus cried out with a loud voice, saying, "ELI, ELI, LAMA SABACHTHANI?" that is, "MY GOD, MY GOD, WHY HAVE YOU FORSAKEN ME?"

[9] Colossians 1:27
to whom God willed to make known what is the riches of the glory of this mystery among the Gentiles, which is Christ in you, the hope of glory.

[10] Ephesians 3:9
and to bring to light what is the administration of the mystery which for ages has been hidden in God who created all things;

[11] Philippians 1:6
For I am confident of this very thing, that He who began a good work in you will perfect it until the day of Christ Jesus.

[12] Revelation 12:15
But the earth helped the woman, and the earth opened its mouth and drank up the river which the dragon poured out of his mouth.

[13] Joel 2:2
A day of darkness and gloom, A day of clouds and thick darkness. As the dawn is spread over the mountains, So there is a great and mighty people; There has never been anything like it, Nor will there be again after it To the years of many generations.

[14] Luke 17:28
"It was the same as happened in the days of Lot: they were eating, they were drinking, they were buying, they were selling, they were planting, they were building;

[15] Luke 17:26
"And just as it happened in the days of Noah, so it will be also in the days of the Son of Man:

[16] Genesis 15:16
"Then in the fourth generation they will return here, for the iniquity of the Amorite is not yet complete."

[17] Colossians 1:12
giving thanks to the Father, who has qualified us to share in the inheritance of the saints in Light.

[18] Numbers 13:33
"There also we saw the Nephilim (the sons of Anak are part of the Nephilim); and we became like grasshoppers in our own sight, and so we were in their sight."

[19] Judges 2:10
All that generation also were gathered to their fathers; and there arose another generation after them who did not know the LORD, nor yet the work which He had done for Israel.

[20] Numbers 14:9
"Only do not rebel against the LORD; and do not fear the people of the land, for they will be our prey. Their protection has been removed from them, and the LORD is with us; do not fear them."

[21] Isaiah 54:17
"No weapon that is formed against you will prosper; And every tongue that accuses you in judgment you will condemn. This is the heritage of the servants of the LORD, And their vindication is from Me," declares the LORD.

[22] Hebrews 4:12
For the word of God is living and active and sharper than any two-edged sword, and piercing as far as the division of soul and spirit, of both joints and marrow, and able to judge the thoughts and intentions of the heart.

[23] 1 Peter 1:23
for you have been born again not of seed which is perishable but imperishable, that is, through the living and enduring word of God.

[24] 1 Peter 4:11
Whoever speaks, is to do so as one who is speaking the utterances of God; whoever serves is to do so as one who is serving by the strength which God supplies; so that in all things God may be glorified through Jesus Christ, to whom belongs the glory and dominion forever and ever. Amen.

[25] John 1:14
And the Word became flesh, and dwelt among us, and we saw His glory, glory as of the only begotten from the Father, full of grace and truth.

[26] 1 Thessalonians 5:5
for you are all sons of light and sons of day. We are not of night nor of darkness;

[27] James 1:17 Every good thing given and every perfect gift is from above, coming down from the Father of lights, with whom there is no variation or shifting shadow.

[28] John 3:19
"This is the judgment, that the Light has come into the world, and men loved the darkness rather than the Light, for their deeds were evil.

[29] Daniel 2:35
"Then the iron, the clay, the bronze, the silver and the gold were crushed all at the same time and became like chaff from the summer threshing floors; and the wind carried them away so that not a trace of them was found. But the stone that struck the statue became a great mountain and filled the whole earth.

Section 3

Prepared to Rule

Chapter 10

The New World Order

Many Christians may not be aware of what we call the "new world order", which is a movement that has been happening in the earth now for the past several decades. There are two schools of thought concerning this new world order, and we will address both of them here, separately.

First of all, there has been a movement in the rank-and-file of the satanic seed, to create what is popularly known as the "new world order". You can search on the internet and find thousands of listings that speak about the coming new world order, or the plans of the Nephilim[1] in bringing about a new world order.

In summary, the "new world order" is an attempt by the satanic seed to literally consolidate the countries of this world under one canopy of authority, and to consolidate the money and methods of exchange under one canopy, one denomination. And eventually, to consolidate the control of the countries of this world under one leader.

This has been something that has been on the table with the satanic seed for a very, very long time. A lot of people refer to this as the plans of the global elite. They will say the agenda of the global elite is the "new world order". The global elite are primarily comprised of those who have great wealth and money, and in their own mind, have their own agenda of what they want to see happen in the earth.

It is interesting if you look at the consolidation of wealth in the last decade or two; a very small percentage of the population own the vast majority of wealth in the world. You could probably reduce this down to a number of two or three hundred families that have upwards of 90% of all the wealth. A very precarious position, but one that has been astutely planned by the satanic forces to bring about the ability to execute a new world order agenda.

Those who are tracking on this type of information, and who are very much against the establishment of a new world order, really have no way to approach the issue except to believe that some sort of open dialogue could intervene and bring a solution to this direction. Most everyone in the world views the new world order as a conspiracy led by the elite families of the world who control the wealth and, literally control the economies and commerce of all the countries, and so it is, on one level. For the most part, no one is able to see beyond that which is right in front of their face, concerning the issue of this new world order.

We know in the past we have spoken about a race that is on ... *a race between the manifesting[2] of the sons of God and the manifesting of the sons of Satan.* I know that we have not seen it that way. We have a tendency to believe that everything is going to work out, and we have not been that aware of the part the sons of God are to play in the wrap up of the end time events. The initiative that rests upon God's sons determines how quickly some of this end time agenda will wrap up.

We haven't realized the mantle[3] that has been put upon those who have been called to sonship. Literally, there is a mantle upon the sons to become, and if this word is alive to you, then you are one of those whom the mantle has been placed upon. It is interesting how the Father is orchestrating this, because He is not just going to do everything for the sons—laying everything out where it becomes just a mop-up operation for them. It really is not. God is directing the sons, but there is a great deal of initiative upon the sons to both become, and to do. They must complete and finish what they have been sent to do.

You might look at this and say, "Well, how can it be a race? We know the sons of God will manifest first." And I would say that is what I believe as well, but we are yet to see what the path will be from point A to point B in this scenario. The satanic seed has an inclination of what is coming. They know, in part, about the judgments of the Father that are coming, and this makes it interesting.

You have probably seen how there have been a lot of preparations; a lot of conspiracy theories about bunkers being built underground and all kinds of strange things. In a real sense, the satanic seed is preparing themselves for what is coming, for they see it as a judgment coming from God upon this age. In their deception, they believe that they can side-step that judgment, and so there has been a drive in the sons of Satan to manifest.

I know that for the sons of God to manifest, that we are talking about resurrection life. We're talking about authority; the administration[4] of the authority to be specific. And we're talking about bringing down every kingdom. That is what we speak of when we talk about the manifesting of the sons of God. We are also talking about the freedom for all creation that has been tied into the release of the sons. So there is a great deal at stake concerning the manifesting of the sons of God.

Concerning the sons of Satan, or the seed of the satanic beings, I can't tell you exactly what their intent is in manifesting, but it obviously would be to side-step the judgments of God that are coming and to move into a realm of power ahead of the sons moving into the realm of authority.

You must understand that in the spirit realm you have both power, and authority. Satan has a great deal of power but he has no authority, unless he can usurp it from a son; because authority comes from God. And authority is born out of the submission of the son to the Lord Jesus Christ, in whom all authority[5] resides.

Satan has no authority; but he does have power. And as the satanic hosts begin to manifest, more and more they will wield a great deal of power. The Word talks about deceiving signs and wonders as the man of sin manifests, or what they would call the "antichrist". A lot of this is tied to the exertion of power over the masses living in this vast darkness. As the scriptures mention .... if it were possible, even the very elect[6] would be deceived.

The antichrist manifests with a great deal of power. And we've spoken about the antichrist within us, which is the soul-flesh nature that has been at odds with the spirit. But there is also that which exists externally in what Satan is looking to bring forth.

We are in a very interesting time right now because a great deal is coming to a head, and this is the time that everything is accelerating. More than we understand, we are in a drive to manifest sonship and to become. Unless this is vividly real to you, you will not feel that drive or intensity in the spirit.

It can seem like you plod through one day after another, dealing with a little battle here, a little skirmish there, and not realize how much of a player that you are in the final wrap up of things. We know the admonition is constantly in front of us ... out of Isaiah; "Behold I will do something new[7]. Will you be aware?"

The human nature has a very arrogant tendency to assume, "Well, of course, I will be aware. I am aware. I am a son." But there is a point when confidence can be overridden by the arrogance of the soul, and you make assumptions that are not entirely complete. The admonition is, "Will you be aware[7]?", because we exist and live under a vast cloak of darkness during this time. The people of the world are asleep. Many of the sons are still asleep. The problem is that they don't know that they are asleep. They don't know that they no longer have eyes to see. They don't know that they no longer have a heart to understand. They don't know that they are under deception. All of this is a very fine line, and unless the Lord reveals it, you really have no idea.

You can go and talk to a brother that you see a calling of God on, and yet they are asleep. They don't see what's happening. They don't understand the time that they have come to. They are not tracking in the realm of spirit. They are not acutely aware of what is happening. They are asleep.

This is the parable of the wise and foolish virgins, which I have spoken of many times. Who are the virgins? Are the virgins Christianity? Are the virgins the people of this world? Or ... are the virgins those who have chosen to really walk on with God; those who have a call upon their lives? These are the virgins. They have separated themselves from the whore, and yet within the scope of the virgins, you have those that are wise, and those that have fallen asleep.

Many of the sons have fallen asleep, even though the sound is going out in the spirit; **"Wake up![8] Wake up! Remember!"** If you were to tune into the spirit realm, you would hear a constant beat of the drum; **"Wake up! Remember!"** If you were to stand in the middle of the desert and prophesy, there would be only one, very simple prophecy to make - "to you who have been called and marked for this time, wake up and remember! Wake up and remember!"

What is happening? God is bringing forth something new, and it will not be built upon the foundation of something old.

> **"No one sews a patch of un-shrunk cloth on an old garment; else the patch pulls away from it, the new from the old, and a worse tear results." Mark 2:21**

God will not build the kingdom based upon the foundation of that which is passing away.

The kingdoms of this world are fraught with evil, and God will not build a kingdom from a foundation that is fraught with darkness. He will remove it and bring a new thing. Behold He removes the first[9] in order to bring the second. God must tear down that which exists, in order to bring a new thing in the earth. He is not going to patch up the countries of this world, and just make it work. He is going to bring something new.

We are in the time of Daniel's vision[10] when the stone cut out of the mountain hits the image at the feet, and the last image is destroyed, and brought down. God is not going to take what we have known on this earth, and bring forth a kingdom built upon that foundation.

In the midst of this tumultuous time, the Nephilim seed is seeking to establish a new world order; a kingdom that pervades the entire planet - directed by Satan and those minions that serve under him. When you say "new world order", this is pretty much what comes to mind. People may not think of it in the scope of the satanic input, as much as they would think of it in the scope of the global elitists that control great wealth, and who have an end goal of a new world order that they would control. That is the new world order which is perceived in the world.

This, however, is not the new world order that we are talking about coming. God is bringing forth a whole new thing. At this point we may not understand the depth of it. The new world order that is happening is not a new world order of the satanic seed, but a new world order by virtue of the ascension of the sons.

The true, new world order which is coming, is that which is being introduced by the sons as they enter into the administration of the kingdom. An administration[4] suitable for the fullness of time has been reserved for the sons of God to move into, and this is the true new world order.

The administration of the kingdom is already resting upon God's sons, but the problem is that they have not been aware that that kingdom is already resting upon their shoulders. There can be a tendency to believe that when you have ascended, and been fully caught up and are sitting at the right hand of the Father, that then you will function and begin to subject every kingdom back to the Father and to the Lord. But that is a misnomer.

The administration of the kingdom is already resting upon the sons of God. The authority to bring forth, and to tear down, is already here. Most of the sons are not aware. They see the kingdom coming forth as something in a future tense, rather than realizing that it is here now. Similar to the book of Thomas, where he speaks about the kingdom[11] of God being spread over the earth and men see it not. That is a problem.

The word has come many times in the spirit, "What you seek is already here. You just don't see it." We have been reaching and crying out for God to bring something forth, when He has already done it. It's already here. We have to embrace it, embrace the authority, and begin to move accordingly.

It can feel like you are living like Paul. In the book of Philippians 3 the word says of Paul; "living[12] or reaching with neck stretched out." Paul was reaching with every facet within him to embrace the vision and the reality of what he saw.

We are here now, positioned at the time of completion, and the provision is no longer at arm's distance. The new world order is the administration of the kingdom resting upon the sons of God who carry out the command: go and make[13] disciples of the nations; bind the principalities[14] and powers, and subject them to His lordship; every knee[15] is going to bow and every tongue will confess. Those are the present realities that are set before the sons to implement.

More than ever, the sons of God are living in two worlds at the same time. This has been both a blessing, and a headache. It is a problem because the transition out of the soul is still in the process, and there still is a tendency to look at everything around you and make decisions through the agency of the mind, rather than understanding that everything about you is being effected by the realm of spirit - because you are living in both worlds at the same time.

God's sons are the kings[16] and priests of this age. We have seen this a number of times, as governmental leaders of countries have come in the spirit saying, "Who are you? What are you?" And yet something within their spirit was recognizing that this is where the true authority is.

In a very mystical sense, you might say the day[17] star is arising in the hearts of the sons ... the day star, the morning star; Christ the Lord. This is what is happening. The day star[17] is arising and with that comes a deep quickening, or epiphany, that this is your time. 2 Peter 1:19; "*So we have the prophetic word made more sure to which you do well to pay attention as to a lamp shining in a dark place until the day dawns and the morning star arises in your hearts.*" The arising of the day-star is no different than talking about resurrection life, or the manifesting of the sons of God ... it all comes together at the same point.

As the indwelling of the godhead[18] comes to completion, so the physical bodies of the sons will change. It would be impossible for that not to happen; for the body will have to reflect the spirit. The spirit of the Father, and the spirit of Christ, that dwells within the sons, will cause a transformation of their physical bodies. We are very close to that, and in many ways, we are already here ... we just have not recognized that the indwelling is here - *that what we seek is already here.* We are still coming out from beneath the veil. We have still been in the process of pulling the curtain back.

Whether we have realized this or not, the sons are being pulled into the spirit as quickly as they are able. And, they are being pulled into the warfare of the kingdom. This is very much happening, and it is part of the new world order, the order of the sons of God.

Life on this level is getting more and more complex, and a little more difficult to deal with day by day, because you are living with one foot in the natural plane and one foot in the spirit. Sometimes it can feel like you don't know whether you are coming or going! You may not even know what day of the week it is! But you know, and feel, the energy of the conflict that you're carrying, as it reflects itself in your body at times.

Sometimes it is hard to form the words to explain what is really unfolding, because you have not walked this way before. There isn't a book you can turn to that will explain exactly what's happening to you, except you feel the changes happening within you, as your body continues to go through changes. The closer you get to the completion of sonship, as the word came sometime back, the more intense everything is going to become.

Very few[19] have been called and chosen of the Lord for this path. Very few. But once you have tasted of this, there is no other life for you than living in His presence; continuing to move out of this body of death[20] into a new body of life. This transition is here now, and it is happening to the sons.

There is so much happening in the world within the realm of darkness, for it is pervading the earth on every level. So much effort is being exerted that is trying to control the masses, but that is not what is happening. What is happening is the kingdom is coming and the times we are in have been even more complex, because we are indeed living in the time of the book of Revelation. Satan is being cast out, and this has been going on now for quite some time - it is not a single event in time.

Satan being cast out is a progressive, unfolding truth. The more this accelerates, the greater the influx of the demonic world on this natural plane. It is happening. We have watched this for the last ten years and the greater the influx of the satanic entities into the natural plane, the more we see the rise of violence, and many other things occurring, that were not present before.

Sometime back the word came that as this demonic intrusion into the natural world accelerates, that you will see a rise of mental health issues and a lot of other medical issues that really didn't exist before this time. On one plane you can look at this and say, "Well, I see all of this happening." And yet these are just strings being pulled by the demonic world behind the scenes. If you go up to a higher level in the spirit, then you find that this is really where the action is happening. Because what is happening right now is not that which you see on the natural plane, but that which is happening in the realm of spirit, for the balance of power is continuing to shift.

Even if people do not have eyes to see what is happening; people can look around and see the confusion, the hatred, the anger, and the hostility that is arising in the earth. They may not know exactly what to credit that to. You could just say, "It is something happening in the Middle East, or it is this group or that group." And all of that would be leaves[21] and branches, because it is really the root spirit behind the scene that is the real problem.

The last several years have seen the increase of the satanic spirit world into the natural plane greatly. And correspondingly, we have seen a huge increase in the flow of violence in the earth. This will continue and accelerate even more, because the prophecy has been from the start - as it was in the days of Noah[22] and the days of Sodom and Gomorrah, so shall it be at the time of the coming of the son of man. It's only going to get more interesting.

Wall Street can manipulate their money. They can manipulate the economy of the world, but it will all come to naught, because the rising of the sons of God is what is going to change everything now. A lot of people—Christians even—may look at the passing scene and say, "Well, let's pray about it. Let's go talk about it." They don't know how to address it. But there is only one answer---one answer to this age. And it will not be praying about it. It's not going to be about talking to someone about it. You will stand as the sons of God that you are, and you will move with the authority and dominion of Christ. You will bring down that which has resisted God. Authority is the only answer for all of the issues happening right now, and that authority is relegated to the sons. The sons are beginning to awaken to their calling, at last.

As I have said, there are many levels happening, simultaneously. At the same time that you see the true new world order beginning to be established in the sons, you are also witnessing the travail[23] of all creation, because creation is travailing to become free. Their freedom is tied into the manifesting of the sons of God. The administration of the kingdom - the true new world order - is tied into the manifesting of the sons of God. Everything is tied into the sons becoming what they were sent to do and to be.

God is catching you up as quickly as you are able to let go and become. Now is the time for the true new world order to begin to manifest, and it will confound the masses. No one will understand what is happening. But it's here in our midst. We are in the throes of this. And it's going to get darker before it gets light, and that is only because the sons are moving into doing what they have been sent to do.

Scriptures (NASB)

[1] Genesis 6:4
The Nephilim were on the earth in those days, and also afterward, when the sons of God came in to the daughters of men, and they bore children to them. Those were the mighty men who were of old, men of renown.

[2] Romans 8:19
For the anxious longing of the creation waits eagerly for the revealing of the sons of God.

[3] 2 Kings 2:13
He also took up the mantle of Elijah that fell from him and returned and stood by the bank of the Jordan.

[4] Ephesians 1:10
with a view to an administration suitable to the fullness of the times, that is, the summing up of all things in Christ, things in the heavens and things on the earth. In Him

[5] Matthew 28:18
And Jesus came up and spoke to them, saying, "All authority has been given to Me in heaven and on earth.

[6] Matthew 24:24
"For false Christs and false prophets will arise and will show great signs and wonders, so as to mislead, if possible, even the elect.

[7] Isaiah 43:19
"Behold, I will do something new, Now it will spring forth; Will you not be aware of it? I will even make a roadway in the wilderness, Rivers in the desert.

[8] Ephesians 5:14
For this reason it says, "Awake, sleeper, And arise from the dead, And Christ will shine on you."

[9] Hebrews 10:9
then He said, "BEHOLD, I HAVE COME TO DO YOUR WILL." He takes away the first in order to establish the second.

[10] Daniel 2:34
"You continued looking until a stone was cut out without hands, and it struck the statue on its feet of iron and clay and crushed them.

[11] Gospel of Thomas saying 113
(113) His disciples said to him: On what day will the kingdom come? <Jesus said:> It will not come while people watch for it; they will not say: Look, here it is, or: Look, there it is; but the kingdom of the father is spread out over the earth, and men do not see it.

[12] Philippians 3:14
I press on toward the goal for the prize of the upward call of God in Christ Jesus.

[13] Matthew 28:19
"Go therefore and make disciples of all the nations, baptizing them in the name of the Father and the Son and the Holy Spirit,

[14] Colossians 2:15
When He had disarmed the rulers and authorities, He made a public display of them, having triumphed over them through Him.

[15] Romans 14:11
For it is written, "AS I LIVE, SAYS THE LORD, EVERY KNEE SHALL BOW TO ME, AND EVERY TONGUE SHALL GIVE PRAISE TO GOD."

[16] Revelation 5:10
"You have made them to be a kingdom and priests to our God; and they will reign upon the earth."

[17] 2 Peter 1:19
So we have the prophetic word made more sure, to which you do well to pay attention as to a lamp shining in a dark place, until the day dawns and the morning star arises in your hearts.

[18] Colossians 2:9
For in Him all the fullness of Deity dwells in bodily form,

[19] Matthew 22:14
"For many are called, but few are chosen."

[20] Romans 8:10
If Christ is in you, though the body is dead because of sin, yet the spirit is alive because of righteousness.

[21] Daniel 4:14
'He shouted out and spoke as follows: "Chop down the tree and cut off its branches, Strip off its foliage and scatter its fruit; Let the beasts flee from under it And the birds from its branches.

[22] Luke 17:26
"And just as it happened in the days of Noah, so it will be also in the days of the Son of Man:

[23] Romans 8:22
For we know that the whole creation groans and suffers the pains of childbirth together until now.

Notes

Chapter 11

Passing Through the Heavens

It is such a privilege and honor to be raised up during this time to walk with God and come to know Him. There is no greater honor, no greater pursuit, than to know Him - even as Paul sought to know the Lord, as he referenced in the book of Philippians, that he might know[1] Him and the power of His resurrection. Paul had that insatiable desire to know the Lord.

Stop and ponder with me for a minute. What separates you? What genuinely separates you from everyone? It is that insatiable hunger that He has put within you to know Him. The Lord has touched you, and He has brought you alive. And there is nothing that can satiate that hunger and drive that He has put within you, but to know Him.

The scripture also speaks in the New Testament how He earnestly desires[2] the spirit that He has placed within us. The Father and the Son earnestly desire a communion and relationship with you, which is your spirit. It's really who you are. Especially as the spirit within you moves into the ascendency over the soul, for the soul is dying out and your spirit is coming forth. And as you come forth, each son will be unique in their manifestation. This may be dictated by your level of abiding in the Father's house, or it could have some relationship to your unique calling. *We will see....*

39 All flesh *is* not the same flesh: but *there is* one *kind of* flesh of men, another flesh of beasts, another of fishes, *and* another of birds.

40 *There are* also celestial bodies, and bodies terrestrial: but the glory of the celestial *is* one, and the *glory* of the terrestrial *is* another.

41 *There is* one glory of the sun, and another glory of the moon, and another glory of the stars: for *one* star differs from *another* star in glory.

42 So also *is* the resurrection of the dead. It is sown in corruption; it is raised in incorruption:

43 It is sown in dishonour; it is raised in glory: it is sown in weakness; it is raised in power:

44 It is sown a natural body; it is raised a spiritual body. There is a natural body, and there is a spiritual body.

45 And so it is written, The first man Adam was made a living soul; the last Adam *was made* a quickening spirit.

46 Howbeit that *was* not first which is spiritual, but that which is natural; and afterward that which is spiritual.

47 The first man *is* of the earth, earthy: the second man *is* the Lord from heaven.

48 As *is* the earthy, such *are* they also that are earthy: and as *is* the heavenly, such *are* they also that are heavenly.

49 And as we have borne the image of the earthy, we shall also bear the image of the heavenly. 1Cor.15: 39-49

As it speaks in the book of Hebrews, God is saving you to the uttermost[3]; spirit, soul and body. You are destined to be an integrated being - spirit, soul and body. You are destined to have a physical manifestation, not just to be a spirit, but one that has a body. However, your body will not reflect the soul, which is being regenerated in Christ, ***but your body is going to be a spiritual body, reflecting your spirit.***

We may not yet understand the privilege and honor that we have been given. How do you explain that to anyone if they have not been quickened on this level? Even to fellow Christians, no one really can understand what it is that drives you. God has destined you to come into a relationship with Him beyond anything.

We are in the process of stepping outside of ourselves and letting go of that which has defined us by virtue of our mind, by virtue of our physical experience, and appearance. We're literally stepping outside and stepping into a whole new creation that God has destined the sons to be. We have been living in a cocoon, so to speak, since we came here during our present sojourn. We have been waiting for the time that we would emerge as who we truly are; the sons of God, a new creation - the royal priesthood; God's kings and priests.

Isaiah saw it when He said, "*Behold*[4] *I will do something new.* The sons are constantly being admonished; *will you be aware?*" The problem that has plagued His sons in their sojourn has been unawareness; coming up to a level where you really are able to understand what God is doing within you, and what you are becoming. Progressively - more and more - that awareness is opening up.

We have chosen not to settle on this level of existence. We have chosen not to accept the good, or the better, but we have chosen the best. Like Paul, God's sons are living on tiptoes, and you really can't even live that type of lifestyle unless the reality of the provision has been quickened to you on a deep enough level.

The kingdom is coming forth, but it is coming forth on a plane of spirit. The kingdom is coming forth on many different levels, many different dimensions, and one of those which is probably the most difficult to understand and grasp, is the word; the kingdom[5] is within you. As the kingdom comes forth, you are coming forth. And as the kingdom moves in to displace every other kingdom on the face of the earth, you are the physical manifestation of that. Very mystical, and without a real spirit of revelation, it is hard to understand, much less identify yourself with that.

You are the kingdom. Ponder on that for a minute. You are the kingdom, and every place that you walk, as the prophecy goes, *the sole of your foot[6] doth tread upon,* belongs to you. The sons are walking out, on a very practical level, the kingdom of God right now. We are in this unique time of transition. We are in this unique time that the preparation of the kings and priests is being completed.

Who are the kings and priests? As I just mentioned, that is who you are. You are the kings and priests of God. And you are the kingdom of God. But it is a very mystical thing that is happening. It is not with outward signs that you can point to and say "there's the kingdom", or "here's the kingdom", or "here's His appearing". It's not that discernible. It's a hidden work that God has been doing ... hidden even to the sons themselves of what they are becoming, have become, and of how the Father truly sees them.

God is raising a nucleus of sons around the globe, and they are coming into a flow and oneness of spirit. Some may have a connection on the natural plain, but most probably will not; for we know that the oneness of the kingdom is a oneness of spirit.

The word speaks about God setting everyone, individually, into the church as it pleases Him; and God is doing that at this time. He is setting the body in order. Even though there may not be a church that you could look to and say, "Well okay. It is in this church or that church."

It is a church that is on a global scale, and on a spiritual level, and God is bringing His sons together in a level of oneness - in the spirit - that most are not aware of yet.

As God establishes the functioning of the church, it will not be your choice to determine what your job description is going to be. You could say, "Well I want to be an apostle, I want to be a prophet." It doesn't really matter. God places[7] you as He wills. And so we find a very unique thing happening because the body is coming together; each part so very unique and so necessary to the whole; even if the sons are not yet aware of what is happening. The true spiritual church is being set in place, as God takes one from here and another from there. You might be alone in Ireland, in England, somewhere on the plains of the Midwest; it doesn't matter.

You might marvel and say, "I don't understand. I don't know how this is happening. I'm not aware." And yet God is moving; not limited by the natural. He is raising up the sons in the realm of spirit, and their connection is a spirit-realm reality, not a natural plane level of agreement. This is transcending our understanding, for oneness has nothing to do with an agreement, mentally, of doctrine.

Oneness is a spirit realm reality, and oneness has to do with an inter-penetration and blending of spirits together, like the Father and the Son. Christ said, "I pray Father that they be one[8] even as you and I are one". So the body is being raised up in a spirit of oneness that is not dictated, defined, or limited, to this natural plane.

You might be living on the top of a mountain, in the middle of nowhere; it doesn't really matter, because what is happening is in the realm of spirit. As God brings the sons into the ability to function in the realm of spirit, this oneness will have already been set. The sons will begin to interact and function together on a plane of spirit; not a plane of soul.

I understand there are groups that like to get together and review the word and prophecies. I think that's great. That is the commandment to not cease[9] meeting together as the day draws nigh. And so you're walking in obedience to the word. But this is not oneness. This is not even agreement. This is the partial, because the fulfillment for God's sons is in the realm of spirit. It's in the realm of the Father's presence. It's in the realm of the kingdom.

This is why it can seem very disconcerting, because what is happening, is happening in the plane of your spirit. You are in a transition coming out of an awareness that is still pretty much anchored in the realm of the natural, into a plane of spirit. Your plane of reality is getting completely re-defined.

The oneness that God is establishing is an experience beyond anything we've known. I think that you would agree that when Christ said; "The Father and I are one[10]", that this was an experience for the Lord Jesus Christ. That was a reality that far transcended the disciples understanding. And God is establishing something that is a spirit realm reality that will involve the sons across the face of the globe - and perhaps even those from different levels and dimensions within the Father's house.

It's good to have prophecy. It's good to meet together and rehearse the word. It's good to do those things. That is only the partial, and the day of fullness is upon us. As we spoke in the first book, the oneness that God is establishing is going to release a "dunamis", or power, that we have never seen before. Never seen before. We're not looking at a thimbleful, we are looking at a torrent of fulfillment, born out of a oneness, within the sons that God has raised up, as they begin to function and move together.

This will happen as the sons are progressively pulled up higher and higher into the Father's presence, where they truly transition out of the realm of the natural plane and soul, and into the realm of the kingdom. I wish we were there—and in many ways we are there—but we're still catching up to the reality of it.

The word has been a great delight to us, both the word that has come and has been spoken, and the word that has been revealed to us in the night hours.

> Read Revelation 10:8-11. **[8]Then the voice of the Lord which I heard from heaven I heard again speaking with me and saying, "Go take the book which is open in the hand of the angel who stands on the sea and on the land." [9]And so I went to the angel, telling him to give me the little book. And he said to me, "Take it, and eat it; and it will make your stomach bitter, but in your mouth it will be sweet as honey." [10]... and when I had eaten it, my stomach was made bitter. [11]And then he said to me,**

"You must prophesy again concerning many peoples, nations, tongues and kings." Revelation 10:8-11

I believe that we understand that as the word becomes imbedded within us, that it begins to challenge our belief system; it begins to uproot the roadblocks and the log jams; it begins to send the soul into a deeper work of the cross. That is what is meant when you think of the word being bitter. You must go through the process where the word becomes written on your heart; that word becomes you; and you become the word.

What is fascinating is that as the word becomes you, and you become the word, that you are brought on to another plane of life, another plane of existence; another level, if you will. As that happens, this new level begins to yield up to you the mysteries[11] and treasures[12] that God had set aside for you, for that day of maturity, when you would arrive on that level. As your eyes open to this new level, the wonders and mysteries set aside for you, open right up.

We have been experiencing and living this for quite some time, even if we haven't understood that this was what was happening. We now see it more clearly, because we are passing through the heavens, much more quickly. The Word says that when Christ died on the cross and was raised from the dead, that He passed[13] through the heavens, and sat down at the right hand of the Father.

What happened to Christ, as He passed through the heavens? He was going up higher and higher in the Father's house, He was passing through realms, dimensions and levels of created reality, that we are presently not that aware of. He ascended and sat down at the right hand of the Father; but not before releasing the captives from level to level in His ascension.

The sons are passing through the heavens, in like manner. And as they ascend into the Father's house - as the work is completed within them - they pass through the heavens, through levels and dimensions that you previously had not been aware of, and are also setting free the captives. You are passing through levels of the Father's kingdom ... and as you do so, you will encounter those who live on those various levels of the Father's house, and you will be their release. They are part of "creation" that you are destined to set free.

It is an amazing time to be walking with God, and we should be living with great expectation, day by day. The enemy would seek to discourage you, to create heaviness, to dull your senses through bonds and contacts, relationships — any of a number of things that we have talked about before. But now, more than ever, is a time to be expecting, because you are passing through the heavens much more quickly. You are unlocking the treasure[12] chests that have been ordained for you as you ascend into His presence. You should be expecting more experiences to happen; a great deal more.

As we have talked about before; the kingdom is here. Our paradigm has not fully embraced it, so it has been held at arm's distance. We have still seen resurrection life outside of us, rather than realizing that we already have it. And because we don't see that, it still remains at arms distance. There is so much that God is doing that He has already done within the sons; so much that has already been finished, but the sons have yet to come up to a plane of awareness where they know that it's been done within them. As a state of knowing encompasses them, they will be able to bring the realities and provisions of what is already here, into full manifestation[14].

Our destiny — and that destiny is pretty much on top of us right now — is to know the Lord, to really know Him. It's not about being vessels, about doing healing, about the prophetic anointing or discerning of spirits. It's about knowing Him; knowing Him in every facet of our being that when He speaks, every part of you is quickened. You may not hear an audible word, you may not see a vision, but every part of you is quickened to Him and you hear Him in a capacity of spirit that is both hard to define, and completely new to you. Do you understand. We are talking about hearing Him with every capacity of our being.

We love the word, and we continue to embrace the word, but we also understand that the word is the very agency that throws us into the dealings of God. This purifying of God will bring us into a plane of functioning that hitherto we were not able to attain to. The change that we are looking for comes by this level of exposure to Him.

The words that Anne and I bring, however anointed of God, will profit nothing unless you see Him in the word. And if you see Him, then you're changed. Our change comes by exposure; we know this. God is not looking for a bunch of sons to take up the cross on their back and grab hold of a few books and revelations and go stand on the corner and start preaching away, as so many do. That is just a product of the soul.

God is looking to transform His sons into the spirit beings that they are. And wherever they go, and every time they open their mouth, the presence of God and the power of God flows from them. They are not standing on the corner passing out tracts. They are just walking through the hospitals and healing the multitudes, without even laying on hands. Their destiny is that their presence brings both the healing and the judgment upon this age.

Revelation talks about the trees[15] that are given for the nations that grow up along the river. The trees are given for the healing of the nations; and in many ways, that is the sons. The sons are the healing for the nations, they are the healing to this age. To the degree that people can open up to God (you), to that degree they can be healed and made complete and whole.

We are in the company of so many great men and women of God who have laid everything down to fulfill the will of God in their generation. They are right here. We call them the Cloud of Witnesses. They broke through and established a beachhead in their generation, and they are the reason that we stand here, at this last leg of the race, holding the baton - destined to break the tape.

They have gone before us and paved the way, enabling us to run and finish the race. Everything that was done in the past, all of the groundwork that was laid, all of the judgment that was issued, was done so that the sons at this time would be able to finish the race, and complete what they were raised up to do.

The Lord has so many mysteries, so many truths, so much that He has destined to be revealed within us. It's right here at the door. We keep embracing the word. We keep letting the word effectually[16] work within us. And we understand that there is no path to sonship that is void of the daily work of the cross[17] in our life.

Paul said that he died[18] daily. So the sons die daily. But with expectation – for you are right here at the door, the door of the greatest breakthrough and release ever seen.

Scriptures (NASB)

[1] Philippians 3:10
that I may know Him and the power of His resurrection and the fellowship of His sufferings, being conformed to His death;

[2] James 4:5
that I may know Him and the power of His resurrection and the fellowship of His sufferings, being conformed to His death;

[3] Hebrews 7:25
Therefore He is able also to save forever those who draw near to God through Him, since He always lives to make intercession for them.

[4] Isaiah 43:19
"Behold, I will do something new, Now it will spring forth; Will you not be aware of it? I will even make a roadway in the wilderness, Rivers in the desert.

[5] Luke 17:21
nor will they say, 'Look, here it is!' or, 'There it is!' For behold, the kingdom of God is in your midst."

[6] Joshua 1:3
"Every place on which the sole of your foot treads, I have given it to you, just as I spoke to Moses.

[7] 1 Corinthians 12:18
But now hath God set the members every one of them in the body, as it hath pleased him.

[8] John 17:21
that they may all be one; even as You, Father, are in Me and I in You, that they also may be in Us, so that the world may believe that You sent Me.

[9] Hebrews 10:25
not forsaking our own assembling together, as is the habit of some, but encouraging one another; and all the more as you see the day drawing near.

[10] John 10:30 ... "I and the Father are one.

[11] 1 Corinthians 4:1
Let a man regard us in this manner, as servants of Christ and stewards of the mysteries of God.

[12] Colossians 2:3
in whom are hidden all the treasures of wisdom and knowledge

[13] Hebrews 4:14
Therefore, since we have a great high priest who has passed through the heavens, Jesus the Son of God, let us hold fast our confession.

[14] Romans 8:19
For the anxious longing of the creation waits eagerly for the revealing of the sons of God.

[15] Revelation 22:2
in the middle of its street. On either side of the river was the tree of life, bearing twelve kinds of fruit, yielding its fruit every month; and the leaves of the tree were for the healing of the nations.

[16] 1 Thessalonians 2:13
For this reason we also constantly thank God that when you received the word of God which you heard from us, you accepted it not as the word of men, but for what it really is, the word of God, which also performs its work in you who believe.

[17] Philippians 2:
Being found in appearance as a man, He humbled Himself by becoming obedient to the point of death, even death on a cross.

[18] 1 Corinthians 15:31
I affirm, brethren, by the boasting in you which I have in Christ Jesus our Lord, I die daily. I protest by your rejoicing which I have in Christ Jesus our Lord, I die daily.

Chapter 12

The Passkey into the Kingdom

In the New Testament the Word talks about how we are God's inheritance[1] in Christ Jesus. We are His inheritance; and it is more than just belonging to Him; there is something so profound when you just think of what you are. You are God's inheritance. It is very special what He is doing with the sons, and what the sons are to Him.

2 Corinthians 6:17 it says; *Separate yourself. Come out from her, My people.* God is purging the defilement of this age out of you. He is purging it out of your mind, and the identification that you have had to the human race - literally to the Adamic nature; to mankind. It's a complete, not partial, deliverance that God is doing, and we are in the process of it right now. We are seeing bits and pieces of it, glimpses if you will. At times you may realize, for a moment, that something has changed within you. It may seem so minute, yet it is more important than we realize.

The changes that are happening can seem almost imperceptible, but they are going to become more apparent, as we finish this last phase of the preparation of God's kings and priests.

You have been called outside the camp, but there is yet another level of experience, deliverance, and transformation awaiting you. There is another level of change, right here, knocking on the door. God is completely extracting you from this world system. He is breaking off of you the ties to the human race, the ties to a way of life, and a mentality of thinking that has attempted to define you and to limit you. You are not merely another human on this planet, amongst millions of others. You are a pre-destined son of God, who has been sent for such a time as this. This is who you are.

Your calling is very unique, and the fact that your awareness is quickening is testimony, in itself, to the preparation that is being completed within you. The calling of sonship has been upon you, and you are unique and different from mainstream Christianity, not to mention the world as a whole.

God was not playing games when He commanded His sons to separate themselves. And I believe that is how the scripture goes ... *if they separate themselves unto Me then I will be a God to them and they will be sons and daughters to me and I will be a Father to them*[2]. However, the command is - **separate yourself.**

We haven't realized how much defilement exists in the world, and in all the peoples of this current age. It is a defilement of soul and spirit. It is a defilement that goes deep within the mental belief systems and paradigms of people. It is very pervasive, and this is why God says; "Separate yourself - come outside the camp and let Me wash you in the word." God is cleansing you in the blood of Christ, so that you might see; and in seeing that you might know; and in knowing that you might change. We do not yet know how unique and special the sons of God are to the Father .. but that awareness is coming.

The Lord is establishing within you a relationship to Him unlike anything that has ever existed. We have seen bits and pieces of it in His relationship to the Levitical priesthood, all throughout the Old Testament. That was just a "sign", a token, of what His intent was towards the sons, who would come to birth at this time.

The Lord is calling for His sons to separate themselves on a much deeper level. It is more than just trying to keep your act clean; trying to be careful as you sojourn through the day not to pick up the uncleanness of the pervasive iniquity that is in the earth. Let me be more specific .....

You remember the story in the New Testament when the disciples met with Jesus. He stood before them and wanted them to remove their sandals; He was going to wash their feet[3]. And of course they didn't realize what was happening, and they were ready for the Lord to wash their feet, hands, head; give them a whole bath[4]. But He just wanted to wash their feet; to get rid of the defilement that they had picked up in the course of that day, as they walked through the streets and picked up the filth.

Now this is an example. It is more of a physical example but it's a type and shadow of the spiritual defilement that is so easy to pick up. This is why the Lord is calling for the sons to come outside the camp, to separate themselves unto Him, and to break the contacts, the bonds;

literally everything that would be an entanglement to them. As they do this, the Lord executes a surgery on them, as He begins to remove from them their ties to humanity, and their ties to the Adamic race. In truth, they are of the order of Melchizedek[5], having neither a beginning nor an end. They are spirit beings; the sons.

The deliverance that God is bringing during this time of completion is far greater, and far more expansive, than we understand. The deeper the deliverance goes, the more empowered and enabled the sons become to move in the authority and dominion of sonship, because they have dropped the baggage they have been carrying.

In some ways it could seem very cold and calculating, because you are leaving behind the bonds and relationships of the soul. There is no other way, if you truly want spiritual sight. You cannot carry the baggage of unequally yoked relationships into the Kingdom. It just won't work. You can fool yourself, and believe you can bring the baggage along, but that is only an illusion. **Your ability to see will be hindered, and that is the passkey into the kingdom.**

Perhaps you need a revelation of "unequally yoked relationships"; I don't know. But now is the time to have faith, with your eyes open. We may feel that we are not being loving and sympathetic; and if that is the case, then we do not understand the love of God. We look at it from the perspective of our mind and the soul; but to understand it from God's perspective, is quite a bit different than how we perceive it to be.

How much did God love Jesus? God so loved the world that He gave His only begotten son[6]. He gave Him up to the cross. And God so loves His sons, that He scourges[7] every one of them whom He receives. There is no entrance into kingship, sonship, or the priesthood, without a deep scourging of the spirit. In plain English, this is what it means for the Father to receive you unto Himself.

This is nothing new to you. This is the path you have lived for a long time. The only difference is that we are in the last leg of this race, and God is finishing the work within you. It can feel quite lonely, if you're honest, but you must let go of the last ties; reaching deep within your being, and allow God to pull the last cords off of you. Understand, these little cords of the flesh both suck off you and feed you on the soul level. He must yank them off of you - like little feeder tubes. If you are able to do this, then it can feel very lonely, because nothing else will feed you, but Him.

There are very few who understand these principles; certainly not those close to you on the soul plane. If you are able to make this shift, then most likely they won't understand. It could be misread that you don't care anymore. You don't love them. You're not involved. But it is none of that. God is separating the sons, and He must, if they are to enter in through the portal to sonship.

> **"Enter through the narrow gate; for the gate is wide and the way is broad that leads to destruction, and there are many who enter through it. For the gate is small and the way is narrow that leads to life, and there are few who find it." Matthew &:13-14**

It can feel very lonesome because your communion and feeding comes only from Him.

> **He brought us out that He might bring us in and give to us the land that He has sworn to our fathers. Deuteronomy 6:23**

This is what God is doing. He has brought you out and now He is making sure the deliverance is complete; with the cords, the ties, and the bonds, on every level, severed.

<u>You only enter into the kingdom if you see it.</u>

You must see it to possess it. You cannot possess resurrection life, if you don't first see it. You cannot possess sonship, if you don't see it. You go through the work of the cross[8], and all of the dealings that God puts you through, so that He might strip off the dross, the baggage, and the weights. Spiritual eyesight at this time is NOT a luxury; for *without spiritual sight you will not enter the kingdom.*

The change that is happening, and the change that must finish, is not going to happen because we are just in an upper room waiting before the Lord saying; "Okay, here I am Lord". In the New Testament they were waiting before Him - in the book of Acts - and the Spirit fell. This time though, everything is different. To receive what is coming now takes a more aggressive stance and positioning. What is happening is that your eyes are opening, and you are beginning to see. And in seeing, you will become, and you will change. This is time of the Upper Room, but it is an upper room where everyone must be able to see. What are we talking about? The parable of the wise and foolish virgins, only the virgins are the sons – or those called to sonship, and they are awake.

The scripture speaks about changing in the twinkling[9] of an eye. What is that really talking about? Well, we know in Corinthians it talks about *they that behold Him will be changed into His likeness from glory to glory[10]*. What are we talking about here in the twinkling of an eye? We're talking about a change that happens the moment you see Him on that level. The moment you see resurrection life, it happens.

This change will not be a process ... all of a sudden you start going through this process. No. The process is to get you to the point where the baggage is taken off. At that point, your eyes are opened, and you see Him on that level and you are changed. How quickly? In a twinkling of an eye; you are changed in a moment, in an instant.

Everything is tied in to being able to see the Lord and that is why the deliverance has to be thorough and complete. You must be delivered from everything of this age. There can't be anything remaining. It can't be something that you try and work out; try and be a better person; try and pray more. That's not it.

The deliverance God is doing has to be thorough, because in its thoroughness the weights[11], and the sins which have so easily beset you, will be gone. The baggage that you have carried and run the race with - *which has strengthened you in God* - will be gone. God has been in everything that He has done for you. He's brought you forth. He's strengthened you. And it is for this moment that you have been brought forth; that He might complete your deliverance ... a deliverance to the uttermost[12]; spirit, soul, and body. With this deliverance comes eyesight, and with eyesight comes ... ***change.***

I bless this word to the sons of God, for this is the time of their completion; the completion of the kings and priests. It is time for them to transition out of this body of death; out of this realm of strife; out of a life of limitation, and into the unlimitedness of the Melchizedek ministry. The unlimitedness of Christ is a ***freedom beyond what we have known or could define.***

Outside the camp means a lot more than what we have thought. It is a lot more than just leaving a church that was stagnating in the way, and going on to walk with God. Outside the camp means outside of ***everything***. Outside the world system. Outside the Adamic nature. Outside the ancestry of humanity. Outside of everything. Are you ready for this? .... Because here it comes.

God is completing His deliverance within you, and your identification is changing. Change will snowball the more you begin to truly see who you are. This is not a, "I think I can. I think I can. I know I must be." It is a deep inner knowing that comes because He has appeared to you and you have seen Him as He is and in a twinkling[9] of an eye, you changed.

Scriptures (NASB)

[1] Ephesians 1:18
I pray that the eyes of your heart may be enlightened, so that you will know what is the hope of His calling, what are the riches of the glory of His inheritance in the saints,

[2] 2 Corinthians 6:18
"And I will be a father to you, And you shall be sons and daughters to Me," Says the Lord Almighty.

[3] John 13:5
Then He poured water into the basin, and began to wash the disciples' feet and to wipe them with the towel with which He was girded.

[4] John 13:9-10
9"Then, Lord," Simon Peter replied, "not just my feet but my hands and my head as well!" **10**Jesus answered, "Those who have had a bath need only to wash their feet; their whole body is clean

[5] Hebrews 7:3
Without father, without mother, without genealogy, having neither beginning of days nor end of life, but made like the Son of God, he remains a priest perpetually.

[6] John 3:16
"For God so loved the world, that He gave His only begotten Son, that whoever believes in Him shall not perish, but have eternal life.

[7] Hebrews 12:6
FOR THOSE WHOM THE LORD LOVES HE DISCIPLINES, AND HE SCOURGES EVERY SON WHOM HE RECEIVES."

[8] Philippians 2:8
Being found in appearance as a man, He humbled Himself by becoming obedient to the point of death, even death on a cross.

[9] 1 Corinthians 15:52
in a moment, in the twinkling of an eye, at the last trumpet; for the trumpet will sound, and the dead will be raised imperishable, and we will be changed.

[10] 2 Corinthians 3:18
But we all, with unveiled face, beholding as in a mirror the glory of the Lord, are being transformed into the same image from glory to glory, just as from the Lord, the Spirit.

[11] Hebrews 12:1
Therefore, since we have so great a cloud of witnesses surrounding us, let us also lay aside every encumbrance and the sin which so easily entangles us, and let us run with endurance the race that is set before us,

[12] Hebrews 7:25
Therefore He is able also to save forever those who draw near to God through Him, since He always lives to make intercession for them.

Notes

Chapter 13

Ending the Gap

What separates us from the real fulfillment of what God has for us? I know that we are in a time that God is opening the portals of heaven for the sons, and He is bringing them into experience after experience. I know the Lord speaks to His sons in the night hours and He speaks to them of things both to come and, of the provisions that are here now, for each one of them. When those words or visions or appearings come, they have a tendency to throw you into travail, because your spirit bears witness to the reality that the provision you seek, is already here. ... even though the appearance is that you have not yet possessed them.

We know that with every appearing of the Lord comes change. To the measure that you see Him, to that measure you are changed[1]. There is no appearing of the Lord that doesn't come without change. Yet the challenge we often times face, is the initiative that God has put upon the sons to reach in and walk in what He has revealed - to actually manifest it in the here and now.

The appearing of the Lord can range from the quickening of the word to your heart, to a dream, a vision, an actual appearing; any number of things. That is why the process of coming to know the Lord involves more than just one aspect of hearing Him; it involves your entire being that comes alive until you hear Him in any way that He would choose to manifest.

In the book of Proverbs it says that it is the glory[2] of God to conceal a matter, and the glory of kings to seek it out. Whether we like it or not, whether we have enjoyed the process or not, that mantle is upon us. God reveals bits and pieces, line[3] upon line, here a little, there a little, to the sons, as they are prepared and as they are able to bear it.

The Lord spoke to the disciples that He had many things yet they were not yet able[4] to bear it. I believe that is in the book of John. The Lord has a great deal prepared for the sons to walk in and to understand and to know, but it really depends upon whether or not they are ready to bear the exposure to the truth. When Christ spoke to the disciples and said, *"I have much to reveal to you but you are not yet ready not yet able to bear it"*, it was more than just understanding a concept; it was based on whether they were at a place that they had ears that could hear the word. It had to do with their preparation.

Malachi speaks that when He appears[5] who can stand, for He appears like the refiner's fire. For the Lord to appear to you is a visitation of the fire. For the Lord to reveal the deeper truths and mysteries of the kingdom, He must first expose you to the fire. Being able to bear the truth goes hand in hand with the appearing of the fire in your life.

The appearings of the Lord throw you into travail[6] because you see that which is beyond the veil. You see a provision. You see something that has been made available, and yet you have not yet been able to possess it; and so your spirit agonizes and groans within you to come forth.

The promise has always been that they who seek[7] Him with their whole heart that He will appear and reveal Himself. It has always been contingent upon that drive to know Him. That has been the greatest problem with the church in this day. All of the churches, all of them mentioned in the book of Revelation, have to some degree lost their first love. The exposure to the world only brings a dullness, a heaviness; an unawareness. You must be careful, for too much exposure or complacency, will take away that deep drive to know Him. Paul had that drive. And that mark is upon the sons as well.

We must continue to reach in. It is time that the sons reach through the veil, and make this transition from life to life.

Over the years the word has come many times to let go ... *let go of how you have thought, and what you have believed.* The Lord has been working at changing our paradigm and belief system, for without the change in our paradigm, we will not be able to see the truth, and to a great degree, this is tied into the renewing[8] of the mind, as it is referenced in Romans 8.

God has been in the process of completing a deep renewing of the mind; and with that comes a shift of how you have seen reality and how you have believed. I know that we, in ourselves, cannot do this. The Lord must do this. He has to help the sons let go. It's all about a shift of paradigm - out of limitation into His unlimitedness.

We know that we have grown up in a world that has been fraught with a great deal of deception and illusion; propagated by the satanic forces. Part of the baggage that we have comes from having lived under this canopy of illusion and deception, and this must go.

I began to ponder about this whole concept of believing. You can have faith, and you can have belief, and you can have knowing. Knowing is what God is establishing deep within the sons, something that transcends belief; that transcends having to have faith for something.

On the natural level, you do not have to believe in gravity, you just "know" its reality. God is moving the sons into a state of abiding, where the truths and realities of the realm of spirit cease to be something you must believe for; it is something that you just know exists. We have believed, even though we haven't seen. We have seen in part, but we are transitioning out of the realm of faith and belief, and into a realm of absolute knowing. This is the key to the greater works, and to the ministry of the sons of God.

Much of what God is doing has already been done; it is already here. The challenge has been, why haven't we possessed it before now? Are we waiting for a unique time, day, month, or year? Perhaps. But I am not completely sold on that, because I think it has to do with an internal change that is happening within the sons; a shedding of a way of thinking and a paradigm of how they have seen reality and limitation.

For some time now the Lord has been speaking about resurrection life. The word has come continually; "It is here. It is right here. Just reach in and possess it." In the Book of Thomas, Thomas says; "The kingdom[9] of God is spread upon the earth and men see it not." Conversely, resurrection life is here amongst us, but we see it not.

What is the resurrection, but Christ? Christ is the resurrection[10]. And our resurrection is tied into our ability to see and know the Lord; for He is the resurrection. We fully embrace Christ, as Christ fully embraces us, and our bodies have no choice but to respond to that same energy and power - resurrection must manifest. It is hard to quantify how close we are to this, because we have lived with the limitations that we have had for such a very long time. And yet the Lord says, "It is right here. It is right here."

The Lord wants to reveal many things to His people; the deep things[11], the deep mysteries, the wonders of the kingdom and of the age to come. And it's all tied around the renewal of the mind and the change within our own personal paradigm. We're in a countdown. We have been in a countdown. We are in a window of time; a timeline if you will. And God is speaking about believing; not just believing ,but entering into a state of knowing.

We are to enter into a state of knowing. You could say a realm of knowledge, but that might seem too nebulous. It's really a realm of knowing. And the promise is that we shall know[12] even as we are known. For some time the sons have been known, to a degree, even though they have not known themselves, but this is changing.

In the Book of Thomas it talks about poverty. Thomas talks about poverty[13] as a state of being where you do not know who you are. And so therefore you live in poverty, and ... you are poverty. In many ways we have lived on the fringes of a poverty mentality, because we have not known who we are. But this is changing.

We are in a time of what I would call a silent appearing of the Lord. And that silent appearing is something that we are just beginning to be aware of. We are in a time that the Lord is appearing to His sons, but it takes eyes to see, and ears to hear. You would think, "Surely I would recognize the Lord when He would appear to me." But that is not always the case. Unless there is an ear[14] to hear, and an eye to see, you will not recognize His appearing. It will seem as though it is something else, because it will be veiled.

Something within the sons is coming alive, and as you go through your day, more and more, you're becoming aware an appearing that is happening to you. Not with a lot of fanfare or pompous ceremony. It is something like that still small[15] voice. And this time there is an ability to hear and understand the voice of the Lord in a way you have not previously known.

There have been times when the Cloud of Witnesses have come through and said, "Please. Move more quickly." And the response that we feel is, "Yes. We want to move more quickly. What more can we do?" Everything, however, is tied into the timing and the process of the Lord finishing the work in the sons.

God is closing the gap between what He has revealed and spoken to you, and what you are walking in. That has been a challenging situation for God's sons. The only way the Lord has of stretching you beyond what you have previously walked in, is that He first reveals what is coming, and you see it ... *similar to the book of Hebrews where it speaks that they saw*[16] *and reached in.* Once you have seen, then you go into travail to bring it to pass.

You see it, and maybe you experience it for a moment, and you feel the reality of it, yet it remains seemingly at arms distance. There appears to be a gap between what He has spoken and revealed to you, and what you've been able to attain or move into. And this is when the stretching begins! Paul lived on tip toe ... I would say he was being stretched ... and it is no different for you or I. We are living on tip-toe, with neck stretched out, as the Greek literal puts it.

It is the process of being stretched that is the most uncomfortable, and yet it is the way of God. He is constantly stretching the sons beyond their comfort zone, beyond what they have moved into, that they might break into the deeper things of God. That has always been His way.

This is how Paul walked. It says in Philippians 3, if you read the literal Greek, that he lived with "neck stretched out", reaching. And that is a very interesting explanation. Neck stretched out. Paul was stretching, reaching as much as he could. God was stretching Paul; always stretching Paul to move beyond his perception of reality. And so the sons are constantly being stretched. The end product of this will be a closing of the gap between that which has been spoken, and that which His sons are moving in.

The sons are living in two worlds at the same time, and they have been for quite some time. It's becoming more and more evident, as the pull increases from the realm of spirit to draw you up higher. In doing so, you gradually relinquish your hold on the natural plane. We've been tethered, if you will, to the natural plane, far too long. But God is anchoring us in a new realm; the realm of spirit, and He is pulling us up as quickly as He can.

We are coming out of the realm of illusion, and into the realm of truth, more and more. We are moving more deeply into the realm of light, which is the realm of the Father's presence. It is time for the gap to end. It is time to see the completion of what the Lord has spoken over the sons. Resurrection life is right here at the door, knocking. The change is beginning to happen, even if it is imperceptible to the sons, at this point.

In the Book of Revelations the word speaks about delay[17] and that delay should no longer be. We know that the angel stands with one foot on land and one foot on sea and says, "There shall no longer be delay."

Well this is that angel's time, because the delay that has been here in seeing the full manifestation of the sons of God, is coming to an end.

The problem has not been so much with the "spirit of delay", as it has been the sons fully seeing the provision and entering in. This has really been the hindrance; the inability for the sons to realize how deep into the kingdom that the Father has brought them ... so much so that those things which they have believed for, *are here in their midst even now.*

We are declaring an end of the gap ... the gap between what God has spoken, and that which the sons are walking in. The paradigm or mindset of the sons has been undergoing an extensive change since their sojourn began, for God has been delivering them out of this world as quickly as they were able.

The word says that eye[18] hasn't seen, nor has ear heard, those things which God has prepared for His sons, yet the Lord has been speaking to His sons, in the night hours, some very deep things. The deep mysteries[19] of the kingdom come with a demand for the sons to walk in them; to embrace their truth; to embrace their reality.

A word came some time back to visualize yourself on the other side of this transition. Just picture it, see it, put that in your mind as a paradigm, and embrace that truth rather than subtly embracing the illusion that you don't have it, and you're still reaching for it. The paradigm of sonship is one of unlimitedness. It's a paradigm that says; whatever you ask[20] or think - has already been done.

In the realm of spirit, all you have to do is think on something and it is created. There is no limitation. That truth needs to be a manifested reality now, for the sons, that as they think upon something, it is created.

The sons are still throwing off the last shackles of unbelief that have crept in and tarnished their thought processes. Those shackles are being removed. If it must be that God comes with a surgical tool and says. "Okay, I'm going to lay you on the table and I'm going to remove it." Then we simply say, "Lord, do it. Just finish it. Whatever needs to be removed, just remove it." For this is the time the gap is to end.

The sons have been progressively moving out of the realms of illusion and deception and into the realms of light and truth with each deliverance they receive. This is an ending of the gap. The soul has been going through the final work of the cross[21]. Everything is changing, for the real ministry of the sons of God is going to happen on the other side of this transition that is set before them. It is the time for the deep ministry of the sons of God to fully unfold.

It is one thing to say, "Well, I know our spirits are very active," and yes, they are active in the warfare. And they're active in how the Lord directs them. But there's an integration happening, the integration of all that you are; spirit, soul, and body. You are to function as a whole being before God; with an acute awareness of the spirit realm, of the natural realm - literally of everything. God is integrating you so that you're no longer a dysfunctional creation, where you have the soul out here doing one thing, the body is over here doing another, and the spirit is somewhere else.

God is integrating you and that has always been the promise: spirit[22], soul, and body. And as you move, you move by the spirit, but it's all of you. You don't have to go and lay your body down somewhere and then go and function and come back and raise your body back up. And there have been accounts of those types of things over the years. People would lay their body down literally, and then leave the body and go and do the things that they were being directed to do, and then when finished come back; return to the body and arise. Unusual stuff. God is creating sons that are fully integrated; spirit, soul and body - Father, Son and Holy Spirit.

The realities of the promises have been hovering over the sons for a very long time. They've been within them. It's not as though one has needed to reach out to possess the promises, as much as to reach in and embrace what has already been given.

Whatever has been blocking the complete manifestation of the sons of God, is coming to an end. The mindset of the sons are changing from a paradigm of limitation, to a paradigm of abundance and overflowing.

Faith is a spirit level reality. We believe. And we believe, Lord, this is the time. Perhaps it's been the time for a long time. But the sons are now positioned at the door of entrance. And as they go through the door that's been set before them, not only will they find release, but all of creation[23] will enter in through that door of release as well.

Scriptures (NASB)

[1] 1 John 3:2
Beloved, now we are children of God, and it has not appeared as yet what we will be. We know that when He appears, we will be like Him, because we will see Him just as He is.

Or [1] 2 Corinthians 3:18
But we all, with unveiled face, beholding as in a mirror the glory of the Lord, are being transformed into the same image from glory to glory, just as from the Lord, the Spirit.

[2] Proverbs 25:2
It is the glory of God to conceal a matter, But the glory of kings is to search out a matter.

[3] Isaiah 28:19
"For He says, 'Order on order, order on order, Line on line, line on line, A little here, a little there.'"

[4] John 16:12
"I have many more things to say to you, but you cannot bear them now.

[5] Malachi 3:2
"But who can endure the day of His coming? And who can stand when He appears? For He is like a refiner's fire and like fullers' soap.

[6] Romans 8:22
For we know that the whole creation groans and suffers the pains of childbirth together until now.

[7] Jeremiah 29:13
You will seek Me and find Me when you search for Me with all your heart.

[8] Romans 12:2
And do not be conformed to this world, but be transformed by the renewing of your mind, so that you may prove what the will of God is, that which is good and acceptable and perfect.

[9] Book of Thomas Saying 113
(113) His disciples said to him: On what day will the kingdom come? <Jesus said:> It will not come while people watch for it; they will not say: Look, here it is, or: Look, there it is; but the kingdom of the father is spread out over the earth, and men do not see it.

[10] John 11:25
Jesus said to her, "I am the resurrection and the life; he who believes in Me will live even if he dies,

[11] Job 11:7
"Can you discover the depths of God? Can you discover the limits of the Almighty?

[12] 1 Corinthians 13:12
For now we see in a mirror dimly, but then face to face; now I know in part, but then I will know fully just as I also have been fully known.

[13] Book of Thomas Saying 3
(3) Jesus said: If those who lead you say to you: See, the kingdom is in heaven, then the birds of the heaven will go before you; if they say to you: It is in the sea, then the fish will go before you. But the kingdom is within you, and it is outside of you. When you know yourselves, then you will be known, and you will know that you are the sons of the living Father. But if you do not know yourselves, then you are in poverty, and you are poverty.

[14] Matthew 13:13
"Therefore I speak to them in parables; because while seeing they do not see, and while hearing they do not hear, nor do they understand.

[15] 1 Kings 19:12
After the earthquake a fire, but the LORD was not in the fire; and after the fire a sound of a gentle blowing.

[16] Hebrews 11:13
All these died in faith, without receiving the promises, but having seen them and having welcomed them from a distance, and having confessed that they were strangers and exiles on the earth.

[17] Revelation 10:6
and swore by Him who lives forever and ever, WHO CREATED HEAVEN AND THE THINGS IN IT, AND THE EARTH AND THE THINGS IN IT, AND THE SEA AND THE THINGS IN IT, that there will be delay no longer,

[18] 1 Corinthians 2:9
but just as it is written, "THINGS WHICH EYE HAS NOT SEEN AND EAR HAS NOT HEARD, AND which HAVE NOT ENTERED THE

HEART OF MAN, ALL THAT GOD HAS PREPARED FOR THOSE WHO LOVE HIM."

[19] 1 Corinthians 2:10
For to us God revealed them through the Spirit; for the Spirit searches all things, even the depths of God.

[20] Mark 11:24
"Therefore I say to you, all things for which you pray and ask, believe that you have received them, and they will be granted you.

[21] Philippians 2:8
And being found in fashion as a man, he humbled himself, and became obedient unto death, even the death of the cross.

[22] 1 Thessalonians 5:2
Now may the God of peace Himself sanctify you entirely; and may your spirit and soul and body be preserved complete, without blame at the coming of our Lord Jesus Christ.

[23] Romans 8:19
For the anxious longing of the creation waits eagerly for the revealing of the sons of God.

Section 4

The Battle Of the Ages

Chapter 14

Understanding the Warfare

What I want to do is review aspects of the warfare that the sons of God are experiencing during this time, adding just a bit more insight and clarity.

As we have taught over the years, bonds and contacts are a major source of warfare and conflict to the saints, because that is how the enemy gains access to you. This access is achieved through what we call "transference". We have spoken about transference in all of our books, and it is at the core of all of the warfare that comes against the saints. Transference works through bonds. We have taught about bonds, and that they function out of sympathy, obligation, and the emotions of the soul.

We have been consistently looking to the Lord for ways to gain immunity in the conflict which comes against the saints, for the conflict from this point on, *as we have been told a number of times in the spirit*, is only going to increase. This is why the function of the cross has been so important, for the cross in a believer's life brings greater and greater immunity. How? As Christ spoke, "*the wicked one comes and finds nothing in Me.*" With the cross comes the removal of the soul nature, and equally, the elimination of the bonds and the cords that have existed in your life.

We have not realized how easy it is to become bound together with an unbeliever[1]. What has Christ to do with Belial? Nothing! Bonds and unequally yoked relationships reside in the realm of the soul. And God has been delivering the sons, one step at a time, as they have been maturing out of that level of access and vulnerability.

There is another aspect to the warfare that we need to understand and that is to understand what we are as human beings. We have a body, we have soul, and we have a spirit. We also have spoken about the fact that we are electrical/energetic beings, and that the whole spirit realm is comprised of energy, frequency, and vibration. In the book of John, the

Word points out; ***"In My Father's house are many dwelling[2] places. If it were not so, I would tell you. But where I go, there I prepare a place for you...."*** This is really talking about abiding places, frequencies and vibrational levels, if you will.

As we continue to make this transition out of the realm of the soul and the physical, and into the realm of the spirit, we understand more and more that we are energetic beings. Anything that has any bearing on us, or the natural plane, comes first from the realm of spirit. God's word brings change first in the spirit, then it filters down to the natural plane. Anything which touches the sons, first emanates from the realm of spirit.

A lot of the warfare against the saints is standing upon the word when God speaks; "Okay, it's done." In the eyes of God, and the Lord, it is done. But it is done on a realm of spirit. And so the fight of faith[3] that the saints have lived under is believing that, so that it can have its fruition and manifestation on the natural plane without being sidelined by virtue of any unbelief. A lot of our contending is in just holding fast, knowing that the manifestation of the truth will come about.

We are spiritual energetic beings, and the true foundation and basis of our functioning is based in the realm of spirit. Because of this, everything that is going on in the realm of spirit, has an effect upon us.

We have been saying for some time now that we are in a transition; and we are in a transition - a transition out of the realm of the physical and the soul and the mind; into the realm of spirit. And that transition is more than just something that we say by faith, "Okay I'm in transition into the realm of spirit." You could say, "Well, what does that mean?" It means that you're coming into a life that is more founded or based in the realm of spirit as your reality, rather than the natural plane.

It's like taking the anchor out of this level, and you throw it up and become anchored in the heavens. And it can be a very interesting experience as this begins to unfold, because all of a sudden you have a hot line on a different level. And your senses begin registering in the realm of your soul and physical based upon the connection of your spirit.

We are evolving into spiritual sons of God, and our whole basis and framework of reality is shifting into the realm of spirit.

Where we are headed with this teaching is to understand a little bit more about the spiritual warfare that we're under. Assuming that you have done your homework, and that the majority of the bonds and contacts that you are aware of have been dealt with, the question arises, "Okay, why, am I still experiencing warfare. What's happening?" You have been birthed into the realm of spirit, even more, and although you may not yet be aware, your spirit is making an impact in the spirit world wherever you go. The spirits of wickedness—the principalities, powers, thrones, dominions—that exist over different areas as you drive through the country, will react to your presence. We understand that different spirits rule or govern over areas, literally towns, regions, counties—they're very, very, real. And they exert a definite power and influence over that area.

This is why you can go into certain areas, and certain countries even, and be aware of the oppression that is there because of the prevailing spirit that is controlling that area, city, or region. As the sons continue to come into their inheritance, and as you continue to make this transition out of the realm of soul and flesh into the realm of spirit, you're going to find that the spirits of wickedness are going to be reacting more and more aggressively against you.

In the book of Isaiah, chapter 52, the word comes; *"Arise and shine, lift up your head*—wake up, wake up! As you come alive to God, then the promise comes that the unclean[4] thing will no longer have access to you.

> **Awake, awake, Clothe yourself in your strength, O Zion; Clothe yourself in your beautiful garments, O Jerusalem, the holy city; For the uncircumcised and the unclean Will no longer come into you. Isaiah 52:1**

What we haven't understood is that by the existence of bonds, we have allowed the spirit world to have access into us. And so when the warfare hits, if it's founded on contacts and bonds, it can have a dynamic effect on you because it has gained access into your being ... *into your energetic field.* There is nothing that is warding it off. You may have the front door bolted, but the back door[5] is wide open and the enemy is able to come into you. And he can blind you, and he can hit you on a physical level, a spiritual level, or a mental level, whatever the case may be. This why bonds have been so important. But the promise is that if you wake up, and come up higher, that the wickedness will no longer have access into you.

Given that, what we're really talking about is understanding that as an energetic being, everything about us is energy, vibration, and frequency. If the enemy coming against you does not have access to you through a bond or contact, then he will not be able to come into you. However, he will still be able to hit you, but with much less effectiveness.

This is why you could walk down the street and someone across the street might look at you and you could just feel them hit you royal, just a zap of energy—wham. It might throw you off your guard for a second, but it cannot stick because you have dominion and authority and you can throw it right off.

If you were dealing with assault that was being channeled through a contact, or a bond, it would not be the same case. You wouldn't be able to throw it right off. Generally, it takes a lot more work, because you've got to really be able to discern how it's coming in.

This reminds me of something which happened many years ago. While in the conflict, I was confronted by a demonic entity with a drawn sword, intent on resisting me. At this point my understanding was very limited regarding energetic beings, and the dimensions of the Father's house, so I was not prepared for what came next. At the point of enacting a judgment upon this demonic entity, all of a sudden it disappeared. The entity had changed its vibration or frequency, and thus was able to move into another plane or dimension of reality and side step the judgment I was going to deliver. Too young in God, I did not know how to change my frequency to follow, nor did I understand, at that time, what was needed.

More and more we will come to understand the realm of the spirit *and the realm of our own spirit,* as God completes the training of His sons. The warfare coming against the sons is going to continue to increase, but this goes hand in hand with coming alive to the realm of spirit. The difference will be that the sons will know what to do, and when it is done. The dynamics of everything is changing right now. Open vision is coming, which is a precursor to the change of your physical body that is coming.

The changes coming are happening in stages. The first stage that has been happening, at a more accelerated rate, is a greater sensitivity to the realm of spirit has been coming. That is the purpose for this word - to understand how the spirit realm can hit you, even though you do not have to accept it. That which is happening right now is all part of your education, you might say.

If you can imagine - and I've seen this many times in vision - that you have someone that can be looking at you with such hate that they can create a ball of negative energy and they can throw that energy at you. Kahunas can do that in the Hawaiian religion. And I've seen it on other levels. That ball of energy may not have a contact point or a conduit or a channel to gain access into your being, but it can hit you externally, just like throwing cold water, except a lot more powerful. And it can hit you, royally, because it is dark, negative energy.

The more that we move on this level, the more you're going to feel the energy around you; the energy of people, and the energy of the spirit world. And they're going to react. Some will be drawn to you, and others will hate you, but know that you have the authority and the dominion to to deal with it. You are learning a different type of warfare, for it is based upon a rejection of the Light that you are, and your presence is becoming confrontational. Whether you like it or not, your presence is becoming more and more confrontational.

The sons are are experiencing these various levels of conflict, but the understanding is coming now. As you are birthed more and more into the spirit, you will have the ways and means to deal with this. God is training your fingers for war. Perhaps it wasn't as crucial to understand as it is now, because the battle of the ages is here.

We are not looking for a detent in the battle, and I' have seen that ... you can get into a battle with witches or other demonic entities, and it's like a detent. They throw something at you and you throw it back. Push and shove. Nothing seems to happen. I've seen that in the past.

What is different now is that the authority has been committed[6] to the saints of light. Now, it may not be the full authority as spoken of in the book of Daniel, but it is coming. You recall where it says that judgment[7] is passed and given into the hands of the saints ... we are in that transition. We may not have all of it, but we have a good measure of it. And that means that we don't have to accept anything that's coming against us. There is an authority resting upon the sons that can route the spirit world as it comes against you, as it peeks out from a closet and seeks to come against the light. You can stand and see that thing brought down. The sons can't hide who they are anymore, because this is the time of their unveiling.

In the past, the Lord had His sons under[8] His wings. Hidden in preparation; maturing and growing. We weren't ready yet for the conflict and the battle that He had raised us up and destined us to enter into. So He allowed the precious[9] fruit of the earth to mature and come to its place of maturity. And that really is us; it is the sons who have come to a place of maturity. Now the Lord has removed some of the veil over us, and we are being seen in the spirit, because now is our time to enter in and complete what He sent us in the earth to do.

Now we have the authority. Now we are prepared. And now we understand and see clearly what is happening and what is coming down right now.

The sons cannot hide the light that they have become. We are the true light, as the Father and Christ are the true light.

You might say, "Well, isn't that an audacious statement? How can you say that you're the true light?" ... only because we are identified with Christ and the Father. In ourselves we are nothing, but He is everything. So we are the Light that has come into the earth. No longer will it be hidden beneath a bushel[10]. The bushel has been removed and the light of His countenance, and all the prophecies of the emergence of the light in the earth, are coming to pass now.

We know the prophecies of how the enemy is slain[11] by the brightness of His rising. We also know that this speaks about the sons of God; for they are the brightness of His rising. It doesn't speak that all of a sudden Christ, somehow individually, is rising and then judgment comes. It is the rising of Christ within the sons that bring the finality of judgment, and we are in this time of the finality of judgment.

And if you have ears[12] to hear, we are the kings and priests of the Most High. This earth belongs to us. We are the administrators of His judgment. We are the caretakers, as we transition from this level of life into a level of sonship that God has fore-ordained for us.

We know the Lord has already done it. We know that we are already into this. All we are doing is identifying it.

Scriptures (NASB)

[1] 2 Corinthians 6:15
Or what harmony has Christ with Belial, or what has a believer in common with an unbeliever?

[2] John 14:2
"In My Father's house are many dwelling places; if it were not so, I would have told you; for I go to prepare a place for you.

[3] 1 Timothy 6:12
Fight the good fight of faith; take hold of the eternal life to which you were called, and you made the good confession in the presence of many witnesses.

[4] Isaiah 52:1
Awake, awake, Clothe yourself in your strength, O Zion; Clothe yourself in your beautiful garments, O Jerusalem, the holy city; For the uncircumcised and the unclean Will no longer come into you.

[5] Joel 2:9
They rush on the city, They run on the wall; They climb into the houses, They enter through the windows like a thief.

[6] Daniel 7:18
'But the saints of the Highest One will receive the kingdom and possess the kingdom forever, for all ages to come.'

[7] Daniel 7:22
until the Ancient of Days came and judgment was passed in favor of the saints of the Highest One, and the time arrived when the saints took possession of the kingdom.

[8] Psalm 91:4
He will cover you with His pinions, And under His wings you may seek refuge; His faithfulness is a shield and bulwark.

[9] James 5:7
Therefore be patient, brethren, until the coming of the Lord. The farmer waits for the precious produce of the soil, being patient about it, until it gets the early and late rains.

[10] Luke 8:16
"Now no one after lighting a lamp covers it over with a container, or puts it under a bed; but he puts it on a lampstand, so that those who come in may see the light.

[11] 2 Thessalonians 2:8
Then that lawless one will be revealed whom the Lord will slay with the breath of His mouth and bring to an end by the appearance of His coming;

[12] Luke 14:35
Then that lawless one will be revealed whom the Lord will slay with the breath of His mouth and bring to an end by the appearance of His coming;

Chapter 15

They Chose the Darkness

How many people really want to know the truth?" In the word we know it says that men are drawn to the darkness, and not the light. The default of the soul nature is to reject the truth, and embrace the lie.

> **This is the judgment, that the Light has come into the world, and men loved the darkness rather than the Light, for their deeds were evil. John 3:19**

Look at the election that just passed. You might say, "Well in the alternate world of news reporting—maybe there's 10% that really desire to know the truth, since the mainstream media seems to be dishing out one lie after another."

So you'd have to kind of look at that and say, "Well, if 10% of the population really wants to know the truth and they're really scouring to try and figure out what is going on, what does that leave you with? It leaves you with 90% who really don't care. People are generally of the mind-set to be easily manipulated by whatever the media chooses to do. And this has been the case for many decades. This is how the satanic world can so easily manipulate the masses.

We have talked about this in all three books that we have written; that the principalities[1], the powers, thrones and dominions, control this world and they control the paradigm of the people that live in this world. They do that by the media, the movies, the TV; all of the elements that have any interaction with the public that could sway them. On a very basic level, all of the world exists[2] under the power of the evil one. The world exists in great darkness, and this we have known.

The prophecy of this time is that it is a time of great darkness. So what is darkness? <u>Darkness is the absence of light</u>. It is the absence of truth. It is the infusion of the lie. And what pervades the world, and America specifically, is this darkness. The darkness is what pervades the world at this time, not the light.

A word from the Lord came recently that what is in men's hearts will be accurately reflected in what comes forth during this time in the earth. The decree is that which people choose shall become manifest.

Research has found that if you speak something often enough, it will eventually be accepted as truth. People pick up a book or magazine, and the thinking is: "Well, this must be true. If it is in print, then it must be true." If you see it enough on TV, then it must be true. Right? No, we are just watching first hand the ongoing manipulation of the masses and this world system.

We have been shown this, many times, that what is happening in the world is that humanity is being herded like sheep into a pre-determined outcome that the satanic hosts are looking to achieve. And the prophecy is that if the time is not cut short, no flesh[3] would be saved alive. We are in this time. This is not speaking about the future, nor the past; we are smack dab in the middle of it.

The manipulation and control over mankind has been going on for a very long time. For thousands of years the spirits of darkness have wielded a control of the earth. The scripture talks about how people will believe a lie; they will call the truth[4] a lie, and the lie a truth. I am paraphrasing, but this is in the book of Isaiah, and this is becoming more and more evident.

This is the time that we are in, and it can be staggering. You could look at it and say, "Okay, it seems that 90% of the population are set to buy into whatever the mainstream media will present." But all you need to do is to look just beneath the surface, and you can see that it is all a lie; an illusion. But no one is really interested. So what do you in effect have? You have a global consciousness that can be easily wielded by the spirits of darkness at a whim.

If you go into John chapter 3, verse 19, it is an interesting scripture. The Word talks about when the light[5] came into the world and that the people rejected the light and sought the darkness. This is the reality for most of the earth. We need to understand that right now we are still living in the time of what I would call, "a downward flow".

In Micah 4, verse 1, it talks about the days of the kingdom, and that it will be a day of a reverse[6] flow. There will be a flow upward; not a flow downward; a flow upward into His presence, upward into the kingdom.

In Zechariah the Word talks about appearing before the Lord, and if the people of the earth do not do homage[7], then it won't rain on them. But if they do, then it will rain. We are in that time. People that open their hearts to the Lord **(you)**, it's going to rain upon them. It's going to bring forth fruit and change. But they that do not, what little[8] they have will turn to even greater darkness. And that is a prophecy as well.

At the recent election in America you could say, "Well, it was all about this candidate or that candidate," but it was really not about either. It was about that which is in the hearts of men and women being made manifest, that the judgments of God might come forth.

This presidential election, and what follows, will eventually reflect the will of the people. And by and large, that will is the darkness. And it just staggers you to think about that. How could someone choose darkness over light? But that is the time we are in and what we are facing. This is pervading the entire earth. As it was in the days[9] of Noah so it will be in the days of the Son of Man ... and in the days[10] of Sodom and Gomorrah. The iniquity was so pervasive, it was beyond imagination, yet here we are.

As it was in those days, so shall it be in the days of the coming of the Son of Man. We are in the time of the coming of the Lord, the Parousia of the Lord. And that Parousia first starts within the sons that have been called out, before we see a Parousia that will happen where every eye[11] will see Him. Right now the appearing is happening within the sons, and to a large extent, this is veiled from the eyes of the world, for they have not eyes to see.

We are in a secret coming, you might say. We are in that time. We do not have a clue how pervasive the evil and darkness has become in the world, and I don't think we would be able to sleep at night if we really knew how great the darkness has become. But this is not our focus.

We are focusing on the transformation and change of sonship; what God is bringing the sons into. God doesn't want you going off and focusing on all of the darkness, but He does not want you to be unaware, either.

America is like a microcosm of what is happening in the earth, and it can stagger you. You can look at it and you can say, "How can these people believe this stuff?" And yet they do; hook, line and sinker. What we see unfolding is country after country has turned its heart against God, and the judgments are lining up. The countries and nations of this world are beginning to fall apart; the image in Daniel has been struck, and it is only a matter of time before it all implodes.

If you see what is happening in Germany and in France; those countries are descending into chaos. Those countries don't even know what they're headed into. Britain is on that path. Russia and China, of course. And there are other countries.

The world system is imploding, for its time for the emergence of the kingdom of God. They have rejected the Lord of Hosts, and the Lord of Hosts has rejected them. Countries are beginning to implode - almost like a black hole - and taking with it everything surrounding it. This is what is happening with Germany, France, and it is going to happen with the remaining countries of this vast darkness. America; just one microcosm of what is happening on a global scale.

It's really all about the light verses the darkness. Men love the darkness[5] and have rejected the light. That is the default at this time. The default is that people love the darkness. That is why a word came recently about beginning to relate and see and walk by virtue of the energy; by virtue of the light or the darkness that you see. That's the only way to really tell what you're dealing with in the realm of spirit; the energy of a person cannot be hidden.

It's hard to fathom at times how much the soul is given to the darkness. But that is the case, for the soul is enmity[12] to God. And we haven't really given that the accord that we need to. That is really where the antichrist is. The soul vacillates towards the darkness, and that is what we see in the earth.

The pervasive temperament in the earth and America is vacillating to the darkness. It doesn't seem to make sense and you can't look at it from your perspective and say, "How can these things be?" They are.

Men love the darkness[5] and reject the light - and that is the situation. As it was in the days[10] of Lot and Sodom and Gomorrah, so it is now.

You can say, "Well, I don't see it." Look down the street ... everyone has nice homes; they're all outfitted; people go to work, everyone smiles. It doesn't seem on the surface to equate to that prophecy." But if you just go one step beneath the surface, it is staggering; the pervasiveness of evil and wickedness in the earth right now.

So we'll see what happens. The people of this world have chosen the darkness. And now God is giving them an opportunity to cast their ballot, so to speak. The word goes out in the earth, "Choose whom you will serve[13], God or mammon?" God is allowing people to make their choice; this is the time of decision, and this time of decision will initiate a level of God's judgment that has been waiting in the wings.

Scriptures (NASB)

[1] Ephesians 6:12
For our struggle is not against flesh and blood, but against the rulers, against the powers, against the world forces of this darkness, against the spiritual forces of wickedness in the heavenly places.

[2] 1 John 5:19
We know that we are of God, and that the whole world lies in the power of the evil one.

[3] Mark 13:20
"Unless the Lord had shortened those days, no life would have been saved; but for the sake of the elect, whom He chose, He shortened the days.

[4] Isaiah 5:20
Woe to those who call evil good, and good evil; Who substitute darkness for light and light for darkness; Who substitute bitter for sweet and sweet for bitter!

[5] John 3:19
"This is the judgment, that the Light has come into the world, and men loved the darkness rather than the Light, for their deeds were evil.

[6] Micah 4:1
And it will come about in the last days That the mountain of the house of the LORD Will be established as the chief of the mountains. It will be raised above the hills, And the peoples will stream to it.

[7] Zechariah 14:17
And it will be that whichever of the families of the earth does not go up to Jerusalem to worship the King, the LORD of hosts, there will be no rain on them.

[8] Matthew 25:29
"For to everyone who has, more shall be given, and he will have an abundance; but from the one who does not have, even what he does have shall be taken away.

[9] Luke 17:26
"And just as it happened in the days of Noah, so it will be also in the days of the Son of Man:

[10] Luke 17:28-29
28It was the same in the days of Lot: People were eating and drinking, buying and selling, planting and building. 29But on the day Lot left Sodom, fire and brimstone rained down from heaven and destroyed them all....

[11] Revelation 1:7
BEHOLD, HE IS COMING WITH THE CLOUDS, and every eye will see Him, even those who pierced Him; and all the tribes of the earth will mourn over Him. So it is to be. Amen.

[12] Romans 8:7
because the mind set on the flesh is hostile toward God; for it does not subject itself to the law of God, for it is not even able to do so,

[13] Luke 16:13
"No servant can serve two masters; for either he will hate the one and love the other, or else he will be devoted to one and despise the other. You cannot serve God and wealth."

Chapter 16

Spiritual Entities

The casting down of Satan and his hordes during this time is creating a unique set of dynamics in the earth plane right now; one that we need to review. We are seeing the completion of the preparation of the kings and priests[1] of God. These are two aspects of the ministry of the sons of God during this time; the priest ministry that goes before God on behalf of different ones or situations, and the king ministry that moves in the administration[2] of authority and dominion to begin to tear down and build up.

With the king ministry of the sons of God, we understand that we are dealing with entities constantly. You could say principalities[3], powers, thrones, and dominions ... a host of entities, you might say. We could probably spend an entire book talking about the various orders of demonic entities, but that is not the point of this teaching. I think we really understand that there are a lot of spiritual forces that we are dealing with, and that need to be brought down.

I believe that we understand that these spiritual entities, in many cases, demonic spirits, all have a name. Often times that name is born out of what they are. These entities are an embodiment of energy, like a demon of hate, a principality of fear, or a spirit of oppression. Even though these entities have a specific name, they are as well the embodiment of exactly what they were created to be. You don't generally find a spirit that manifests two or three different types of aspects to them. They are usually one. It is a spirit of this. It is a spirit of that.

Everything in the realm of spirit right now, is in a state of fluidity, because we are walking out Revelation, chapter 12. You recall the scripture, I'll read just part of it here.

9And the great dragon was cast out, the serpent, called the devil and Satan, who deceives the whole world; *(who deceives the whole world... except the very elect.)* ***and he was cast out into the***

earth, and his angels were cast out with him. (Revelation 12:9) I think that probably suffices it to stop right there.

This can seem like a singular event; they were cast out. But I believe what is being portrayed is a state of action; Satan is cast out and being cast out. The satanic forces of this darkness have been cast out of the presence of the Father, and they have been cast out of the highest levels of the realm of spirit. But, they are in the process of being cast down. It's not just a singular event that in one moment they are in the heavens, and in the next moment they are on earth tormenting those who inhabit the earth.

No. It is a liquid state that we are talking about. It is a state evolving. We have touched on this before. The state of being cast down has a direct correlation to the sons being caught up[4]. There is no co-existing of the saints and the satanic hosts occupying the same time and space, per se. As the sons are caught up, they displace the satanic hosts who are then consequently being cast down.

We have watched this for the last ten to twelve years. As it was first shown to us, we saw a tear in the veil in the realm of spirit that separated one dimension from another. And with this tear we have seen a progressive shift of the satanic entities, falling from the heavenlies, down to the earth plane.

Let's take a brief detour, for a moment. As a point of interest; when Christ died, He passed[5] through the heavens. He had access, and He passed through the heavens. So you would think, "Well, is that how it exists? Once you die you have the ability to just move about freely from level to level to level?" No. I don't believe it works that way.

As you mature, as you are refined[6], purged and purified, whether it is on this side of the veil, or on that side. Then, you move forward deeper into the presence of God and higher into the realms of spirit. The progress on the other side of the veil is slower, because they are not in the body. They still are in the process of becoming, and as they go through the refining, they are able to ascend further up as well.

It is interesting that even though someone may be on the other side of the veil, they do not have access like Christ did, when He passed through the heavens and set the captives[7] free. We always thought of "setting the captives free" as just those here that arose from the graves and began to walk about Jerusalem. Those captives were set free, but there is more to it than that.

We have yet to expand our consciousness or our awareness of how vast and all-encompassing the kingdom of God is. The kingdom of God, the kingdom of the Father, encompasses many levels, many realms, and, many worlds. When Christ passed through the heavens, He began to set the captives free on every level. We are yet to understand just how important the ministry of the sons of God truly is. Their ministry is not relegated to just the earth, and the planes of the earth, but their ministry encompasses ALL of creation, regardless of dimension or world.

We are beginning to understand that all of the Father's creation is intrinsically tied into the sons of God. And that has been very, very hard to fathom and understand that such an anointing, such a mantle, would be placed upon such earthen vessels of clay, as the sons are. The release of the captives spans worlds and dimensions. And I have seen that numerous times. And I have seen the preparation going on, brief glimpses if you will, on different dimensions, different worlds, where they have been readying themselves for the final showdown. They have known that the culmination of the ages was imminent, and that it was tied into the release of the sons of God.

If this gets to be a little too much for you, then put this on the shelf. But I have had times when I have spoken with different ones who represent civilizations that have evolved on other worlds. I can't even say exactly where or how. And within their cultures they have had prophecies speaking that a time would come when these anointed ones (the sons of God) would come and set them free. They don't know how it will happen, but they are expecting.

I had one young girl approach me once and ask, "Are you one of those that will come and set us free?" So there is an awareness, as well as prophecies, and a consciousness out there of the emerging of the sons of God that is in the midst. And furthermore, the impact it is going to have. So when Christ passed through the heaven; you have to think outside the box.

Christ began to set the captives free. We don't understand how extensive the Lords ministry was at that time, but we know that Christ's ministry is being completed through the sons. If you are a scholar of the Bible, then you know that His ministry was cut off three and a half years of the seven (half way), as was prophesied, because the second three and a half year ministry of Christ was to be completed through the sons.

Now a lot of people can look at that and say, "Well, I understand that prophecy and that was done. The second three and one half year ministry of Christ through the sons has already been done"; and I would just say, "No. It hasn't. It hasn't even begun. But the sons of God are to complete the ministry of the Lord Jesus Christ that began." Where are we in the time frame of that? We are very close if not already into it. But it is hard to quantify at this point.

So going back to what we saw a number of years ago ... the tear in the veil. As this tear began to emerge in the veil, we saw a progressive falling down into the natural plane of the satanic hosts. This encompassed thousands; legions, upon legions. It is even hard to imagine the various orders that exist in the realm of darkness. But they began to be cast down and with that the word came; "watch what is going to unfold".

As the agents of darkness began to manifest more and more in the earth, we saw more inexplicable things happening on the human plane: diseases that were never heard of, mental conditions that all of a sudden have gone off the charts. A lot of things began unfolding, not to mention a huge increase in the acts of violence in the earth. This is where it is all coming from.

What is happening in the earth is not coming from the ideology of people and their desire to be free, it is coming from a spirit realm that is exploding as they are progressively cast down. It is very difficult, at this point in time, to look at anyone and not see spiritual attachments that are already happening. There are very few people that we see that aren't, on some level, carrying entities.

This may be something that you have already noticed. We are not talking necessarily about demon possession, which in itself is definitely on the rise. We are talking about entities that just attach themselves to people. They could be people that are in between the realms, who passed over, but never really made the transition, so they are kind of wandering. They could be evil people that died and definitely made no transition. They could be those from the realm of darkness, the spirit realm, being cast down who seek embodiment.

The one thing that we need to understand is the spirit realm seeks embodiment. I can't explain what that feeling is. Remember when Christ cast the demons out of the oppressed man and they beseeched Him to cast them into a herd of swine? And so He did. And subsequently the swine jumped off the cliff. So, the spirit world seeks embodiment. And so the number one agenda is embodiment, some sort of attachment—that they find some way to manifest.

We have seen a huge influx in this over the last several years. Most people are very much unaware. And it is hard to explain exactly what causes these entity attachments to happen. But in most people, their auras are not complete; there is like a tear in it. This is hard to explain, but most people's auras have gaps, caused in their sojourn, and because of that entities are able to attach themselves in the aura. However, let's not go down this road for now. We just know that there is a huge influx of entities into the natural plane, and more and more the dynamics of the natural plane are changing.

A word came a year ago, after the blood moon, that we would see a huge influx of a very dark and hostile spirit or energy, that would affect literally all of mankind. And, unless you were walking with God, you would not be able to withstand it. Over the last year we have seen a huge rise in violence, acts of aggression, and murders. Across the board. And people can point the finger and say, "Well, it's this movement or it's that movement." But it is a lot more than a movement here or a movement there. There is something that is entering into the earth that people cannot withstand, and they have no awareness of it, unless they are walking in the spirit. It is part of what is happening, as we see this age wrap up.

So what are we talking about? We are talking about the ministry of the kings and priests[1]. We are talking about what the sons of God are already entering into, prior to their completion. This is part of the ministry of the king, and this is an awareness that needs to be cultivated within you, because more and more you are going to be dealing with this.

As we have said before, ***what you see is not what is***. People have a tendency to look at things and draw a conclusion that what you see, at face value, is what is. And I tell you, it is easier said than done not to be drawn into that mindset, because you have functioned this way all of your life. The automatic response, in any given situation, is usually to respond to the circumstance as though it is valid, or real, because there it is, right in front of you. And yet it is all part of the illusion of this age. It is not what you think it is.

It becomes very important to understand the infiltration of the satanic presence on the natural plane, because more and more you will be dealing with a host of spirits that have painted an illusion. And you will be tempted to respond, or react, or be drawn into a battle or a skirmish, with something that is an entire illusion propagated by the entities and spirits of darkness that are behind it. It is something that we need to understand more and more, because this is part of the ministry of the king.

What is sad is that the stage has been set for the last ten to fifteen years for so much of this to come to pass now. People are accepting aspects of what is happening, without thinking about it. If you have followed the books that have been written for the young children, ages 5, 6, 7, and 8 ... much less the movies that have been put out through Hollywood in the last ten to twelve years, you will see how there has been a progressive programming going on. Everything is about light and dark and demons and witches and warlocks, and a lot of other darkness.

You might say, "Well, that is just harmless." But it is not, because there is an impartation coming through these books and movies; an impartation from the spirit world that is beginning to form how people think, how they view reality, and how they view what is acceptable and what is not. There is a rising consciousness of a world of evil that is becoming more and more acceptable. And consequently, this is enabling the levels of possession and entity attachment to move much more quickly down the road.

There was a reason why they burned[8] the books at Ephesus. It wasn't just that they were about a certain subject matter that was not the most desirable; that is not why they burned the books. They burned the books because of the energy that was on them and the ability for the spirit world to transfer darkness and blindness through those books.

We have to get out of thinking in linear terms, if you will. Everything about you is energy. Everything. You cannot function any longer from the perspective of your mind evaluating and drawing conclusions and looking at your life and your reality from that perspective, because everything about you is energy. It is not black and white; it is not linear or mentally definitive. As you come up to this level of release and manifestation, the energy of everything about you has a much more dynamic effect than it ever had in the past.

The books of darkness being written today, and the movies being produced, convey more than just concepts, they convey spirit. Emails, believe it or not, can convey a blessing or they can convey an oppression.

A spirit of oppression can touch you, and many times it can be very difficult to get rid of - unless you really understand. It especially becomes more difficult if you have a bond or some sort of attachment to the person emailing you.

Everything is energy. I can't say that enough. And we have repeated it over and over and over again. But it needs to go deep. We need to understand that our frame of reference is switching from the natural plane and the carnal analysis, into realizing that we are a people of spirit and everything that touches you has a spiritual energy or force, vibration or frequency.

Look at it from this perspective; forget about demons or a bad vibe, if you will. Just understand that everything in creation, even if it is a keyboard, has a frequency, has a vibration, because all matter vibrates at various frequencies. This, in itself, warrants a book to study and understand.

Christ knew who He was. He could change His frequency or vibration and pass through the walls. Is that difficult for us to do? It shouldn't be. Honestly, at this point, it should not be, because you are beginning to understand that you are frequency, you are vibration; you are spirit. More and more the Lord is training and teaching the sons about the realm of spirit, and how to come into a functional reality within the realm of spirit. This is just one aspect that needs to be understood. Remember the Lord passed[9] through walls and passed through a crowd? It's not that difficult; we just need to understand who and what we are.

Many years ago it was shown to me that we are tuning forks. Now for some of you that may make sense. You understand that a tuning fork is what tunes a piano, or any musical instrument, to come into correct sound. But what God was saying is that the sons are tuning forks and you can manipulate or modify your sound. And you can tune right into whatever you need to tune into. That is just one aspect of it.

When we come to understand more and more of what we have the capability of doing, we will realize that we can change our vibration, change our energy and literally appear any place we want to be. Not limited by time or space. These things are happening, and they will increase, for this is the time that God is equipping the sons.

It's one thing to go through the process of refining, go through the fire, and come out purged[6], purified, and refined. It is another to understand that God is equipping the saints for the work of service that they are to enter into, and the prelude to this functioning has been, and will continue to be, the purging process.

God is not going to turn you loose one day, and all of a sudden everything just rains down upon you as a massive experience, and all of a sudden you are birthed into the spirit realm 100%, and you know everything. I don't think it happens that way. I haven't seen it happen that way.

He brings you into progressive experiences and He teaches you. Wasn't that what the Lord did? He would first teach them? No. He would first bring them into an experience, and then He would teach them about it. The Lord is preparing the sons for what they must do. And in that preparation is the experience of functioning in the realm of spirit, understanding it, understanding what you are and understanding how to move in the realm of spirit. And this will be more and more important as we move into the time of judgment[10].

The judgment that will be brought forth through the sons is more than just a ministry; it is an aspect of what you are. As you move into that expression of what you are; which is the Father's judgment upon this age[11], it will be necessary for you to know how to do it. God isn't going to bring His sons forth without having taught them and brought them through what they need to know and understand.

Aside from having the demonic spiritual entities that we are warring against, as I said, there are entities that really have been lost in the whole translation process. And these, as well, must be dealt with. Oftentimes, as you wait upon the Lord, you will find them pop up. Curious, but oftentimes mischievous. And you've just got to send them packing. The only ones I allow in my presence when waiting on the Lord, are those whom He sends.

Oftentimes you will find that in your home, if you are not aware of it, spirits and entities are drawn, because they are being drawn to the light[12]. And so they come and oftentimes they end up just occupying space, even within your home. Sometimes all they need is just to be sent on, and they just need a little help.

Part of the ministry of sonship[13], and this would be as the Lord leads you, is to help them. There are those that have genuinely been caught in between. And we have seen this a number of times. And you just need to speak a healing and send them on. And that is what they come for. That is what they are looking for. And this is just another aspect of ministry of the sons of God.

There are those, who are more evil in their nature, and have been caught in between and when they come, they bring darkness and a rather negative energy with them. And those, they need to be sent packing. We don't necessarily judge them, but we don't allow them to be in our presence either. If they start coming against us, then that becomes a different issue. If you start picking up witchcraft that would emanate from them, then that really draws the line.

There is a rise of this type of entity in the earth plane more than we ever have had. It is hard to explain exactly why that is. But a lot of people are having a difficulty in their transition when they pass over, even those who are Christians, who are God-fearing and God-loving have difficulty at times making the transition. So the Lord will lead you, but it is just something to be aware of.

The path of the sons can be a difficult path to navigate, especially when you read in the New Testament that it says a man's enemies[14] will be the members of his own household. This is why the teaching on bonds has been so critical, and why so few have really understood it. Because it is hard to conceive that a family member could become such a channel and yet on the surface appear just fine as ever. This is an issue that is of great concern to us, because we have seen the blindness that exists on people and the difficulty for them to open up and really understand what is happening to them and where it truly is coming from.

It is interesting with Christ that in His relationship to Peter, as much as Peter loved Him, and much as the Lord loved Peter, that He was not bonded to him. He was not corded to him. And when they were on their way and Peter counseled the Lord as far as going into Jerusalem, Christ turned to him and said, "Get behind[15] me, Satan." Because the Lord did not have a bond to Peter, He was able to immediately discern the presence of Satan. And He knew exactly what was happening. It was probably devastating for Peter, but I am sure it was a learning experience for both Peter and the disciples. There is much in the word that is not expounded upon, but I would not be surprised if the Lord did not sit the disciples down and explain to them what just happened.

As we have said before, the stakes are a lot higher now than they were ten years ago, or twenty years ago. Now, more than ever, the spirit world has one desire, one focus: stop the manifestation of the sons of God.

To stop your manifesting any way they can. So they work over-time through your bonds and connections, and your unawareness.

Bonds or cords can be very subtle, because a bond is not necessarily a two-way street. An attachment can just happen because someone reaches out and projects an energy and seeks to attach to you. And if you are not aware of that attachment, it can just hang there and can be a source of oppression.

You might say, "I'm not bonded. I don't have any bond with this individual or that individual." It can even be someone walking down the street and you have nothing to do with them and yet somehow an oppression, a cord, a conduit is created and projected on you. And you might say, "Well, I'm not bonded," but you have got to realize that it doesn't necessarily have to be two-way street.

This reminds me of a story. Many years ago a man of God that we knew was walking down the street. On the other side of the street, walking the other direction, was a man walking. He looked over and saw the man but didn't think much about it, until all of a sudden he felt a hit in the spirit. He turned and realized that the individual had projected witchcraft at him and had successfully hit him. The more he looked at the man, the more he realized that the person really didn't even have a spirit, at least not as we would define. Some sort of alien-thing he thought. It was a wake-up call for him, and he began to watch his backside a little bit more closely.

For the sons of God during this time there is a burgeoning awareness that we are walking in the midst of a sea of spirit. We are walking in the midst of millions and millions of people. We can have a tendency to just think that everyone is normal, these are all humans, everything is just as it seems, just as it appears. But it really is not. You've got humans. You've got hybrids. You have Nephilim[16]. You have those that are human but with a satanic input. And you have aliens and God knows what else is out there. I will say this, **nothing is at it appears.**

And therefore, you need to continue to cultivate an awareness, because the king ministry is a threat to the spirits of darkness. You are a threat. The manifesting of the sons of God are the greatest threat that the spirit world has ever known since the fallen angels fell; since the whole thing began.

We are at the culmination of time, and the sons of God are the agencies that the Father has raised up to bring down these messengers of darkness. Now, more than ever, there is a realization that the Light has come and is here.

I love the scriptures in Joel[17] chapter 2. It talks about the army of the Lord and how they go forth. Behind them is a desolate wilderness, and fire proceeds out of their mouth. It's very descriptive. It also speaks about how they leap through the windows and so on. Although this is figurative, it speaks of the sons ability to take down the forces of darkness. The sons of God are no longer to be behind the eight ball, they are coming to know the realm of spirit and how to function in it.

It says in the scripture that the sons of darkness[18] have been more adept in the ways of the world and spirit than the sons have been. But that was only for a season. And that season is over. The sons are quickly being trained how to function and move in the realm of spirit.

Leaping through the windows[17] speaks of the access the sons have to the enemy, where the enemy is no longer able to stand protected by the demonic hordes. Their shadow has been removed, even as it was in the days of Joshua and Caleb, where the protection[18] was removed from the giants. So the shadow, or protection, has been removed from the spirits of darkness.

What goes out of the mouth of the sons? Fire. And a desolate wilderness behind them. When you open your mouth what shows forth? Light? Blessing? Anointing? Mixed with a good dose of fire.

The train of thought in this day is peace and safety. Everything is just fine. But it is anything but that. The warfare of the kingdom is gaining momentum even if no one is aware of what is happening. And the ministry of the kings and priests has arrived. More and more you will function with an awareness of what you are doing, and how to deal with that which comes against you.

The first step is to be aware and to understand that everything is changing, both in the realm of spirit, and in the natural. The sons are coming forth and this is changing the playing field. What you are dealing with today, will not be what you must deal with tomorrow ... the level of infiltration of the spirits of darkness today is on one level, but it is going to continue to unfold more and more. And tomorrow will be different. The day after that will be different. The challenges of change, the challenges of moving into the realms of judgment and authority, are upon the sons of God.

You are the kings and priests[1] of God, and He is finishing your preparation.

Scriptures (NASB)

[1] Revelation 5:10
"You have made them to be a kingdom and priests to our God; and they will reign upon the earth."

[2] Ephesians 1:10
with a view to an administration suitable to the fullness of the times, that is, the summing up of all things in Christ, things in the heavens and things on the earth. In Him

[3] Ephesians 6:12
For our struggle is not against flesh and blood, but against the rulers, against the powers, against the world forces of this darkness, against the spiritual forces of wickedness in the heavenly places.

[4] Revelation 12:5
And she gave birth to a son, a male child, who is to rule all the nations with a rod of iron; and her child was caught up to God and to His throne.

[5] Hebrews 4:14
Therefore, since we have a great high priest who has passed through the heavens, Jesus the Son of God, let us hold fast our confession.

[6] Daniel 12:10
"Many will be purged, purified and refined, but the wicked will act wickedly; and none of the wicked will understand, but those who have insight will understand.

[7] Luke 4:18
"THE SPIRIT OF THE LORD IS UPON ME, BECAUSE HE ANOINTED ME TO PREACH THE GOSPEL TO THE POOR. HE HAS SENT ME TO PROCLAIM RELEASE TO THE CAPTIVES, AND RECOVERY OF SIGHT TO THE BLIND, TO SET FREE THOSE WHO ARE OPPRESSED,

[8] Acts 19:19
And many of those who practiced magic brought their books together and began burning them in the sight of everyone; and they counted up the price of them and found it fifty thousand pieces of silver.

[9] Mark 16:14
Afterward He appeared to the eleven themselves as they were reclining at the table; and He reproached them for their unbelief and hardness of heart, because they had not believed those who had seen Him after He had risen.

[10] John 3:19
"This is the judgment, that the Light has come into the world, and men loved the darkness rather than the Light, for their deeds were evil.

[11] John 12:31
"Now judgment is upon this world; now the ruler of this world will be cast out.

[12] Isaiah 60:3
"Nations will come to your light, And kings to the brightness of your rising.

[13] Ephesians 1:5
He predestined us to adoption as sons through Jesus Christ to Himself, according to the kind intention of His will,

[14] Matthew 10:36
and A MAN'S ENEMIES WILL BE THE MEMBERS OF HIS HOUSEHOLD.

[15] Matthew 16:23
But He turned and said to Peter, "Get behind Me, Satan! You are a stumbling block to Me; for you are not setting your mind on God's interests, but man's."

[16] Genesis 6:4
The Nephilim were on the earth in those days, and also afterward, when the sons of God came in to the daughters of men, and they bore children to them. Those were the mighty men who were of old, men of renown.

[17] Joel 2:2-11 **Army of the Lord**
2A day of darkness and gloom, A day of clouds and thick darkness. As the dawn is spread over the mountains, So there is a great and mighty people; There has never been anything like it, Nor will there be again after it To the years of many generations. 3A fire consumes before them And behind them a flame burns. The land is like the garden of Eden before them But a desolate wilderness behind them, And nothing at all escapes them.

4Their appearance is like the appearance of horses; And like war horses, so they run. 5With a noise as of chariots They leap on the tops of the mountains, Like the crackling of a flame of fire consuming the stubble, Like a mighty people arranged for battle. 6Before them the people are in anguish; All faces turn pale. 7They run like mighty men, They climb the wall like soldiers; And they each march in line, Nor do they deviate from their paths. 8They do not crowd each other, They march everyone in his path;

When they burst through the defenses, They do not break ranks. 9They rush on the city, They run on the wall; They climb into the houses, They enter through the windows like a thief. 10Before them the earth quakes, The heavens tremble, The sun and the moon grow dark And the stars lose their brightness.

11The LORD utters His voice before His army; Surely His camp is very great, For strong is he who carries out His word. The day of the LORD is indeed great and very awesome, And who can endure it?

[18] Luke 16:8
"And his master praised the unrighteous manager because he had acted shrewdly; for the sons of this age are more shrewd in relation to their own kind than the sons of light.

Chapter 17

The Battle of the Ages

The Light vs. The Darkness

If you're wearing glasses, take them off. We're going to put a different pair of glasses on. I want us to see reality from a different perspective. Right now the way that we view reality is through the process of the intellect. It is the mind/body connection; what your eye sees is then filtered and interpreted by the mind, based upon your preset belief system.

Your view of reality is in a constant state of change, because you are in the midst of the renewing of your mind. To be absolutely free from this whole evaluation/judgment level of what your eye sees and your mind interprets, isn't really possible until you have experienced the completion of the renewing[1] of your mind. So we constantly wrestle with how we perceive everything around us.

As much as we are commanded not to know one another after the flesh, but after the spirit, I don't believe that it is possible until we are on the other side of this transformation of the mind. We are still caught in this web where we see people after the flesh[2]. And it's hard to admit that. We don't want to. It's not our desire. We're not looking to limit someone by their limitations, or by how they present themselves. But, it's still a function of the how the mind works, and how it assimilates what the eye sees and what the emotions sense. And so, you're constantly working at throwing that type of perception off, while we are in this transition. The whole realm of relating can be very challenging.

What I want to do is talk about our "body of Light". This will all come together, so stay with me on this. The word has been coming that we need to be eating for the new body that we're being given; even though the resurrected body isn't going to be dependent upon food. Food will not be the issue that it is now, once the changes come. You recall that Christ saw the disciples when they were on the seashore and he ate[4] and broke fish with them. He didn't have to eat, but he could.

Christ wasn't of the same order of Peter and James and John and the other disciples. He had a glorified body. It was a whole transformation. And we're in that process. While we are in this transition, for whatever period of time it will be, we will have to be more careful and realize that *our body is becoming more and more light.*

Now I want you to understand what I'm saying. It doesn't mean that we are losing weight. We're talking about a body of light[5] that is energy, and that is something completely different. And we know that everything in the realm of the kingdom of God is energy. We are energy, even though we are still coming to understand that. There is so much about the Father's kingdom that we don't understand, yet we have seen bits and pieces. We are coming into a functional relationship in the realm of spirit, and we are getting a new set of eyes and a new set of ears to be able to understand the truths of the kingdom.

Our bodies are in the process of a physical change. I don't know how that lines up with everyone's doctrine and revelation of what it means to be changed in the moment, in the twinkling[7] of an eye, from a worm to a butterfly, but this is where we are headed. We are experiencing, almost imperceptibly, changes on a physical/DNA level that we are not even aware of, yet. We have lived in a cocoon all of our life and haven't known it .... a cocoon from which we will see emerge a new creation; the sons of God.

We know that as He appears[8] that we shall be like Him. And 1st Corinthians 15 talks about how each son that comes to birth is going to be very unique[9]. Each body will have a slightly different manifestation as it comes to maturity.

So we are in this transition and our bodies are changing. And I wish to God that we could understand that. I wish that we could grasp it; that the reality of what I just said could sink in. First and foremost we have to break our bonds with everyone, because everyone projects all of their ideas of who you are and what you are, until the waters can get rather muddied. Relationships have a way of cluttering you, along with contacts and obligations.

So we've been talking about this for a long time. Perhaps not as long we have been talking about breaking the bonds with yourself, and how you see yourself. There can be a tendency to not see, not understand, not grasp, not realize that something is going on inside of you and you're changing.

So the first question I would have to those reading this: is Christ in you? Is the Father in you? That's a very basic tenant of what we believe. However, it's gone far beyond believing. I don't believe that. I know that! I know that is a reality! Christ in us the hope[10] of glory. We're still coming to understand what that means: *the hope of glory.*

Stop and ponder on this for a second. Is Christ in you? Is the Father in you? Okay, we agree. They are. What's happening? Well, you could say the great takeover is happening. The Father, the Son, and the Holy Spirit are taking over until there is nothing left[11] but Christ. You're a unique expression and manifestation of Christ. It can be challenging to talk about these things, because I know that the truth of them need to hit us on deeper and deeper levels. As we come up higher, our energy changes; and we are able to progressively grasp more and more truth.

We realize that just because we are walking with God it doesn't mean we are able to grasp the truth in its entirety. "Got it! Got it! Got it!" No. Not at all. God's sons are on the path of change and transformation into sonship, and their capacity to absorb the truth, to hear the truth, is conditional upon their change and transformation, *i.e. the work of the cross.* As you change, as you come up higher in God, you have a greater capacity to hear the truth.

That is why the scriptures are a constant, unfolding experience. With each level in God, the scriptures come alive on deeper and deeper levels. What has limited our ability to comprehend is tied into our maturing in God, which is in an ever-evolving state of change.

The sons are being caught up to the throne right now. I know, it doesn't seem to match your concept - perhaps. It doesn't match my concept either, but that doesn't matter.

This is what is happening. And as we go from plateau to plateau in God, we are becoming lighter and lighter and lighter. We are becoming more and more like our Father, who is the Father of Lights. Who are you? You are a child[13] of Light. Everything about you is Light. It's very mystical to just grasp this.

We may think of ourselves as these finite beings, with these bodies, and we know that our destiny is resurrection life, but I don't know how much it's really grasped us of how much we are and how much He is in us. It really comes down to the Light, and what we are truly becoming during this time. The Word says that no one can approach the Father for He dwells in unapproachable[14] light.

Why is the light unapproachable? Because of the sin and the iniquity that still exists within the soul. As the refining comes to a completion, our access to the Father, will also come to a point of total access. Who are the we? We are the Light ... and the brilliance of our rising is beginning to be noticed throughout the spirit world.

I saw this once on a map in a vision. I was in space, looking at the earth. This was about five years ago. I began to see bright pin points of light emerge; first one and then another one. Then as I watched, more and more pin points of light began to emerge around the world. I went, "And Father, what is this?" ... *the sons are coming to birth and as they recognize who they are, the light that they are is beginning to emerge.* Nothing could cover it any longer.

We know the word talks about when Christ appears[8] that we shall be like Him. Every time He appears to you in the word you are changed into His likeness; you are no longer the same. We are still grappling with our mind to understand what is happening within us as our spirits are changing, because everything about us begins to have a dynamic. Your sensitivity becomes greater; the warfare seems to be greater; just so many things about you is changing, because you're literally being pulled into walking in two worlds at the same time.

You're being pulled more and more into the realm of spirit, because of the changes that are happening. Even though your carnal mind has you anchored down here and you're kind of slugging it through on the physical level dealing with more and more physical issues; but that really is a positive thing. What is happening to you is because of what your spirit is tuning into and what you truly are becoming ... the bearers of the Light.

If you have ever gone back to look at the subject matter of the Hollywood movies throughout the eras, you will notice the ongoing theme of the light verses the darkness. Hollywood has been obsessed with it. But, in truth, we are in the battle of the ages, and it is the battle of light verses dark. Now. As the sons emerge as the true bearers of the Light, the dynamics in the earth will go through a huge shift, because, as I have said, the balance of power in the spirit is shifting now towards the sons.

So going back to what I said at the very beginning, let's put on a different set of glasses. Now I want you to imagine for a second looking at reality from an entirely different perspective. We lose the ability, for a moment, to see matter and atoms and the formation of molecules that represent our physical reality, as anything. Reality becomes something of energy. You no longer have the ability to see a person. In the past you have known people through the registry of your eyes. Now things have changed. You do not see their physical body, you see energy.

Imagine, as you look around, that you don't see anything that makes any sense on a physical level. All you see is energy. You can see the Father, because there is this bright light of energy that radiates and you feel His love and His essence. And you see Christ. But otherwise you look about you and everything is energy. I know this is kind of hard to visualize maybe, but instead of seeing people, you begin to see the energy that the people emanate.

As you see this, you find that you begin to relate to people by virtue of the energy that they manifest. And not so much the energy of the soul, but the energy from their spirit. It is important that we begin to see everything around us from an energetic point of view—from a whole different paradigm, or perspective. When people speak, you see the energy. And with that sight, you are able to read them. You know what is Light, what is dark, what is confusion, and so on. You have set your mind aside, and you are navigating only by virtue of the energy field that you see around people and coming from their mouth.

This may feel like we are stretching things a bit, but this is how we must begin to function.

What was it like for Christ when He turned around to Peter? And what would have happened if He would have stopped and said, "Hey, Peter. Let's go sit down for a second now. I want to talk to you about some contacts that you seem to have and we've got a channeling thing coming through here, and you've got some ideas that are hitting me in the spirit." He didn't. Christ was very black and white in that respect. You could almost call it cold. How cold that must have been. He turned around and looked at Peter—looked. He didn't say, "Hey, Peter." He looked at Peter and said, "Satan, get behind[15] Me." He saw the energy.

I think this is a great deal how Christ functioned in the world about Him as He walked. He saw people physically, but He also saw an overlap of energy ... two or three realities overlapping simultaneously. And He responded to the energy. He didn't respond to the person, He responded to the energy. Or you could say to the spirit that was really reaching out. Both are very closely akin to energy.

I believe that as we progress further down this road in the next six to twelve months, that we are going to be facing greater and greater challenges. These challenges are going to determine whether or not you are able to break forth into sonship, ***or not***. They are going to determine what is going to happen to you - because in the word it says if the elect[16] could be deceived they would be.

The deception that is so prevalent in the earth is staggering. I am not talking about the obvious, because there is a great deal of exposing going on right now of the evil that's been going on behind closed doors—a great deal of it. You can see it in the American political arena. You can see it in the governments of the world. It's all over the place. God is exposing on a level that we've never seen. But what I am talking about is the deception that is not obvious, that is so subtle, that without eyes to see, you would not see it. If you see the energy, or spirit, then you have a chance, but if you see only that which is being projected on the natural plane, then there is a great probability that you could be deceived ... that is ***if*** you are walking primarily on the plane of the soul.

The scripture speaks about the time being cut short ... that if it is not cut short, then no flesh[17] will be saved alive. What is happening is a need for us to be able to really see the energy of everything that is happening in the earth.

We must get out of the mind, and into the spirit.

How interesting it must have been for the Lord. He loved everyone, but He wasn't sympathetic. He loved everyone. But He wasn't sitting there trying to reach out and nursemaid. He was very careful in His relating, for He trusted no man ... for He knew what was in man, as the scripture goes. He could have appeared cold and calculating, because He saw the spirit. He saw the energy, and that is what He was dealing with.

We've got to come to the next level where we begin to see the energy that is coming out of people. Coming out of their mouths. Coming out of what they project. We cannot be locked into a pair of eyeglasses (or paradigm) ... that would keep us in a mode of seeing reality as we have known from the past.

Maybe we have never met someone before and all of a sudden we meet them. Maybe we have never met them and we see them on TV or in the paper. And they look good. They've got the nice tie on. I mean they've got the power tie, the power shirt, and even though their energy is as dark as midnight, the mind would have filtered what you saw based on your previous paradigm, and you would not realize what they truly are.

It takes the scripture to a much deeper level when it talks about how Satan transforms his ministers as ministers[18] of righteousness. And I'm not talking about churches. That's the obvious one. You can say, "Oh, yeah. I know what you're talking about. All of these churches out there, and all those minsters that have got 5,000 in their congregation. And the congregation is blind as blind can be ... blind leaders of the blind. And that pastor who is dressed up to the 'T'. He's got it down. He's the mojo man." That's not what I'm talking about. That's obvious. To us that is obvious. Obvious to the people in the congregation? Apparently not. When we speak about Satan dressing up his ministers as ministers[18] of righteousness, these "ministers" are not relegated to churches. These messengers of Satan are on every level, every profession, and every governmental institution.

Without true discernment, you could face a real problem moving forward from this time on, in the earth.

The word that God is speaking is to the elect, it is to the chosen. The word that is coming is not to the masses that are perishing or that have some other level of life that God will provide for them, in their long sojourn. The word that is coming in the earth at this time is a word to the elect and to the chosen. This is not a word to the church. This is not a word to the millions of Christians. This is only a word to the wise[19] virgins.

It is imperative that we make a change here—call it another set of eyes—something much deeper than what we've had that overlays this world of reality that we've known. It all has to go onto a much deeper, deeper level. If it were possible even the very elect[16] could be deceived. Even the very elect, the chosen. We are talking about a level of deception that, without a great deal of transformation and discernment, the very elect would not see it.

As much as we see, we must realize how much we do not see. We have to be able to see people purely by the energy that they project. You've got to be able to discern light and dark to get through the waters that we are facing right ahead of us. We might be in a rowboat. We might be in a speedboat. We could even be in a naval destroyer, but we're coming into some rough waters. And there's no way to navigate these rough waters that are coming, without the ability to see the energy behind everyone and every situation.

You could be talking to someone, "Oh, this is wonderful." You feel the light, then all of a sudden, boom! "Where did that come from?" Some darkness came in that was an undercurrent to everything that had happened in the prior ten minutes. All of this great light and then all of a sudden darkness starts flowing in. And if you don't catch it, it will blindside you.

We have to be able to function this way. Christ functioned that way. Christ knew what was in man[20] and He gave Himself to no one. He gave Himself to no one. I wish I could say that of the sons at this time, but I can't. Everyone is a bit guilty.

We must give ourselves to no man, only the Lord. We can say that, "Yes. Yes. Yes. I do. I do. I do." But there's a much deeper level here that we have to see. You give yourself to no man. It's almost like getting up in the morning and saying, "I give myself to no man! But I give myself to You, Lord. I give myself to the light not the darkness."

There are a lot of scriptures that we could dive into about the coming darkness. The coming darkness is here. The darkness in the earth is the darkest it's ever been. They equate this time to the days[21] of Sodom and Gomorrah. We can read about it, but you don't really know it until you walk it out first-hand.

And the mind struggles with that. "Well, how is that possible? I'm still enjoying myself. Everything's great." You're doing whatever you do. Ministering to people, if that's what you do, "How is it that what you say could possibly be here? This level of darkness?" And yet if you read through the scriptures they all point to this time. A time of great darkness[22]. Even Joel talks about it in the earth.

Read 2 Corinthians 6, verse 14-15. *Don't be bound together with unbelievers; for what partnership has righteousness with lawlessness, or what fellowship has light with darkness? Or what harmony has Christ with Belial?* We have to be so careful.

When the Father looks down at the sons coming to birth, who does He see? Well, ideally He sees Christ. But not always. And the problem is the Father has a hard time looking on unconsecrated flesh. And so the reason the words have come on bonds for the last 15 years is because as long as bonds remain, then you have a strong potential of carrying the very darkness of someone else that is not yours ... by virtue of transference.

And the Father looks down on you and what does He see? He doesn't see Christ. He sees darkness. And this cannot be. The differentiation between light and dark is coming much more to a head because the sons of light are coming to birth. It has become imperative that we are able to see, for the darkness coming is greater than what is even here now.

I can't tell you how it's going to come individually and touch you. Certainly it's not going to come because you go to some old order church and some preacher is out there spewing his darkness and everyone is just eating it up. It's going to be very personal. It's going to come in the back door of your life, that you won't even realize. The book of Joel talks about how the army of God is going to leap through the defenses and they're going to go through the back door[23] and the windows and they're going to take a prey.

Well, there is a flip side to that. The enemy has already been doing that to you.

> **Awake, awake, Clothe yourself in your strength, O Zion; Clothe yourself in your beautiful garments, O Jerusalem, the holy city; For the uncircumcised and the unclean will no longer come into you.**
> **Isaiah 52:L1**

When you separate yourself from the unclean, and break your bonds, you come up higher in the spirit. And the promise? The unclean[24] will no longer come into you. Think about that ... no longer come into you. Do you realize how unclean and how filthy bonds are? The relationships of the soul/flesh are very unclean. The darkness is going to parade as light and seek to have access, and bonds are a perfect breeding ground.

What is it like for someone to come into you? The closest thing I can parallel this to is the relationship of Adam and Eve. Adam went into Eve. I would say that was pretty close. Well, Isaiah 52 is speaking of something very similar. The darkness has had access through the back door[23], through a window, through your unawareness, to come into you. We have not been aware of how filthy bonds, unequally yoked relationships, contacts, cords ... you name it, are. And all of a sudden your light has become a little dim—not so bright. That's the jeopardy that we're facing right now.

The promise pertains to separating yourself. You come up higher. You wake up! I think that's how the word goes. Arise! Wake up! Wake up! Wake up! Wake up! Now let me say it again. Wake up! Get out of your slumber. Wake up! Come up higher. ***And the promise is that the unclean[24] thing will no longer come into you.***

We are in the battle of the ages, the battle of light verses dark, on a scale and a level that we have never understood, and which pervades the earth on a level that people have no understanding. People are so absorbed with all of the obvious corruption that is going on in the world, in the American politics, and in the governments, and they do not see what is right in front of them.

As much as you see happening in the earth - the governments, the politics, the corruption, corporate America — it is the tip of the iceberg. The corruption is so far greater. The darkness is so great in the earth, that if the Lord was to show you how deep this darkness was at this point, I don't know if you'd be able to sleep at night. I've seen it and the Lord has graciously removed some of it from my memory, because the darkness is so pervasive and the acts of darkness are just staggering. And what you see on the surface is just the tip of an iceberg of what is so evil.

We need to face what is right in front of us. We need to get Isaiah 52, and stop the unclean input going on into our lives.

What is coming is an ability, within the sons, to see the overlapping of the spirit world and the natural world at the same time. This is coming; I would call it - open vision. It is imperative that we begin to see reality from this perspective of energy.

Until open vision fully comes, we must transition out of relating by what our eyes see, into what we perceive, energetically, in the realm of spirit.

Last summer were the presidential debates. They had not yet begun, and the Lord said He didn't want us watching it. And He explained why. He said, "everything coming out of their mouths is snot. And everyone that is watching it is eating this snot. It is foul and it is disgusting, and that is all it is. It is just spewing out everywhere, and people are just eating it, eating it and eating it." And so He didn't want us connected very close, and we were not. But we've been certainly watching it, as close as we can, because the darkness is just running rampant.

This is the change that we must press into. We need to go over this word a number of times and we need to let it really sink in, for God is changing our paradigm. A paradigm has to do with how you see reality, and the sons are changing again.

We're talking about something a little bit different than just a paradigm. We're talking about having a different set of eyes that overlap the one set you have where everything begins to have a dimensional feel to it. Light and dark, good energy and bad energy; and in all of this the darkness is not going to be able to hide.

I know the days right ahead of us are going to see many that have been called - perhaps not make it - because they are not able to separate[25] the darkness from the light. And this is all about the conflict of light verse darkness, that is unfolding right now against the sons.

We are changing on a level that we don't understand. It's hard to even understand what we are. It's almost like getting up in the morning and it's not saying, "Who am I?" but it's almost like, "What am I?" Because there are changes that are outside the scope of your knowledge, outside the scope of the dictionary that your mind has. We don't know how to relate to where we are at - much less what we are, but we know the end product will be sonship.

May this word go deep, because the issue of light and dark has to be separated out. We have to understand that the warfare has gone up several notches, and the darkness in the earth is getting greater. We have to be aware of anything touching us, and we have to separate[25] the darkness and nail it at the gate. There can no longer be any back door, or back window, for the enemy to come in, because of a lack of awareness on our part of the energy that is coming.

Satan will not able to work in darkness any longer - not concerning the sons. This new ability comes forth, ***now***.

Scriptures (NASB)

[1] Romans 12:2
And do not be conformed to this world, but be transformed by the renewing of your mind, so that you may prove what the will of God is, that which is good and acceptable and perfect.

[2] 2 Corinthians 5:16
Therefore from now on we recognize no one according to the flesh; even though we have known Christ according to the flesh, yet now we know Him in this way no longer.

[3] Luke 24:39
"See My hands and My feet, that it is I Myself; touch Me and see, for a spirit does not have flesh and bones as you see that I have."

[4] Luke 24:41-42
While they were still in disbelief because of their joy and amazement, He asked them, "Do you have anything here to eat?" So they gave Him a piece of broiled fish,

[5] Luke 11:38
"If therefore your whole body is full of light, with no dark part in it, it will be wholly illumined, as when the lamp illumines you with its rays."

[6] Philippians 2:13
for it is God who is at work in you, both to will and to work for His good pleasure.

[7] 1 Corinthians 15:52
In a moment, in the twinkling of an eye, at the last trumpet; for the trumpet will sound, and the dead will be raised imperishable, and we will be changed.

[8] 1 John 3:2
Beloved, now we are children of God, and it has not appeared as yet what we will be. We know that when He appears, we will be like Him, because we will see Him just as He is.

[9] 1 Corinthians 15:39-41
Not all flesh *is* the same, but indeed one flesh *is* of men, and another flesh *is* of beasts, and another flesh *is* of birds, and another *is* of fish. **40**And *there are* heavenly bodies and earthly bodies. But truly the glory of the heavenly *is* one *kind*, and that of the earthly *is* another. *There is* one glory

of *the* sun, and another glory of *the* moon, and another glory of *the* stars; for star differs from star in glory.

[10] Colossians 1:27
to whom God willed to make known what is the riches of the glory of this mystery among the Gentiles, which is Christ in you, the hope of glory.

[11] John 3:30
"He must increase, but I must decrease.

[12] Revelation 12:5
And she gave birth to a son, a male child, who is to rule all the nations with a rod of iron; and her child was caught up to God and to His throne.

[13] 1 Thessalonians 5:5
for you are all sons of light and sons of day. We are not of night nor of darkness;

[14] 1 Timothy 6:16
who alone possesses immortality and dwells in unapproachable light, whom no man has seen or can see. To Him be honor and eternal dominion! Amen.

[15] Matthew 16:23
But He turned and said to Peter, "Get behind Me, Satan! You are a stumbling block to Me; for you are not setting your mind on God's interests, but man's.

[16] Matthew 24:24
"For false Christs and false prophets will arise and will show great signs and wonders, so as to mislead, if possible, even the elect.

[17] Mark 13:20
"Unless the Lord had shortened those days, no life would have been saved; but for the sake of the elect, whom He chose, He shortened the days.

[18] 2 Corinthians 11:15
Therefore it is not surprising if his servants also disguise themselves as servants of righteousness, whose end will be according to their deeds.

[19] Matthew 25:2
"Five of them were foolish, and five were prudent.

[20] John 2:24
But Jesus, on His part, was not entrusting Himself to them, for He knew all men,

[21] Luke 17:28
"It was the same as happened in the days of Lot: they were eating, they were drinking, they were buying, they were selling, they were planting, they were building;

[22] Joel 2:2
A day of darkness and gloom, A day of clouds and thick darkness. As the dawn is spread over the mountains, So there is a great and mighty people; There has never been anything like it, Nor will there be again after it To the years of many generations.

[23] Joel 2:9
They rush on the city, They run on the wall; They climb into the houses, They enter through the windows like a thief.

[24] Isaiah 52:1
Awake, awake, Clothe yourself in your strength, O Zion; Clothe yourself in your beautiful garments, O Jerusalem, the holy city; For the uncircumcised and the unclean Will no longer come into you.

[25] Genesis 1:4
God saw that the light was good; and God separated the light from the darkness.

Chapter 18

Overcoming

Probably many of you are familiar with the word "mantras". They have a deep and storied history in the annals of mankind. The whole concept of the mantra is to speak, over and over again, the same word or phrasing, until that concept permeates your subconscious.

The reason there has been such focus given to mantras, is because people are only now realizing how much the subconscious controls them. It would be like the example given with "Pavlov's dog", do you recall? Pavlov would ring the bell and serve the dog food, at the same time. Over time, a pattern was developed – bell ring equals food. All he had to do was ring the bell, and the dog began salivating. Our subconscious is similar; over time you develop patterns, patterns that are not of God; patterns that must change. In many ways these "patterns" are like your mental paradigm, they define how you see the world.

> **"the book of the law shall not depart out of thy mouth; but thou shalt meditate therein day and night, that thou mayest observe to do according to all that is written therein; for then shall ye prosper and then thou shalt have good success." Joshua 1:8 kjv**

Mantras are very interesting because it ties back into Joshua 1:8 literally. The commandment that God gave to Joshua was the key.

A simple example of the concept of "mantra" can be seen in the commandment from the Lord to Joshua. Joshua was commanded to meditate on the word day and night. Why, you ask? That the word of God would go deep into his subconscious and spirit. When he would go up against the enemy, his subconscious would already be tracking with the word of God; and therein was his success.

As much as people might think that mantras are some evil thing, the "mantra" really is not. It is just a way of rehearsing something, in our case it would be the truth, over and over, until your subconscious throws off the conditioning of limitation.

Why do you think we are not moving in more of the power of God? Raising the dead. Walking on water. You name it. It has everything to do with the conditioning within the subconscious mind. The renewal[1] of the mind, or mind of Christ, goes hand in hand with the removal of the subconscious limitations. You can chant, you can sing, you can read, it does not matter. It is just a matter of getting the truth to replace the lie that we still have, to some degree, within our subconscious.

So what was Joshua's key to success? Was Joshua a great military commander? No. Did he have a lot of experience? No. What were his qualifications? Well, that was simple. He stayed in the tent in the presence of the Lord, while Moses went up the mountain and did the various things that Moses did. Where was Joshua? ... in the tent waiting before the Lord. Those were Joshua's credentials.

He was not a trained general. He did not have strategies and knowledge along that line. But then God wasn't looking for that type of credential. God was looking for someone that He could relate to, that He could guide and speak and lead.

And so the word came to Joshua ... "*thou shalt meditate on My word day and night* (Joshua 1:8). But the real part of that scripture is the first half—*The book of the law shall not depart out of thy mouth (Joshua 1:8).* It was more than just meditating and rehearsing the directives, **it was the fact that *the word did not depart out of his mouth.*** (Joshua 1:8)

So we are dealing with two aspects here; meditating on the word so that the word re-programs the subconscious, and speaking the word. It was a double-edged sword for Joshua. It had to be both.

> **"And they overcame him because of the blood of the Lamb and because of the word of their testimony, and they did not love their life even when faced with death." Revelation 12:11**

The sons are going from plateau to plateau, as they rise into His presence. More and more, the word in their mouth becomes the big X factor. We need to recognize the importance of what we have become and what God has become within us. All through the Book of Revelation it talks about how you overcome by the word and the blood of the Lamb. But it's by the word ... <u>the word out of your mouth; not some generic word.</u>

Over the last ten to fifteen years the word has come many times: "You shall not prevail by man's wisdom; you shall not prevail by navigating around the hurdle; you shall prevail by speaking the word into every situation." The word is what breaks the oppression. The word is what breaks the lie and the illusion and the deception.

The Lord keeps saying; "Understand what I've become in you. Because if you understand what I am in you, you will know that as you speak the word, that you are speaking God and the authority cannot be withstood."

The key is speaking the word from the highest plane. As you come up higher in your vibration, then you speak the word. You take dominion over the lie. You take dominion over the illusion, because it is all about Christ in you. It has always been about Christ in you; not the hope of glory but the reality of His glory being made full and manifest in the time of His presence. And we have spoken about this. We are in the time of His presence, but we are still coming to grips with the deep reality of what we are in God.

As you go from victory to victory, from battle to battle, from glory to glory, the truth of His word will go deeper and deeper into your being. There is nothing that can withstand[2] the word out of your mouth. There is not one wall that can withstand it.

Sometimes it can feel like we are in a situation similar to Daniel and Gabriel. It took Gabriel twenty-one days to break through the ranks of the resistance in the realm of spirit, and deliver the message to Daniel. As he said, "Oh Daniel, man of high esteem, your words were heard the minute you spoke." But it took him twenty-one days[3] to break through the resistance.

Sometimes it might take twenty-one days. Sometimes it might take a little longer to break through the resistance, but breaking through the resistance, you will do. In some ways it is very similar to the principle of isometrics, which is a type of weight training where you exude a great deal of force without much movement. Call it spiritual isometrics, if you will. You are put in situations that will try you until you are digging deep into Him, deep with all that you are.

As you come through these times, you will find that you are much stronger in Him. That word is seared in you. The only way we can move forward at this time is by the word; no other wisdom is going to do it for us. As you speak the word, the resistance will break.

Scriptures (NASB)

[1] Romans 12:2
And do not be conformed to this world, but be transformed by the renewing of your mind, so that you may prove what the will of God is, that which is good and acceptable and perfect.

2 Luke 21:15
for I will give you utterance and wisdom which none of your opponents will be able to resist or refute.

[3] Daniel 10:13
"But the prince of the kingdom of Persia was withstanding me for twenty-one days; then behold, Michael, one of the chief princes, came to help me, for I had been left there with the kings of Persia.

Section 5

Possessing the Kingdom

Chapter 19

The Sons Birth the Kingdom

As we've said many times before, there is no charted map that tells us exactly how to navigate the waters in front of us. No one has walked this way before. We know there have been many who have died in the faith, and who have helped to pave the way for us, upon whom the ends[1] of the ages have fallen.

Unto us has been given the baton to complete the last leg of this race. No one has walked this way before, and we have to be very careful not to draw conclusions from what our eyes see or our emotions dictate, for we are walking through this realm of illusion into the realm of light. This is our destiny, and we are quickly moving in that direction. These are very tumultuous times to say the least. But the Lord has laid a path before His sons and they will not err[2] therein.

More than we understand, we are birthing the kingdom of God on every plane of existence. We understand that we live on more than one level; and the kingdom of God is comprised of more than just one or two levels. There are many levels[3] in our Father's house, many dwelling places; many mansions as the word speaks in the King James. And as such, we yet don't realize the huge effect that we are having on the realm of spirit as we come forth.

We have spoken about Romans 8, and the deliverance of all creation[4] into the freedom of the glory of the sons of God, and we know that the deliverance of creation is tied into the deliverance of the sons. But when you think of that, are we just speaking about something on the natural plane? And if so, what would that mean to deliver the trees, the seas and the oceans?

We understand that we are talking about a level of creation that, for the most part, no one is aware of ... a level of order on an elemental scale that controls and holds in balance so many things that we see on a natural plane. The arrogant atheist looks about and figures that what he sees with his eye is indeed what is, but that could not be further from the truth.

All of creation, as we know, is comprised of the elemental spirits that exist not only on this plane and this world, but on many different dimensions and many different worlds that exist in the Father's kingdom. The impact of the release which the sons are moving into is far more expansive and outreaching, than just this natural plane that we know.

God is birthing the sons. In many ways, He has already birthed them, as we read in the book of Revelation[5], but the dragon is there attempting to devour them, as they come to birth. And out of this comes a birthing of the kingdom - they go hand in hand.

As we said, we have not been this way before, and this could sound rather profound. More than once we have been aware of the feeling of carrying something deep within us — almost like a child, something that you know you're in the midst of birthing — but you don't quite understand it. For the sons to break into greater and greater liberty is for the kingdom to be birthed, progressively, on every level of creation.

As the sons are birthed on every plane, the kingdom is birthed on every plane, as well. Wherever your presence is - there the kingdom is - and there the kingdom will continue to move and break forth. I am sure there will be a point that we can look back and really define what it means to birth the kingdom of God. We know that the kingdom of God is within[6] us. We also know that in some way it is outside of us as well. Perhaps we have not seen the deep correlation of what we are to the entire kingdom of God, for the birthing of the kingdom of God happening within you - is affecting the kingdom on every level of existence. And that is a very mystical statement.

And as you are birthed and as you come forth into progressive liberty upon liberty, so the kingdom is birthed progressively deeper and deeper. This does not happen without a cause-and-effect scenario. For the greater the kingdom of God is birthed into the natural plane and into the realm of spirit, so everything on the natural plane will be progressively more and more affected.

You do not have a birthing of the sons without which the whole realm of the spirit and the natural are not affected. You do not have a birthing of the kingdom of God without which every realm is shaken. Right now the heavens are being shaken[7]. Hebrews speaks about the word that will come that will shake both the heavens and the earth. This is happening. The heavens and the earth are being shaken. But without eyes to see it, you are not able to recognize it.

You would think surely the shaking of the heavens and the shaking of the earth and all of the chaos in the earth would be so easy to discern that anyone would be able to see it and understand, but that is not the case. The birthing of the kingdom, however volatile and tumultuous it is, is still very hidden, because it appears as though it is this thing or as though it's that thing, or this event or that event—unrelated, unconnected. And yet they are all very related and very connected.

You could look at the events going on right now in the earth and they may seem to feel unconnected—even though there are similarities of violence and terrorism. It might seem like what is happening are unrelated, distant acts—one over here, one over there—nothing really connected. All kind of random, but they are not. They are all connected. They are all an outcropping of what is happening in the realm of spirit and what is happening in the whole realm of the birthing of the sons of God - and the kingdom of God.

It takes revelation to see this. It takes eyes to see. It takes revelation to understand that these are not random events, but they are all connected. And in a very real sense they are all part of creation[4] that is travailing. We've spoken of all of creation travailing and you could look at that and say what does that mean in real time? In real time this points to geophysical events happening on the face of the earth. This points to the acts of violence that are happening as well. They are all connected. This planet is so inter-connected with the birthing of the sons, and the transition of power taking place in the heavens, that it could be hard to fathom. Even the minutest of events are connected in. This is how important the sons are to the will of God happening during this time.

Whether it is an earthquake, a tsunami, or any other geophysical event happening, or anything in the scope of the acts of violence that are going on worldwide ... and I have seen this ... They are all connected. They are not random events. But it takes revelation to see it and to understand what really is happening.

In this whole process of the birthing of the sons and the birthing of the kingdom, we are finding that the word is ceasing to be a theory or a concept, or something ethereal - apart from you. We are beginning to understand that the plan of the Father in redeeming the sons to Himself involves many different levels and many different steps. One very important step is the absolute identification of all that you are with all that the Father is, all that the Son is, the Lord Jesus Christ, and the reality that you have, and are becoming, the word made flesh.

Now to the sons this may still seem a bit ethereal. We know in the book of John it says; *and the word came and it was made flesh*[8] *and dwelt amongst us.* We know the Lord Jesus Christ was the word, and is the word made flesh. We know that He is the first born[9] of many brethren. What does that mean? That we are to be as Christ, but we haven't understood the full import of what this means. There is a new identity coming to you. It is the last vestige of the breaking of the bonds with your carnal nature. The breaking of the bonds within you to humanity, to your genealogy; to everything that has defined or tried to define who and what you are.

God has been bringing a progressive deliverance and we have spoken about this many times. He is delivering you; spirit, soul, and body[10], from the genealogy of mankind. You are of the order of Melchizedek[11], perhaps you have not known that. You must understand that we are the incarnation of the word and the further we go down this path of redemption and manifestation, the more that we are going to experience a very deep mystical awakening. You are beginning to recognize that there is a oneness with the Father and the Son happening within you, and your awareness of this is dawning upon you.

There is another aspect to this. It is the deep recognition that you are the manifested word, in the flesh, as was Christ. It is not what you speak that is the word. It is what you are. You are the word. This epiphany will happen to us on deeper and deeper levels from this point on.

Many years ago someone came and appeared to me in the spirit and was talking to me about the judgments coming and said to me, "You are judgment." Not that you will have a ministry of judgment or a spirit of judgment. Simply said, "You are judgment."

Carry that forward to this timeline. The sons will not have a ministry of the word. They are not going to just speak the word. They will be the word. And the depth of grasping that is still unattainable to the carnal mind, but there is an experience here that will unfold. And you will realize that you are the word. And it's something so beyond the scope of our present grasp of reality. It's outside of any box that we could possibly have. It's outside of the capability of the carnal mind to comprehend. You are the word made flesh[8]. And that realization is going to hit you like a tidal wave, the deeper you press into this transformation.

The duplicity of the mind has constantly warred against your manifesting. Because the mind says, "I know who you are. We have a history. I know who you are." And it's so very subtle (this is the warring of the soul and the spirit). And yet God is breaking the ties even within yourself; even to your carnal mind. I don't know if we understand what a unique bond is here that must be broken, but this too shall be removed from us.

This is a deliverance from your connection with your mind. We have allowed our mind to define who and what we are. I know these things that we are talking about are a little difficult to grasp, because they must be experienced, but what I am talking about is an experience that is going to happen to us. We're in it at some level. But it's going to fully grip us, and there is no other way to explain this. I can't explain you into the experience, I can just tell you that it's going to happen to you.

As the mind goes through the final steps of crucifixion and redemption, you will find that the mind of Christ comes forth fully within you. You will see the bond broken that you have had with yourself; with your thinking, and where you have allowed yourself to be defined by virtue of how the mind has processed the information and then delivered up a judgment to you. This is another deliverance.

We have not realized how much the mind, both conscious and subconscious, have controlled our ability to manifest the truth of who and what we are. Everything is escalating during this time. The spirit world, as I have said before, is in chaos because everything is changing right now.

In the word it speaks of the travels of the disciples .... and they said to the disciples, "Are you they that have come to turn the world[12] upside down?" The disciples were turning the world upside down at their time. Was that by virtue of them going and speaking and witnessing?" No. It was more than that. It was what they were that was affecting everything - on every level. Now, even more so, the world is being turned upside down as the sons continue to come to birth, and move more deeply into the manifestation that they have been destined for.

In the book of Revelation, chapter 21, John made a statement; *And I heard a great voice out of heaven saying, "Behold the tabernacle[13] of*

God is with men. And He will dwell with them and they shall be His people and God Himself shall be with them and be their God."

The third feast that we have been commanded to observe is the Feast of Tabernacles[14]. It is typically in September/October. Tabernacles represents the last phase of the redemption of the sons which culminates in the full indwelling of the godhead. More than we understand, we have moved into this. The indwelling of the Father and the Son are so much further within us than we have been able to understand.

Reflecting back on what we have said about the Word; the manifesting of the word of God, (you), can only happen because this deep indwelling has been coming to a point of fruition.

In Revelation 12 it talks about the sons being birthed and caught up[15] to rule and reign. In many ways this has been done and is being done. The sons have been birthed and they are being caught up. And this is part of the experience of what is happening. If someone were to ask you in the future, "What does it mean to be 'caught up'?" ... you might say that it has everything to do with the indwelling of the godhead where you cease to be, and you become literally the manifestation of the Father, the Son and the word, once again.

We are still writing this last chapter concerning Revelation 12:5. The sons are being caught up[15], and the mantle and administration of authority is resting upon them. The more they realize that the mantle is upon them, the more they will be able to move into the administration of the kingdom, that is so necessary at this time.

There is a great deal of work to be done, both on this side of the veil and after the transition into sonship. A great deal has to be done. But we can't sit back and wait for it, when we feel the time of fulfillment is here. We have to understand that the word of authority and dominion is already resting upon the sons (you). And we must move into a deeper level of the administration the kingdom. And the more the move in it, the more it will become real, and the more you will know what to do and what is being required of you.

The mind could say, "Well, you're not ready. You're not ready." Just like Christ, when Mary came up to Christ and He said, "Woman, it is not My time" — you know the story of the wedding of Cana[16]. Her response; "Whatever He says, just do it." Stop and think about that.

We know that the Lord Jesus Christ went through so many things similar to what God has put us through, and is putting us through, and will put us through. But where was the Lord coming from when He said, "Woman, it is not My time". I believe that is what He felt and yet it was Mary's faith that saw past that and the disciples' obedience that brought forth the truth. It was His time.

In many ways we can all stand and say, "Lord we are believing. I know we are on the path. I know it is close. I sense the anointing and so on and so forth, but it is not my time yet." Because we don't seem to be walking on a level that we think we are supposed to be walking on before our time is here.

I think we are looking at it backwards. I think that we must realize that it is our time, and that as we move accordingly, all of the releases will follow. I know that the realm of spirit, t*he cloud of witnesses*, concur that this is the time. They are here encouraging us as it speaks of in the book of Hebrews. They are pushing us, because they want to get into the releases that are destined for the sons of God and they know it is tied into us, and we can't drag our feet any longer.

We must say, "Yes it is my time." And whatever is needed in the scope of an atmosphere or faith will be provided, and is being provided. The last grave clothes are being taken off of the sons. We cannot say; "I'm not ready. It's not my time. How is it possible? Look at all my limitations." God doesn't define you by that. He is just looking for those that say, "Yeah and verily, Lord. As You Have spoken, so it is."

For many of you ladies, you know the experience of birthing. It's pretty serious. It's pretty aggressive and violent. It's very demanding. And so - can it be anything less for the birthing of God's sons? Honestly. Think about that. God is birthing the sons and He's catching them up. And all that we have to draw a parallel to is the birthing experience that a woman goes through in birthing a child. We see how intense the process is; can it be any less for us?

Hopefully this explains why your path has been so intense. Intense is probably a good word. We could use a lot of words to describe this. But your life, especially as it has come down to this targeted focus of the last several years, has become more and more intense, because it is the birthing process. And we haven't understood, and we haven't seen the correlation, but our birthing is the birthing of God's kingdom. And that is a big responsibility that God has put upon the sons.

Someone can say, "Well, how do you bring the kingdom forth?" All I can say is you have entered into the labor and travail to manifest it. The sons have been in labor. They have been in travail, both to be birthed, and to birth, the kingdom of the Father. And yet the last one to be really aware of it are the sons themselves.

In the book of Thomas it says, "The kingdom[17] of God is spread out upon the earth and men know it not." The sons are still transitioning out of a realm of unawareness and into a realm of sight and understanding. The more the birthing process continues, the more chaos is going to unfold in the earth, and the greater the sight and understanding that will come to the sons.

Hopefully this helps to shed some light on what you have been going through: the battle, the warfare, the inner conflict, the drain, your energy levels. There have been so many things happening, until it just seems like you struggle to get out of bed in the morning. But you have to be careful not to judge yourself based on what you are feeling or seeing, because it is only the partial[18]. We are being birthed, and the kingdom is being birthed - simultaneously. And as this happens it will fill all the earth and it is going to affect every level of existence, both seen and not seen.

With the emergence of the kingdom of God through the birthing by the sons, we will see a principle of displacement. The kingdom of God is beginning to displace the kingdoms of this age. You won't have two things occupying the same space and time. As the kingdom of God manifests, it is going to progressively displace more and more of that which has existed here; the kingdom of darkness that has been on this plane for so very long. The kingdom of God does not come forth without which it replaces[19] that which was.

It's the same thing as the change happening within you. Everything is about the principle of displacement. As Paul said, "I die daily." As he diminishes, God increases. And so as the last vestiges of your soul is removed, it is replaced by the Father, by the Son, and by a burgeoning awareness of who and what you are. This is how it happens. One displaces the other. You don't have just two coming on board and all of a sudden you have to go get a new cup because a 12-ounce cup doesn't hold it all. You've got to go get a 16-ounce cup? No. One replaces or displaces the other.

The kingdom of God is happening right now in the earth. And it is displacing those kingdoms which have existed up until now. Right now it may be barely perceptible. It may not be visible. You may not understand it or see it without a spirit of revelation. But I can tell you this. Look at the kingdoms of this age. Look at the countries. Look at everything that is going on and realize that there is a principle of displacement happening right now.

The kingdom of God is being birthed. The sons of God are being birthed, and they are displacing the darkness. It happens no other way. You don't bring the light in and leave the darkness to abide in the same time and space. It cannot. There is only so much you can put in a 12-ounce cup. The darkness is being displaced by the light. And that is happening. And it is happening right now, across the face of the earth, and probably on many spiritual dimensions. But - you must have eyes to see it.

Like I said earlier; you can look at random acts that are happening, random acts of violence, and random acts of geophysical manifestations. And you would think, "Well, they are random." But they are not random. They are all interconnected to this convulsion that is going on. The emergence of the kingdom of God that is coming now and beginning to displace the kingdoms of this age. And they don't like it. The chaos is growing, and it is going to get greater.

A lot of prophets out there—or they want to think they are prophets—may look at this time and say, "Well, peace and safety. We're going to have times of prosperity. The money is growing. Everything looks good." But that is all an illusion. Every bit of it is an illusion. The kingdom of God is coming forth and it's gaining steam like a train going down a railroad track. And the more steam it gets, the more displacement is happening until we're going to hit a point in the book of Revelation where they are going to seek to hide[20] underneath the rocks because of the appearance of the kingdom on such a level.

A number of things are happening simultaneously. The birthing of the kingdom. The birthing of the sons. And the displacement of the kingdoms of this age. And that is why it is imperative that the sons move in the mantle of authority and dominion and not wait for when they think an acceptable time is that they are ready. You are ready now. The Lord Jesus Christ was ready at the time of the wedding of Cana. There was just a little something that had to be done. And there may just be a little something here that has to be done. But it's time for the sons to move and to understand that they must move. They must manifest the mantle of authority. As Ephesians says, "The administration suitable to the fullness of time."

We are at the fullness of times, and the administration suitable is the mantle of authority that rests upon the sons to go in and bring down the kingdoms of this age. We know the end result will be that they will give them back to the Lord Jesus Christ, who will then present it back to the Father.

This is where we are. The displacement is happening concurrently with the sons moving into the mantle of authority to begin to administer the kingdom. Very mystical. Many different things happening right now on many different levels. Pray for eyes to see. I know that the deeper the renewing of the mind happens for you, the more you are going to be able to see ... and the more it will all come together.

Everyone else lives in darkness. They will not be able to understand anything. It will be so random and not connected and it will make no sense. But to the sons of God, they will see how it is all connected. They will understand what is happening and what they are doing. The sons are beginning to understand their part in God's plan, right now.

In many ways we're finishing up Daniel 2. The stone[21] cut out of the mountain hits the image at the feet. That's happening right now. You could say, "Well, that was fulfilled 500 years ago." Maybe it was. Maybe it wasn't. But in the realm of spirit this is happening now. The stone cut out of the mountain hits the image at the feet. The last kingdom. And it is absolutely destroyed - *the world system that we have known.*

The birthing of the kingdom is accelerating, just as your birthing process right now is accelerating. Be expecting. **This is your time. This is the time for resurrection life.**

Scriptures (NASB)

[1] 1 Corinthians 10:11
"Now these things happened to them as an example, and they were written for our instruction, upon whom the ends of the ages have come."

[2] Isaiah 35:8
A highway will be there, a roadway, And it will be called the Highway of Holiness. The unclean will not travel on it, But it will be for him who walks that way, And fools will not wander on it.

[3] John 14:2
"In My Father's house are many dwelling places; if it were not so, I would have told you; for I go to prepare a place for you.

[4] Romans 8:22
For we know that the whole creation groans and suffers the pains of childbirth together until now.

[5] Revelation 12:4
And his tail swept away a third of the stars of heaven and threw them to the earth. And the dragon stood before the woman who was about to give birth, so that when she gave birth he might devour her child.

[6] Luke 17:21
nor will they say, 'Look, here it is!' or, 'There it is!' For behold, the kingdom of God is in your midst."

[7] Hebrews 12:26-27
At that time His voice shook the earth, but now He has promised, “Once more I will shake not only the earth, but heaven as well.” The words, “Once more,” signify the removal of what can be shaken — that is, created things — so that the unshakable may remain.

[8] John 1:14
And the Word became flesh, and dwelt among us, and we saw His glory, glory as of the only begotten from the Father, full of grace and truth.

[9] Romans 8:29
For those whom He foreknew, He also predestined to become conformed to the image of His Son, so that He would be the firstborn among many brethren;

[10] 1 Thessalonians 5:23
Now may the God of peace Himself sanctify you entirely; and may your spirit and soul and body be preserved complete, without blame at the coming of our Lord Jesus Christ.

[11] Hebrews 6:20
where Jesus has entered as a forerunner for us, having become a high priest forever according to the order of Melchizedek.

[12] Acts 17:6
When they did not find them, they began dragging Jason and some brethren before the city authorities, shouting, "These men who have upset the world have come here also;

[13] Revelation 21:3
When they did not find them, they began dragging Jason and some brethren before the city authorities, shouting, "These men who have upset the world have come here also;

[14] Deuteronomy 16:16
"Three times in a year all your males shall appear before the LORD your God in the place which He chooses, at the Feast of Unleavened Bread and at the Feast of Weeks and at the Feast of Booths, and they shall not appear before the LORD empty-handed.

[15] Revelation 3:5
And she gave birth to a son, a male child, who is to rule all the nations with a rod of iron; and her child was caught up to God and to His throne.

[16] John 2:1-5
1On the third day a wedding took place at Cana in Galilee. Jesus' mother was there, 2and Jesus and His disciples had also been invited to the wedding. 3When the wine ran out, Jesus' mother said to Him, "They have no more wine." 4"Woman, why does this concern us? Jesus replied. "My hour has not yet come." 5His mother said to the servants, "Do whatever He tells you."

[17] Book of Thomas saying 113
(113) His disciples said to him: On what day will the kingdom come? <Jesus said:> It will not come while people watch for it; they will not say: Look, here it is, or: Look, there it is; but the kingdom of the father is spread out over the earth, and men do not see it.

[18] 1 Corinthians 13:12
For now we see in a mirror dimly, but then face to face; now I know in part, but then I will know fully just as I also have been fully known.

[19] Daniel 2:44
"In the days of those kings the God of heaven will set up a kingdom which will never be destroyed, and that kingdom will not be left for another people; it will crush and put an end to all these kingdoms, but it will itself endure forever.

[20] Isaiah 2:20-21
...20In that day men will cast away to the moles and the bats Their idols of silver and their idols of gold, Which they made for themselves to worship, 21In order to go into the caverns of the rocks and the clefts of the cliffs Before the terror of the LORD and the splendor of His majesty, When He arises to make the earth tremble.

21 Daniel 2:44-45
...44"In the days of those kings the God of heaven will set up a kingdom which will never be destroyed, and that kingdom will not be left for another people; it will crush and put an end to all these kingdoms, but it will itself endure forever. 45"Inasmuch as you saw that a stone was cut out of the mountain without hands and that it crushed the iron, the bronze, the clay, the silver and the gold, the great God has made known to the king what will take place in the future; so the dream is true and its interpretation is trustworthy."

Notes

Chapter 20

The Kingdom ~ One Level At A Time

We have talked many times about going into another level as you mature in God, and the need to deal with the demonic resistance that is associated with that level. We have said before that one of the first things you must do is to clean[1] it out.

When you hit a new level how do you clean it out? Just exactly what are we saying?" As you come to a new level in God - *a new abiding level or vibration* - you will find an entrenchment of demonic spirits. The enemy has inhabited that level and has usurped your freedom[2] and the provision that God has for you on that level.

Perhaps an easy way to visualize going from one level to another would be borrowing a scene from the movie *Star Trek,* when they're beaming up from one space ship to another. In essence that is how it works. Your vibration changes as you mature in God and you come up to higher and higher levels. You actually enter into new planes of reality that you did not have access to before.

Were those realities present around you? Yes they were, but you were just not cognizant of them. A higher level in God is just a new sphere of functioning in the realm of spirit for you. We've always talked about how fulfillment unfolds as you go from level to level.

As you move into another level in God there is more to it than just taking dominion over the squatters[5] that have existed there. It is about accessing the provision that God has for you there. And this is how we have walked as sons.

When we speak of cleaning out a new realm that you come up to, what we mean is that there has been a degree of the presence of the enemy on that vibrational level. And they have literally been squatting on your provision. As you come to that new level in God, you now have the access and ability to bring down the demonic entrenchments and to move into your inheritance.

As you progress to each new level, you will be met with lies, illusion and resistance. Understand that you're dealing with the spirit world. This is not something that is ethereal that you can't put your finger on. You're dealing with a host of spirits that have been existing on that plane that you have come to possess. And the first thing that you do is you clean[1] it out. This is simply done by taking your rightful position in God, and pushing through the resistance of the squatters who would try to bluff you out of possessing and functioning as you are meant to. In each level you will be met with a resistance that will try to intimidate you and cause you to back off. As sons, we just push right through, because it is all an illusion.

It used to be in times past that it would take a long time to go from one level in God to another, because it is linked in with the maturing of the sons. You could go back in the annuls of history, the times of the restoration—the 1500s, the 1600s—and you can see how long it took for people to break through into new levels and experiences in God.

But this time that we are in, is a time that the kingdom is hastening. And God's sons are moving through portals of change much more quickly. As we come closer to this time of fulfillment and the completion of sonship, it can seem difficult at times to get your sea legs, so to speak. Why is that? Because you're passing from level to level much more quickly. And it would seem just the moment you had a handle on one level, God propels you into the next. As soon as you come into a new level in God and you begin to move with the authority over that realm which has been resisting God in you, then it seems like you're shot into the transition of another level.

The kingdom is being brought forth - *one level at a time.* **You must understand that in a very mystical sense you are the kingdom.** I understand that we may not fully grasp the depth of this truth, or shall I say that we have not fully experienced the reality of it, **but the fact remains that you are the kingdom.** And as you go from level to level in God, you are bringing forth the kingdom - with you.

Be careful not to be drawn into distractions and battles which you have already won. The enemy would seek to pull you into conflict after conflict; dealing with this issue or that issue, when the truth is that you have authority and you have dominion; all you have to do is speak the word, and the lie and illusion must give way.

You can look right in front of you and see something that seems to be so real, yet it is just an illusion. One word breaks it, whether it's a wall or whether it's issues that you seem to be dealing with. It doesn't matter. It's all an illusion.

The sons are in the process of ascension. And as they go up higher and higher, their vibration (or dwelling place) in God changes, and as their vibration shifts this literally unlocks the provisions that God has for them on that level.

What does this mean? In plain English, it means that you are a fluid being. Right now your vibration, your frequency in God, is at one specific level. But as you ascend higher, you become more and more one with the Light, and your frequency or vibration continues to go up higher.

You need to understand that the realms of light are realms of vibration in the presence of God. You could say vibration; you could say frequency. It is pretty much the same thing. As you go higher in God, your personal frequency changes because you are becoming more and more the Light. And your frequency will continue to change, and change again, and change again. This is simple to understand, and this is what it means to go from level to level.

We have taught in the past that God has provisions for His sons, realms of functioning, administrations that they are to move in, that are earmarked for certain levels in God that they attain. Their presence in that new level literal unlocks the provisions that God has for them on that level. You become, as it were, the key that opens the doors to the mysteries[3] and the treasures[4] that have been reserved for you for the time that you come to that level.

This is really all about the maturing of the sons. You could also say it's about the time set by the Father. People may think that the time set for the maturing and the manifesting of the sons is a specific given date. But it is really related to your functioning and maturing in God. And as you attain new levels in God, your presence unlocks the provision and the bounty that God has reserved for you.

There are so many levels in God; I could not even imagine how many there are. However, we have been moving consistently higher and higher up into the realm of His presence. We are truly being caught[6] up.

This may be the first time in history that a people can actually explain and understand what this experience of being caught up is. You are living the book of Revelation right now, and you are being caught up. Your abiding; your vibration — everything about your presence, is continuing to change.

What we're talking about is something that is a constant, and has been a constant for us as we have walked before the face of God. There are a number of scriptures that talk about the word; both the spoken word and the word of authority. In the last days My word shall judge[7]. And they overcame[8] by the word. And they loved not their lives unto death[8]. And the enemy is slain by the brightness[9] of His rising (in you). These are all scriptures that we've known, but we now are living them.

The word has come for a number of years to us that the kingdom will move forward by the word that we (the sons) speak[10]. It's different than prayer. Prayer and supplication is one thing. You're going to entreat the Lord to release something. But speaking the word is acting upon what has already put within[11] you - for you are more than just a channel to speak the word.

We have seen the level of conflict in the last several months accelerate. The spirit realm is like a finely woven matrix, and you can't move your foot one inch one way, or one inch the other way, without which you are affecting the spirit world and meeting resistance. It can be disconcerting, because you're trying to rightly discern what is unfolding. The word that has come, time and time again, is: "You will prevail by the word, and you will be sustained by the word that you eat." It is important that we understand that possessing the kingdom, one level at a time, has both to do with the level of the word that you are speaking, but it also has very much to do with the word that you are eating and digesting.

One thing that we're coming to understand more and more, is that the word cannot be hindered[12]. It cannot be withstood. The way that we are going to continue to prevail is that we speak the word into every situation, even if we don't have an accurate discernment of what seems to be going on.

The spirit realm would love to keep the sons off balance just enough that they are always trying to figure out what is going on or, they are consumed with trying to come up with answers. The only way that the sons prevail in this battle of the ages is that they just speak the word.

Go back into the New Testament. There are so many promises about the freedom[13] and the liberty of the sons of God and the anointing[14] that the sons are to move in. Often the Lord has revealed to you very specific promises that you are destined to walk in. And as you begin to stand upon those promises and upon those revelations and speak that word, the truth coming out of your mouth begins to break the illusion and the lie.

You must realize that so much of our warfare, if not all of it, really comes down to dealing with illusion. The enemy is real, and so you can say that we're fighting against principalities[15] and powers and thrones and dominions[16]. We must understand that the tools and tactics of the enemy are deception and illusion. You either cave into the lie and the illusion, and start trying to find solutions, or you speak a word that cuts right through it like a sharp knife. And that is where we stand. We stand speaking the word of God, which cannot be withstood.

In the Book of Isaiah it speaks that His word is sent out and does not return void[17]. We look at that as the Father and the son speaking the word - not returning void. But we need to internalize this for a minute. You are the extension of the Father. You are the extension of the Lord. You speak the word by the spirit, and that word does not return void. When the Father speaks, look in the mirror. Your mouth is moving and that word will not return void ... and we speak the word into the spirit realm and we break the impasses.

God tears down that which seems to be a wall of iron around the sons where they can't seem to break through. The word shatters[18] it and lays it bare. The breakthroughs, the promises and the provisions are loosed to the sons because that is the word, and it's by the word that we prevail. There is no other way that you're going to prevail. You won't have enough wisdom or insight to figure everything out.

We are not like those that walk in the earth. To them there is no resistance. Fruition and fruitfulness seem to just happen without any difficulty. But it doesn't work that way for the sons. The wisdom of the world will not make a difference. But it's the word that you speak, the word of authority, the word of dominion, and the word of power. For God has ruined you for any other life and any other way of functioning.

Transference may come in like a flood, but you will stand and send it all back. This is how we move forward. Someone may say, "Well, the kingdom moves forward on your knees." Well, yes, it does. But the kingdom doesn't really move forward with prayer and supplication—not when God has already created the sons.

The kingdom moves forward when the sons move with the initiative of faith to speak a word that breaks the barriers, that breaks the lie, that breaks the illusion and that breaks the wall. And this you do almost on a day-by-day basis, for you are quickly ascending[6] into the presence of the Father.

You are the voice of God in the earth. And you are prevailing[19] by the word you're speaking. If you don't speak the word then it may be a little rough going. And maybe this is a paradigm shift for some of you where your natural course is to go in and begin to either pray, or sit down and scratch your head and try to figure it out.

You can't figure it out, and you can't go before God and say, "Help me," when He's already said, "I've given it to you. Just walk in the word." Maybe you don't see the whole picture yet, but that's okay. You've got enough to work with. Just speak the word and understand that as you go from level to level, that it is the most exciting experience a son can have, because each level in God is like a whole new place of abiding.

It's like traveling from one country to another. All of a sudden you've arrived and there you are. On a day-by-day basis it may seem hard to relate to that; you look at yourself in your human form and the battles that you go through. And you may not realize that you are changing and that everything seems to be a little bit off kilter , but it is only because you are growing into new levels much more quickly.

In the past you may have gone from one level to another and it may have taken months or years. Now we're talking days and weeks. So it can seem a little off balance. But that's okay, because you're moving into a new land and God has set before you a provision; a bounty for you, just waiting.

The only condition is that once you get to that new level, then just take dominion over the lies and the illusions and know that there is a provision, a treasure chest of His mysteries reserved for you that are attached to that level ... and the roar of the enemy will not bluff you out. The provisions for you on that level will open up, and with that will come an experience in God that will continue to deepen, and your understanding will deepen.

The promise has been that the Lord wants to reveal the hidden mysteries to His sons, the deep mysteries[3] of the kingdom, and the mysteries of the satanic[20] world as well. From level to level are subsequent provisions that will see a releasing of the wisdom, of the insight - of the mysteries. That is what is so exciting. Expect that, because this is what is happening. In a very mystical sense, the mysteries that God will reveal will not be external, rather He will be revealing the mysteries within you.

Right now you don't see yourself as complete in Him, yet that is the promise. Right now you see yourself in a form of limitation perhaps. **But the truth is that all the knowledge, the wisdom, and all of the mysteries in God are already resident within[11] you**. And as you go from level to level, their release in you will open up as your spiritual vibration and level of abiding changes.

So what God is going to reveal to you will not be external mysteries; they will be very much internal. You will see them. You will know them. You will understand them, because they are already a part of you. And this is very mystical. It's not something easy to explain or define.

The kingdom is coming forth - one level at a time - one step at a time - one victory at a time. And you are right in the midst of a great possessing of the kingdom. Be looking for so much to open up. Be anticipating the mysteries, the deep things of God, because they are your provision and they are opening up even as we speak.

Scriptures (NASB)

[1] Numbers 33:52
then you shall drive out all the inhabitants of the land from before you, and destroy all their figured stones, and destroy all their molten images and demolish all their high places;

[2] 2 Chronicles 20:7
"Did You not, O our God, drive out the inhabitants of this land before Your people Israel and give it to the descendants of Abraham Your friend forever?

[3] 1 Corinthians 4:1
Let a man regard us in this manner, as servants of Christ and stewards of the mysteries of God.

[4] Colossians 2:3
in whom are hidden all the treasures of wisdom and knowledge.

[5] Deuteronomy 20:16-17
"Only in the cities of these peoples that the LORD your God is giving you as an inheritance, you shall not leave alive anything that breathes. But you shall utterly destroy them, the Hittite and the Amorite, the Canaanite and the Perizzite, the Hivite and the Jebusite, as the LORD your God has commanded you..."

[6] Revelation 12:5
And she gave birth to a son, a male child, who is to rule all the nations with a rod of iron; and her child was caught up to God and to His throne.

[7] John 12:48
"He who rejects Me and does not receive My sayings, has one who judges him; the word I spoke is what will judge him at the last day.

[8] Revelation 12:11
"And they overcame him because of the blood of the Lamb and because of the word of their testimony, and they did not love their life even when faced with death.

[9] 2 Thessalonians 2:8
Then that lawless one will be revealed whom the Lord will slay with the breath of His mouth and bring to an end by the appearance of His coming;

[10] Jeremiah 5:14
Therefore, thus says the LORD, the God of hosts, "Because you have spoken this word, Behold, I am making My words in your mouth fire And this people wood, and it will consume them.

[11] Luke 17:21
nor will they say, 'Look, here it is!' or, 'There it is!' For behold, the kingdom of God is in your midst."

[12] Proverbs 4:12
When you walk, your steps will not be impeded; And if you run, you will not stumble.

[13] Galatians 5:1
It was for freedom that Christ set us free; therefore keep standing firm and do not be subject again to a yoke of slavery.

Also [13] 2 Corinthians 3:17
Now the Lord is the Spirit, and where the Spirit of the Lord is, there is liberty.

Also [13] Romans 8:21
that the creation itself also will be set free from its slavery to corruption into the freedom of the glory of the children of God.

[14] 1 John 2:27
As for you, the anointing which you received from Him abides in you, and you have no need for anyone to teach you; but as His anointing teaches you about all things, and is true and is not a lie, and just as it has taught you, you abide in Him.

[15] Ephesians 6:12
For our struggle is not against flesh and blood, but against the rulers, against the powers, against the world forces of this darkness, against the spiritual forces of wickedness in the heavenly places.

[16] Colossians 1:15
For by Him all things were created, both in the heavens and on earth, visible and invisible, whether thrones or dominions or rulers or authorities-- all things have been created through Him and for Him.

[17] Isaiah 55:11
So will My word be which goes forth from My mouth; It will not return to Me empty, Without accomplishing what I desire, And without succeeding in the matter for which I sent it.

[18] Isaiah 30:31
For through the voice of the LORD shall the Assyrian be beaten down, *which* smote with a rod.

[19] Acts 19:20
So the word of the Lord was growing mightily and prevailing.

[20] Job 12:22
"He reveals mysteries from the darkness And brings the deep darkness into light.

Notes

Section 6

Kingdom Consciousness

Chapter 21

In A Moment of Time

In this word we're going to delve further into the realm of illusion and the realm of reality. It's a very interesting topic, because as His sons come forth during this time, they will find themselves living in two worlds at the same time. You may not be aware of it yet, but you are living in two worlds; the world of the spirit and the natural plane. And as such your life is being affected by both levels at the same time.

For most people this could sound way outside the box and perhaps difficult to accept; or perhaps seem too much of a New Age type of thing. But we know that we are a spirit, a soul, and a body. And as such, we know our spirits have been made alive and that God has promised and spoken that He will save us to the uttermost[1]; spirit, soul and body.

We have spoken many times about the functioning of our spirit as it goes about to do the Father's bidding, and how much our spirit is involved in the warfare. So this is something that you will have to understand more and more, whether or not you're aware of it, for you are living in two worlds at the same time.

We're going to talk a little bit more about illusion. A number of years ago the word came in vision from the Lord that we are pushing up against the realm of illusion. And as we continue to walk before Him, daily, that we will be pushing, pushing against the realm of illusion, until it gives way.

Perhaps, at times, we may question why we feel so drained at the end of a day, or why our physical bodies seem to be challenged at times to stay up with the intensity of what our involvement is. Just realize that God is delivering the sons out of the realm of darkness and into the realm of His light. This is in transition, as our maturing comes to a completion, and we definitely are experiencing the energy of this transition.

When God speaks the word, it is done, but there is a process which follows to see that word fully manifested in the flesh. God is bringing you through the eye[2] of the needle where you begin to truly manifest the completed reality of that word. As such, we have been in the process of being delivered out of the realm of darkness and into the realm of light. You might say we're in the process of being delivered out of the realm of illusion, and into the realm of truth. It's the same thing.

Illusion can be very slippery, because illusion is both that which the spirit realm can create and present to you - like the manipulation of events in your life - but illusion is also a function of the mind. So it becomes very interesting or challenging, to dissect between that which is being projected at you from the satanic world, and that which is within your own personal makeup and your mind. We have not understood how powerful the mind is, and how it can be swayed and given over to illusion, until you begin to really believe the illusion that has been framed within the thinking of your mind. It's a very deep subject, and God has been delivering us progressively out of the realm of illusion.

The best way to visualize this, if you want to take a moment and visualize with me, would be to personify the spirit of illusion. For example when we speak of death it says, "Oh death[3], where is your sting? Oh death, where is your victory?" It speaks about how we overcome death. Death is not a nebulous entity; death is an entity, a person if you will.

Illusion is not something that is esoteric; illusion is an entity, a person, if we want to use that as an example. And the warfare that you face every day is a level of resistance that pushes back against this spirit of illusion, not taking it on as your reality.

As you continue to pave your way into the kingdom, you are resisting illusion every step of the way. Illusion is resisting you. But you are overcoming illusion, one step at a time. Or like we referenced in a recent word, the kingdom - one level at a time. So you are in a battle constantly. The minute you cease to accept the illusion as your reality is the very moment that the illusion ceases to have any power over you.

It may not seem that way, because you've lived with it and perhaps you've grown accustomed to living in a life of intensity and you haven't really understood exactly what is happening to you. But you are definitely pushing against the realm of illusion every day.

I don't know how much we really understand that this is what we are doing. It's like spiritual isometrics. Every day we push against the illusion that is pushing against us saying, "This is how things are. This is the way they are." The appearance may seem to be a reality, causing your emotions to run wild, but you must be careful ... if you acquiesce to the lie then you have given it power. You take away its power by ceasing to believe in it. It is that simple.

The alternate religions out there call this realm - the realm of Maya. They know that such a thing exists. So even the children of darkness are aware of these things. We know that Satan is the master manipulator within this realm. And sometimes we just need to remind ourselves that what we see is not what is. What you see is an illusion. And unless you see by the spirit, you're not really able to see the truth.

The illusion you face may paint a picture that nothing can change ... that the roadblocks are just too daunting. However, everything is changing, as the sons continue to experience the renewal of the mind, and the capacity to see the truth as it really is. ***A breakthrough can happen in a moment of time.***

In the book of 2 Kings there is a classic experience that happened. If you remember the story about the armies besieging the king in 2 Kings 7, *Elisha went and spoke to the king and said, "Here's the word of the Lord. Thus saith the Lord, 'Tomorrow about this time shall a measure of flour be sold for a shekel and two measures of barley for a shekel in the gates of Samaria.'" Then the lord whose hand the king leaned on answered the man of God and said, "Behold if the lord would make windows in heaven might this thing be?"* And he said, *Elisha said, "Behold you shall see it with your eyes but you will not partake of it"* (2 Kings 7:1-2).

We have the inner challenges that we face where our mind and our paradigm says, "It's taken too long. How can it happen overnight? How can God bring forth a kingdom in a day?" ... because we're so caught up into what seems to be a process. However Isaiah 66 presents a different picture...

***Behold can a nation be born in a day?* (Isaiah 66:8)**

Everything can change in a moment of time. The word came several years ago, and the Lord used the phrase; "In the zing of a moment things will change." He said that "You will hit a wall, and you'll be as far as you can go. But I will reach down and grab you by the nape of the neck and pull you over that wall."

The wall the Lord is going to pull the sons over is not a wall that is made of concrete; it is a wall that exists within our minds. And He will pull us over in it and bring us into our inheritance. So many of the limitations that we have, if not all of them, are those which we still carry as baggage from this age, walls that don't exist, except within our mind.

We have spoken about the power of the mind; the mind to create both the positive and the negative. And as we come into the deep renewing of the mind, we will be able to link up with the truth and literally bring the truth into being.

It's a similar situation that we face right now. We're getting rid of the subliminal programming that we've had deep within our mind that has said that this is going to take a process, a very long time. And that is not the truth.

When the Lord began to speak about resurrection life, He finally just said, "Visualize it. Imagine it. Picture it within your mind." This is a first step to really grabbing a reality that is here and bringing it into being. We have been given a great charge from the Lord, the charge to bring forth sonship, to break the tape, to enter into resurrection life, to open the door for many to follow ... and we know that it's not going to happen by virtue of a rapture.

The rapture mentality is such a religious anchor in so many people, because they're looking for God to do something. You know ... at some point God is going to throw out a line and deliver you ... or the ship is sinking and at some point He's going to throw a line and save you. Even those who are called to sonship and have left the rapture teaching, can still be very prone to a rapture mentality.

You may not be looking for God to pull you out of the tribulation but you are looking for the Lord to pull you into what He's prepared for you. And He is going to do just that, but we would be missing it if we did not realize that this is something that we must do in concert with Him. And that is why the Lord said to begin to visualize the change.

Begin to picture it in your mind - begin to see it here. Begin to relate to yourself as having resurrection life.

I believe that the Lord is reaching down to us, while we are simultaneously reaching up to Him, to grab a hand, but it's a two way street. There is that which we are doing aggressively on our end, and then the Lord reaches down and helps complete that work; but He's requiring the sons to reach in and to see it, to embrace it, to just visualize it, if you will. It is the act of doing that begins to reprogram your mind.

Resurrection life is not in the future; it is here right now and in a moment of time it can be completed.

How is the breakthrough going to happen? We're not certain. But I know that we are in the upper room. I know that we are waiting before Him. But we also know, to a degree, what it is He's bringing. And to that degree we begin to visualize it; begin to picture it, begin to meditate on it like Joshua did. The rest is up to the Lord. He'll bring us into it. But I know that we reach up into Him for it.

We can't cease to forget that we are living in a state of pushing against the illusion of this world, and we are going to break through it with a mighty shout in the twinkling of an eye.

We don't war against flesh[4] and blood, we know that; we war against principalities, powers, thrones and dominions of this vast darkness that we exist in. And progressively we are identifying them one after another. Delay[5] comes to an end with the exposing and subsequent judgment, upon the spirit of illusion.

Scriptures (NASB)

[1] Hebrews 7:25
Therefore He is able also to save forever those who draw near to God through Him, since He always lives to make intercession for them.

[2] Mark 10:25
"It is easier for a camel to go through the eye of a needle than for a rich man to enter the kingdom of God."

[3] 1Corinthians 15:55
"O DEATH, WHERE IS YOUR VICTORY? O DEATH, WHERE IS YOUR STING?"

[4] Ephesians 6:12
For our struggle is not against flesh and blood, but against the rulers, against the powers, against the world forces of this darkness, against the spiritual forces of wickedness in the heavenly places.

[5] Revelation 10:6
and swore by Him who lives forever and ever, WHO CREATED HEAVEN AND THE THINGS IN IT, AND THE EARTH AND THE THINGS IN IT, AND THE SEA AND THE THINGS IN IT, that there will be delay no longer,

Notes

Chapter 22

Dual Existence

The prophecy came that the sons are entering a level of life which will encompass both the natural and spiritual planes, simultaneously. You might ask, "Are we speaking of resurrection life?" That answer would be both yes, and no. The immediate transition we are in will precede resurrection life; however, the complete fulfillment of this transition will only be found in resurrection life.

What we will find, as this transition takes place, is a greater level of immunity in the battle, with a greater level of access to move and function in His presence.

> **But if we walk in the Light, as He is in the Light, we have fellowship one with another, and the blood of Jesus Christ His son cleanses us from all sin.**
> **(1 John 1:7).**

John was speaking of an access and mobility that would come to the sons, as they came up higher, and function from His presence in the Light. No doubt, the Early Church may have walked in a measure of this scripture, but the true fulfillment of 1 John 1:7 has been reserved for the sons, for this day. We are speaking of a life level that is no longer restrained, anchored, or tied to this realm that we have known.

We are being pulled, progressively more and more, into this dual existence, and the mundane tasks that we have known, may become a bit more challenging, as we experience this transition. This is already happening, but it will increase. We are finding that we are walking and functioning on this level, while we are tracking in the spirit, and being drawn constantly, more and more, into the tasks being set before the sons, by His leading.

There are so many levels happening simultaneously, and we will find this tug only grow greater. We may be focused on a certain task, only to find that all of a sudden, we are carrying something else.

Something is pulling us in the spirit, as we are drawn into this level of dual existence. This is something that we have walked in, for some time now, but it has only been on a level of the partial. Now, however, the time is upon us to enter into this life changing experience on a much deeper level. Now is the time for the fullness.

How is this experience happening? What are the spiritual dynamics that are going on within you? It is the merging of all that you are; spirit, soul, and body, in the time of His presence. You are beginning to experience your spirit, and the more we complete this transition out of the soul, the more you will find this transition taking over. It is the ascendancy of the spirit over the soul. We are beginning to have a deeper spiritual experience in the Lord, which is involving the fact that we are becoming more connected to our spirit. This is where everything is headed; the integration of your spirit, soul, and body, standing blameless[1] before Him.

The fact is; we are in this transition. What is the experience of this transition? We know it involves a progressive shift into a deeper level of abiding, and a deeper level of awareness. We are beginning to walk as beings of "spirit", rather than "soul", and this means that we are beginning to walk with an awareness[2] of what our spirit sees, and our spirit hears.

There is a more intense level of this dual existence that is beginning to happen, and as we are drawn into this, it is going change how we have functioned, as both a physical/soul and spiritual being. Why? Because there are different levels, or layers of energy, that we are in, that are beginning to impact our existence and sensitivity.

We are being pulled into another level of life, *which is what we want*, and this is certainly the prophecy. We are literally walking with one foot[3] here and one foot there, and as much as we have been living this experience to a measure, it is going to feel absolutely new. God is doing a new[4] thing, and you are right in the middle of it. How does the word go?

Behold, I will do something new, will you be aware? Isaiah 43:19

We are in the process of ascending to His throne, and the sons are being caught up to His presence, to rule and reign[5]. We are taking this out of the ethereal, and we are beginning to identify what this experience really is. We are in a transition into the fullness of sonship, and into the full mantle of His authority.

This has been a long transition, or so it has seemed, but all of a sudden, we find that we are being drawn up into a life in His presence, and it is happening much more rapidly now. The level of life that you were walking in yesterday, is different today. Maybe you had walked in 20% of a dual existence, but everything is changing now, much more rapidly.

Every change and shift, brings with it, a unique set of challenges that you will face. We might be in the midst of doing something on the natural plane when all of a sudden, we find that we are being pulled into a level of conflict, or some level of activity going on in the spirit, and we will have to adjust to handling the intensity of that connection, with our normal daily existence.

We are coming into an oneness with our spirit, and this was always the promise, that God would save you to the uttermost[6]; spirit, soul, and body. We are coming to know our spirit. That was the word all along. Our spirit has been freed, and consequently, our spirits are so much further down the road than we know.

What does that really mean? And how does that affect us on this level? For one thing, we are finding that there is a shift happening, because the soul is coming to its end. To quote Paul:

"I must decrease that He might increase." John 3:30

So, what is the reality of that? Well, the reality is that the soul begins to truly diminish, and the spirit begins to become more progressively dominant. And how do you identify the experience of that?

As we transition from a life based in the soul realm, into a life based in the realm of spirit, we will experience progressively deeper levels of this dual existence. We literally are walking around in two worlds at the same time, ***all of the time***. And because this level of experience, this unfolding duality, is becoming more and more a part of our present reality, we find that our functioning and tracking before the Lord must change. Deep discernment is no longer a luxury. Spiritual eye salve[7] is a must, if we are to function effectively in both worlds at the same time.

Everything concerning you, is being more effected by the realm of spirit, than you have ever known, because of the connection of your spirit - to your consciousness - to your body. Your spirit is finally beginning to move into a level of ascendency over the soul, which is what we have always wanted.

It may seem like you are experiencing more of the conflict, but if you take a couple of steps back, you will see everything differently. There is a fulfillment happening for His sons; the fulfillment of the ascendency of our spirit over the soul.

There are many ways we can relate to this transition of resurrection life, but it really comes down to the ascension of the spirit over the soul, and that is just one step away from the changing of our bodies. What we have right now, is a body that reflects the soul, and the promise is that we are to have a body that reflects the spirit.

We still have the consciousness of the soul, but now we have so much more of the spirit that is overshadowing, and gaining a presence within us, that we have truly been thrust into a life on both levels, at the same time. However, I believe that this transition will be short, because we are on a dead run to achieve, as Paul called it, the "out-resurrection" from the dead[8]. Resurrection Life.

This is what has been happening. This is the experience that is happening, and it all lines up to the changes that we have been believing for.

Part of our challenge stems from the fact that our bodies are being taxed to stay up with the intensity that is happening in the spirit. I do not know how else to say this except that the more your spirit tunes into and participates in what is unfolding in the spirit realm, the greater the demands will be made upon your physical body, because you are a triune being; spirit, soul, and body.

The prophesy years ago came that our physical bodies would have to change, in order to handle the intensity of the connection coming through the veil; **and this is where we are - now**. Because of this, the body must change, and must conform. Therefore, I believe that this is part of the challenge that we are looking at, as well. We are walking out an experience that we are defining for the very first time. We are beginning to understand what this experience of ascension[9] actually is.

We are beginning to see it, and identify it, and understand that we are right in this - we are right in this channel of change.

As this change continues to happen, we are going to get eyes to see. We already have eyes to see, but our eyes are going to open up more and more, because our spirit sees. This connection within us, is going to bring greater sight, because we are going to begin to see more with the eyes of our spirit, and less with the eyes[10] of the soul. There is a lot to be expected out of this shift, and therefore, we should be watching things very closely, to really understand what this process of ascension is truly all about.

The changes happening within us are going to be so jam-packed into our consciousness, that we will not even have a choice in deciding what comes next. You will know what is going on, because you are carrying it, and it is beginning to have more presence in your consciousness than it has ever had before. The shift is on.

We have already signed on, and given the Lord a blank check over our lives. We are in this, whether we like it or not, but of course, this is what we want. One of the promises that the Lord had given years ago, was that we would come to the point where we would be able to recognize what He was doing in our life. We would link hands with Him, and intensify the fulfillment of that, because rather than resisting it, or being unaware of it, you will be aware of it, and you will be leaning into it as hard as possible. This will accelerate the experience and the process, much faster and deeper, than we can possibly imagine.

This is something that the Lord is making us aware of, because we are in this ascension process that is bringing us into a rapid state of change. We are being transformed into a new creation. We are watching our dynamics change. As the Lord spoke in Isaiah:

> **"I will do something new, will you be aware?"**
> **Isaiah 43:19**

Will you be aware of this new thing that the Lord is doing? Will you? "Yes Lord. We are aware. We want to be aware. We want to be much more aware!"

Our bodies are changing. Our minds are changing. Our eyes are opening. We are being molded and transformed into a new creation[11]. He is drawing His sons higher and higher up. We give ourselves to Him. We have signed the check. "Do it Lord. Do whatever is necessary to bring us into sonship on the highest level." We keep leaning into the Lord on this. "Okay, Lord, I see it. I understand a little bit more of what You are doing here, and I give myself."

I expect that we are going to have a greater capacity to see as each day unfolds, because our spirit already has it! Do it Lord.

Scriptures (NASB)

[1] 1 Thessalonians 5:23
Now may the God of peace Himself sanctify you entirely; and may your spirit and soul and body be preserved complete, without blame at the coming of our Lord Jesus Christ.

[2] 1 Corinthians 12:3
Therefore I make known to you that no one speaking by the Spirit of God says, "Jesus is accursed"; and no one can say, "Jesus is Lord," except by the Holy Spirit.

[3] Revelation 10:5
Then the angel whom I saw standing on the sea and on the land lifted up his right hand to heaven,

[4] Isaiah 43:19
"Behold, I will do something new, Now it will spring forth; Will you not be aware of it? I will even make a roadway in the wilderness, Rivers in the desert.

[5] Revelation 12:5
And she gave birth to a son, a male child, who is to rule all the nations with a rod of iron; and her child was caught up to God and to His throne.

[6] Hebrews 7:25
Therefore He is able also to save forever those who draw near to God through Him, since He always lives to make intercession for them.

[7] Revelation 3:18
I advise you to buy from Me gold refined by fire so that you may become rich, and white garments so that you may clothe yourself, and that the shame of your nakedness will not be revealed; and eye salve to anoint your eyes so that you may see.

[8] Acts 23:6
But perceiving that one group were Sadducees and the other Pharisees, Paul began crying out in the Council, "Brethren, I am a Pharisee, a son of Pharisees; I am on trial for the hope and resurrection of the dead!"

[9] Mark 16:19
So then, when the Lord Jesus had spoken to them, He was received up into heaven and sat down at the right hand of God.

[10] Isaiah 11:3
And He will delight in the fear of the LORD, And He will not judge by what His eyes see, Nor make a decision by what His ears hear;

[11] 2Corinthians 5:17
Therefore if anyone is in Christ, he is a new creature; the old things passed away; behold, new things have come.

Notes

Chapter 23

Illusion or Reality?

We brought a word in the first book, *The Manifestation of the Sons of God,* where we talk about reality and illusion. This teaching will take this chapter to another level.

Hearing and understanding truth is not a product of your ears that you can just say, "Let me go to a conference. I will hear the speaker. He will speak words that are going to resonate and they are truthful and so therefore that is truth. And I assimilate it and I understand it."

Truth is not experienced that way. That is the soul. If you really want to get mystical about it, what is truth? Truth is God. Truth is Christ. He is the truth[3], the way, the life. Right? Isn't that how the scripture goes? You can't even know the truth, unless you are able to assimilate Christ on a deeper level within your being.

Truth is not a concept that your mind can assent to, and process, and all of sudden you know the truth. People get up on their soapboxes and preach scripture and they recite concepts that are truthful—and they think that this is what this is all about. It is not. Truth is about embracing Christ, who is the truth[3], the spirit[4] of truth. We're not talking concepts. And so as you are able to embrace Christ on progressively deeper and deeper levels; which has to do with the work of the cross[5] in your life - which has to do with the renewing of your mind[1] - then you're able to process more and more of what God is revealing and speaking.

It is interesting that people think that to know the truth is just a product of reading something and pondering on it, and meditating and really learning the concept or theory. People leaving universities tend to come out with such an arrogance. They know everything. They think they are so smart, and they don't realize how darkened they really are in their ability to understand. Smart according to the ways of man, according to the natural reasoning, but otherwise very, very lacking.

Truth is an evolving experience. You come to know the truth; progressively. And that is what we seek and desire. We're not just interested in reading scripture and then mentally thinking "I have it." Because you won't get it. You can read it. You can say, "Okay, well I understand it. I got it. I can re-write it down. I can preach it." But that doesn't mean that you have received the truth. If you are able to truly hear the truth, then it will change[6] you.

How does the scripture go? When you know the truth, what happens? The truth sets[6] you free. That is a deeply mystical passage. What is the truth? Who is the way? Who is the life? Who is the truth? Your mind? The mind of the soul? No. It is the Lord Jesus Christ. He is the truth[3]. He is the way. He is the life. And the more you know the truth, the truth sets[6] you free. Very mystical.

This takes it out of the realm of the mind, and out of the realm of the soul. And this is what has been progressively happening.

The months of November and December are the darkest times on the face of the earth. You might wonder, why? It is a very dark time, because people don't understand bonds and contacts. They don't understand the principles that we have taught concerning bonds, because it has to be experienced and heard on a level of the spirit[7]. And so you have all of these relationships going on during the holiday season, and if there ever was a time that bonds thrive, it is during the holiday season, as people gather together and they share gifts and they do whatever they do. I have nothing against giving gifts, and spending time with family, but you must realize that what you have in this time is one massive breeding ground of obligations, bonds, and contacts; a perfect storm for the transference of darkness and confusion. That is why there is such a high suicide rate during this time.

People are just lost. They are lost even in the perception of themselves, because it is so overshadowed with all the projections of friends, family and associates ... and who knows what else. You don't even know who you are. You have no ability to know who you are or even what you are thinking, because transference has just gone into hyperspace. So what little light there is, is so overshadowed by the darkness of transference that is flowing from the realm of soul; not to mention the realm of spirit.

This period of time is a time of great darkness; and we are not even talking about the spirit world. We are not even talking about the spirit of Saturnalia[8].

And so we look at what is happening right now, and you have to ask yourself: Illusion or reality?

As I had mentioned before in one of the books, or maybe all of them; science has made great strides in trying to quantify the existence of God, the existence of the spirit world, and the existence of factors that control beyond your sight, and beyond what you are able to see. This train of analysis has birthed a great rise in the science of what we call, "quantum physics".

We have talked about quantum physics and some of the research that has been done over the years, and it is very, very interesting. Quantum physics is dealing with "reality" on a quantum level. The quantum level deals with matter so minute in size, that it is equated to be at the base level of creation. Scientists have studied and determined that as a person views reality through their given paradigm, that their internal viewpoint can actually influence the reality that they see. And this is all within the scope of what we call, Quantum Physics.

In essence, through your personal paradigm, you are able to create a substantive reality - even if it is an illusion. That is how powerful the mind really is, and how it can affect reality based upon the science of Quantum Physics. And that of course can be substantiated in the scriptures ... ***as a man thinks[9] in his heart, so is he***. So, what am I saying?

As you see reality around you, your reality will come into an alignment with your view. It may be true or not. It may entirely be an illusion, but you have the power to create an illusion as a substantive reality. This is why God has been dealing with the sons so much, to get them out of their limited paradigm - which is your mental freeway, you might say.

Imagine that the mind travels on a freeway. And so your paradigm is on freeway I-95. Someone else is on I-10. Understand, everyone is on a different freeway, or different track, which have been grooved out, carved out, within their mind. And they view reality along that track.

And you might meet someone. "Oh, what's their reality?" "Well, they're on the I-10." "Well, okay. I'm on the I-95 over here." Because that's how they view reality—that's the groove their mind is in. Therefore their reality is the substantive manifestation of how they see. That is quantum physics. And quantum physics says that if you can change your view of reality, then your reality will change to align to your view.

Now that's scary stuff, because you have the power to create what you believe. It's scary. If you believe in resurrection life enough, then that will become your reality. That becomes the truth. Especially if you are aligned to God's truth, and not an illusion. How much more powerful it is when you are aligned to the truth, and not the illusion.

This is why Joshua was commanded, "Meditate[10] on My word day and night and you will prosper." Joshua was aligning his paradigm to the truth of God's word; to the truth of that which existed in the spirit.

The sons are being pulled out of the realm of illusion, lies, and deception and darkness. We have been talking about this. They are being delivered out of the vast darkness that exists on the face of the earth, and they are being pulled up into - *and identifying with and anchoring[11] to* - the realm of truth. Their paradigm is being shifted out of adhering to an illusion, to being anchored in the truth.

The assault that comes against the sons of God is to paint the illusion in front of them of limitation, and lack, until you buckle under that, at times. And then you enter into the warfare trying to just fight it off or deal with it - when it is just an illusion. We call it, "paper dragons". Understanding the power of the mind and the principle of Quantum Physics, we realize how very careful we must be not to respond to the illusion or the lie. Our response gives credence or weight to the lie, and helps to create it into a substantive reality. **Be on guard!**

Let's talk about finances. That's pretty much in everyone's face. You say, "Well I just don't have any money to pay this bill. How can this be an illusion?" And so you are sitting there working it out. And I am saying, "It's an illusion." And the enemy throws illusion after illusion after illusion on the sons and you either buckle under it or begin to try to work it out; or you rise above it and you refuse to let that be your paradigm; and you throw your anchor[11] in Him and your anchor is the truth of His word until your reality has to align to your paradigm.

Quantum physics once again. All of a sudden. "I don't have the money to pay the bills." And that becomes your reality. You don't have the money. But what if your paradigm shifts? ... Quantum Physics then shifts. What happens. All of a sudden you have an abundance. Coincidence? I don't think so.

Well how did that happen? "Well so and so paid me, or I got some money, or I got something in the mail." Maybe. Who knows how it happened? But I can tell you how it was created. It was created because your paradigm stopped adhering to the lie and it began to adhere to the truth. And the principle of quantum physics came into action and boom. "As a man thinks[9] in his heart so is he."

The reality had to manifest according to the truth of what you see and how you perceive. How is it that some people can move in some unusual feats that aren't even Christians? Feats that are beyond human comprehension, human capability. Why can someone do that and others cannot?

Well I cannot explain to you what those individuals may have gone through in their life to create a certain mindset, a certain paradigm, but their paradigm did not accept the illusion of "cannot", but rather the truth of, "Well yes. I can do that." People can materialize stuff out of thin air. How? Because their paradigm accepts that as a truth. They don't believe that its impossible.

How does the word go .... ***"All[12] things are possible to him that believes?"*** All things. "Well, maybe not all things but maybe just this or this." **No. All things**. What about the scripture that says; ***"you have been blessed with every spiritual[13] blessing in the heavenly places"?*** Every spiritual blessing. And the mind says "Well maybe not. Maybe not. Well, I don't have this or this." **No. Every spiritual blessing**.

So then what are you saying? That as a man thinks[9], so is he. And quantum physics helps to put the science behind it.

Do you believe that you are blessed with every spiritual blessing in the heavenly places? Because if you do, and we are all going through this, then every spiritual blessing has to manifest. It cannot help but manifest.

Go back to the Tower of Babel[14]. What happened? They were all together, building this tower. They were of one mind, and God had to confound them. The book of Genesis. Read it. God had to confound them, because whatever they put their mind to, they could do. Wow. Was their paradigm limited? No, it was not.

We don't realize the power[15] that we have to create, to pluck up, to destroy. We don't realize it. And that is why God has been renewing the mind. **This is why the renewal[1] of the mind is so intrinsically tied into the manifestation of sonship**. What's holding us back? Why haven't we broken through into the deep, deep things of sonship? Why? Because we haven't fully believed that we could.

There has been a lack within our paradigm and so quantum physics, once again, is at play here. As you see reality, reality will conform to what you believe, and that will be your manifested truth. "As a man sees in his heart[9] so is he.[4]"

God has been progressively renewing the mind of the sons. We know that this only comes about through the deep work of the cross[5] - as you die out daily. As the soul flesh dies out, the Spirit of Christ comes forth. And the renewed mind, the mind of Christ, begins to have ascendancy over the corrupt mind of the soul. Now, all of a sudden, your paradigms begin to change. You stop driving down the I-95 and the I-10 and you go over to another freeway, and all of a sudden your reality shifts.

You might be able to look at it on the natural plane - "Well it's because this happened and this happened, and I did this. It can seem like cause and effect. That is just one level of perception. What caused the change is the shift internally that happened within you ... and everything had to begin to manifest to the truth of your belief.

This is a very deep word, because this is the impasse. If we were to call this word "What is the impasse to sonship?" ... this is the impasse. And it's why we're constantly admonished to wait upon the Lord, and to let go. You've heard me say that how many times? Let go! Let go! Until I just want to scream it at myself. Let go!

I am tired of creating reality out of illusion. The whole world is doing that. We have talked about the ability for the leaders of this age to create a global mentality that then creates a substantive reality out of it. It sounds like a lot of words, doesn't it? But you get people on a global scale into a certain mindset that can be propagating illusion and false news and God knows what. And you get enough people believing that, and it will create a substantive reality. It is really very simple. You get enough people believing in the same line of thought, it is going to create a substantive reality. And that is how the enemy has controlled the world to a great degree.

And God has said, "Be ye not a part of this age[16]. I'm delivering you out of this age. I'm delivering you out of this world, out of this mindset, and I'm bringing you into the realm of truth, the realm of the kingdom, the realm of freedom and the glory of the sons of God."

What is the freedom of the sons? Romans 8 talks about how all creation travails[17] and groans and suffers childbirth waiting for their release, for the freedom of the glory of the sons of God. You have been destined for freedom, for absolute, unequivocal, freedom. And at this point in time, you don't even know what that is. I don't even know what that is.

I don't mean to be putting you down. We don't even know how totally encompassing and freeing it is, what God has ordained for us and what we're heading into. But He has ordained His sons for freedom. It's hard to imagine. I think it is in the book of Malachi, where the word describes freedom like calves skipping[18] from the stall. I am ready to start skipping!

We don't know this experience yet. We've seen it perhaps, in bits and pieces. I know I have seen the freedom coming, as the Lord has taken me to different realms and I've walked through them. And my first thought was the freedom. It was like, "Oh my gosh. I'm free." I didn't feel the entanglement of the soul/mind, or anything. It was all just stripped off and you felt weightless, like you had just lost 500 pounds and you were free. The experience is beyond, beyond. Yet right now, we are still transitioning, and it can feel like your body is 1,000 pounds of dead weight.

I don't want to put this in the future. It's here. It is here now. The freedom[19] of the glory of the sons of God. All creation is waiting for the sons to break through into freedom, because as they do, they in turn will release all creation by virtue of the act of what they have done.

You're not going to go around and start laying hands on creation saying; "I free you. I free you. I free you. I free you. I free you." No. All you have to do is break into it. Open the door. Kick the door down. Put a piece of C-4 and blow it up. Go through the opening. And when that door is opened, really opened, creation will rush through it like a mighty tidal wave. All we have to do is get that door open; which means the sons have to first get it, before they can give it. And we don't even have to worry about giving it, because it will just be imparted and disseminated out in the spirit like wildfire. Once the sons break into the liberty[19] that the Father has destined them for, that liberty will spread like wildfire.

This is where we are. I just admonish you, be so careful. Don't buckle under the lies and the illusion. Because I tell you, if you are called to sonship, then you are wrestling with this every day, as the enemy continues to throw lies and illusions and the appearance of things at you. Don't navigate through it, don't let it seep into your paradigm, just call it for what it is; "a lie and an illusion, and I am not going to accept it." Reach into God and just throw it off. Align yourself with the real truth, and that will determine your substantive reality.

Believe me, we are all in the middle of this in - to a great degree. A great fight is happening, a great battle. The sons deliverance will change the world, just by virtue of their becoming. The act of becoming is going to change everything.

How do you go up to someone who is buying into the lie and illusion? Are you going to walk up to them and say, "Hey, you're in deception." They're going to look at you like, "What are you talking about? I'm not in deception." Yeah? Interesting. The waters of the world are getting more and more muddied. It is getting pretty dark outside. But the sons are not buying it.

This is the time that the kingdom is to break forth. It's a time that you are to break forth into freedom. And I know that it's tied into the renewing[1] of the mind. Hopefully this word just lays some thoughts out for you to meditate on and just look to the Lord about.

The assault comes to get the sons to give in to the darkness, but it's not happening. The most effective assault is that which cannot even be discerned at all. We're not talking about witchcraft and blatant stuff, we are talking about that which can't even be discerned unless you have revelation. That's where the warfare is. We don't realize how much warfare is focused against the saints to keep them out of moving into the freedom of God, to keep them in a mindset and a paradigm that is constantly creating the illusion rather than creating the truth.

The truth is here to set you free[6]. But you must align and anchor yourself to the truth - within your mind. This is a very deep word and very mystical. "Lord, we have the power to create. You have given us the power to create. And whether we realize it or not, we are creating all the time. We are constantly creating, however, we will not create the illusion any longer.

The promise is that He is delivering His sons out of this age. This is what we are talking about; a thorough and complete deliverance.

People think that when they get a revelation from God that they have been delivered. They have not. They have just taken a little pinky-step in that direction.

God is delivering His sons and daughters in the spirit of their mind. How does Paul say it? *That you be renewed*[1] *in the spirit of your mind.* God is renewing the spirit of your mind, so that you will no longer think along the tracks of limitation or illusion, but you will begin to align yourself and think along the lines of truth.

What Joshua did in his meditation before God was so mystical; and he may have just thought, "Okay, I'm sitting here and rehearsing the words. I'm being obedient, Lord." And he was. But on a higher plane he was aligning to the truth. On a quantum level, he was creating a substantive reality that was in adherence to the truth. And that's what we do.

Scriptures (NASB)

[1] Romans 12:12
And do not be conformed to this world, but be transformed by the renewing of your mind, so that you may prove what the will of God is, that which is good and acceptable and perfect.

[2] 1 Corinthians 2:16
For WHO HAS KNOWN THE MIND OF THE LORD, THAT HE WILL INSTRUCT HIM? But we have the mind of Christ.

[3] John 14:6
Jesus said to him, "I am the way, and the truth, and the life; no one comes to the Father but through Me.
[4] John 6:13
"But when He, the Spirit of truth, comes, He will guide you into all the truth; for He will not speak on His own initiative, but whatever He hears, He will speak; and He will disclose to you what is to come.

[5] Philippians 2:8
Being found in appearance as a man, He humbled Himself by becoming obedient to the point of death, even death on a cross.

[6] John 8:32
and you will know the truth, and the truth will make you free."

[7] Romans 8:6
For the mind set on the flesh is death, but the mind set on the Spirit is life and peace,

[8] Saturnalia
From Wikipedia, the free encyclopedia
Saturnalia was an ancient Roman festival in honor of deity Saturn, held on 17 December of the Julian calendar and later expanded with festivities through to 23 December. The holiday was celebrated with a sacrifice at the Temple of Saturn, in the Roman Forum, and a public banquet, followed by private gift-giving, continual partying, and a carnival atmosphere that overturned Roman social norms: gambling was permitted, and masters provided table service for their slaves.[

[9] Proverbs 23:7
For as he thinks within himself, so he is. He says to you, "Eat and drink!" But his heart is not with you.

[10] Joshua 1:8
"This book of the law shall not depart from your mouth, but you shall meditate on it day and night, so that you may be careful to do according to all that is written in it; for then you will make your way prosperous, and then you will have success.

[11] Hebrews 6;19
This hope we have as an anchor of the soul, a hope both sure and steadfast and one which enters within the veil,

[12] Mark 9:23
And Jesus said to him, "'If You can?' All things are possible to him who believes."

[13] Ephesians 1:3
Blessed be the God and Father of our Lord Jesus Christ, who has blessed us with every spiritual blessing in the heavenly places in Christ,

[14] Genesis 11:6-8
...6The LORD said, "Behold, they are one people, and they all have the same language. And this is what they began to do, and now nothing which they purpose to do will be impossible for them. 7"Come, let Us go down and there confuse their language, so that they will not understand one another's speech." 8So the LORD scattered them abroad from there over the face of the whole earth; and they stopped building the city....

[15] Jeremiah 1:10
"See, I have appointed you this day over the nations and over the kingdoms, To pluck up and to break down, To destroy and to overthrow, To build and to plant."

[16] Romans 12:2
And do not be conformed to this world, but be transformed by the renewing of your mind, so that you may prove what the will of God is, that which is good and acceptable and perfect.

[17] Romans 8:20-22
...20For the creation was subjected to futility, not by its own will, but because of the One who subjected it, in hope 21that the creation itself will be set free from its bondage to decay and brought into the glorious freedom of the children of God. 22We know that the whole creation has been groaning together in the pains of childbirth until the present time....

[18] Malachi 4:2
"But for you who fear My name, the sun of righteousness will rise with healing in its wings; and you will go forth and skip about like calves from the stall.

[19] Romans 8:21
that the creation itself also will be set free from its slavery to corruption into the freedom of the glory of the children of God.

[20] Hebrews 7:25
Therefore He is able also to save forever those who draw near to God through Him, since He always lives to make intercession for them.

Notes

Chapter 24

Extended Consciousness

One of the things that we must realize is that we are experiencing a life change that no one has really experienced before us. We have spoken many times that we are paving the way. We are entering into levels of change and experience that have not happened before. The Cloud of Witnesses and those who have died in the faith, paved the way for us to enter into this change. And so we are paving the way, and we are learning our way as we go.

Everything in this book has to do with the final preparation of the kings and priests. In many ways it is like going in and taking a last minute shower before going out to a special event and you get dressed in your finery and you leave. So the Lord is putting us through the last changes necessary. He is washing us in the water[1] of the word ...washing us in the water of His presence, in final preparation.

He has already measured and fit us for the robes of righteousness. They are right there on the bathroom door hanging. We step out of the shower and we are clothed, not only with the robes of righteousness[2], but the promise of resurrection life. The promise is that we will be clothed from on high. We are putting off the garments of the flesh, and we are putting on the robes of righteousness - a new suit of clothes.

God is beginning to set our garments out before us, and we are beginning to be completed now. It's all very mystical. Without any real deep revelation, it can be hard to identify with what is happening to you during this time.

We have talked about being caught up[3] to the throne, Revelation 12. This is happening. There are many things that we should be expecting, as we move deeper into the transformation that the Father has for us.

One of these changes has to do with an extended consciousness. We know that the Father is omnipresent and omniscient and that Christ has entered into that. There is an aspect of that which the sons are entering into, and we are still leaning into it, because God is still expanding us. We are still writing this book. We are still trying to understand what it is that we are experiencing as we write the last chapters of sonship.

God is bringing His sons into a deep level of living in both worlds at the same time. Taking it out of the realm of just faith, where you believe you are living in both realms, to the daily experience of tracking in both worlds at the same time. Your physical body is responding to the intensity and so you labor through your day. All of these things are very viable and are offshoots of moving into a deeper level of living in both worlds.

But another aspect that is happening concurrently is that God is bringing you into what I would call an extended consciousness; where you can be many places at the same time with an awareness of all of them at the same time. That can sound a little interesting, because it almost sounds like you are a central computer and you are tracking on different levels and so different things are feeding back to you. But they are not just from one level or two; they are from a multitude of realms. And this is progressively happening.

I would say that it is not an overnight experience, because it is something that we have to learn and we have to be able to be brought into, as we are able. A lot of the ministry that is facing us, both right now and on the other side of this change, has to do with the outreach that the sons are to have on so many levels.

You could say that what we are talking about, in many ways, is kingdom evangelism. But it's not just passing out tracts and saving a few souls. It is something that is going out and literally changing multitudes and bringing them into an experience of the kingdom. Kingdom evangelism was never about just evangelizing the word and trying to save a few souls, it is far more expansive. God will bring many people to you who are waiting for change and deliverance, and they will experience sonship as you bring the impartation to them.

As this process of ascension continues to happen, we will find that we are living, more and more, in both worlds. What that means is that your spirit, soul and body is in a state of being integrated. Right now we're a bit dysfunctional. We are not completely integrated. The promise is that He will save[4] us; spirit, soul, and body — that is in the book of 1 Thessalonians.

But there is more to it than just that. God is integrating you, as a unified being: a spirit that has a body with a redeemed soul. And so it is the entire man. As you begin to break into deeper levels of the release of sonship, this whole issue of an extended consciousness becomes a reality that we have to address, and we will need to deal with more and more. And so my answer to you is, "No, you are not going crazy. But God is expanding the tent[5] pegs of your dwelling." I believe that is in Isaiah. He is expanding your ability to track on many different levels at the same time.

A lot of the ministry that is going to come forth will be because the sons will be able to move in the spirit. Not astral projection which is a product of the soul. But a spiritual — I'm not going to call it projection — but a spiritual way of functioning that you are able to move, whether it is your entire being or just your spirit — it doesn't really matter — and minister in a broad fashion on many different levels. God is bringing that and I know many of you have experienced bits and pieces of it. Little breakthroughs here, little breakthroughs there, as God just begins to give you a taste of what is coming. He is preparing you mentally and spiritually, for what He wants to bring you into.

As I have said before, we are so much further down the road than we know. And that has been shown to us many times. The word has come, "You are so much further down the road than you know", and we are still running to catch up with understanding really where we are in God right now. A lot of this has to do with being able to truly let go. We have talked about "letting go" in different capacities; letting go of your concepts, your ideas, and your way of thinking so that God can show you a new thing. Letting go so that God can fill[6] you. These are all aspects of what I would call "letting go".

But there is another part of it, too. Just being able to breathe in deeply, breath out, and just disconnect from everything. It is a type of letting go where God can bring you into the next experience that He has for you. I know that some years back I began to study this and I found that when you entered the theta state—which is the frequency just before deep sleep - that you begin to see and hear beyond the veil. And it is in that type of state that some of these experiences are going to happen or continue to happen.

I recall several years ago, as I was waiting on the Lord, that I fell into this theta state ... almost asleep but not quite, almost awake, but not quite - that I travelled to England. I recall that I could smell the cobble stones. I could smell the moisture in the air. It was all very tangible. And I was led then to minister to a small group of people. As that completed, I found that through my focus and intent I could control where I wanted to manifest my consciousness. Did I want to remain there or return back here?

It was an interesting experience, because often times the Lord has spoken about focus and the importance of focus. We are not just talking about just a basic focus, as when you read something where you are kind of focused. No, we are talking about an intensity of focus that transcends the limitations that we have known.

Peter and John experienced this type of focus, and this is a good example.

But Peter, along with John, fixed his gaze on him and said, "Look at us!" Acts 3:4

When they set their gaze[7] on the man, just outside the walls of Jerusalem, it says they fixed their gaze and healed the man. That focus in the Greek was called "atenizo", and it has to do with an intense, almost violent focus. Literally atenizo, in the Greek, means "a particle of union". What happened when they cast their gaze. <u>A cord, or strand of spirit was extended to the man, and conveyed the healing.</u> So, focus is more than just a mindset, it is an extension of a spirit reality and involves your spirit. This type of violent focus is one of many things God is bringing forth within the sons, and will become part of their reality. It is part of the "extended consciousness" we are speaking of.

We have to understand that we are not looking for a violence of the flesh. It is not a violence of the soul. It's none of that. It's a violence[8] of spirit, that God is bringing the sons into.

So a focus of spirit, that is so violent and intense that it causes an extension of your spirit or essence to reach out to someone, is something that has to be experienced. And this extension is not limited to time or distance. Even though Peter and John were just feet away from the man needing healing, this type of focus/extension knows no limitation. Someone can be on the other side of the planet, it is not limited.

This must be experienced to really be understood. You can't just say, "Okay, well I'm going to be violent in my focus." It is something God brings forth within you, so that as you wait before Him, even if just for a moment in time, you can summon this intensity of focus on Him that can literally slice through the limitations, slice through the illusion, slice through the perceived barrier that you might think you have, and really reach in and touch the Lord. This is a part of the functioning of the sons of God that He is bringing forth, and is a tool that you will use more and more.

I have had a number of people come in the spirit and try to teach me about this violent focus and what could be achieved with it. And I understand that we are talking about something here that is more than just what we know of focus in our definition. We are talking about an aspect of God that is being created within the sons, where you can manifest; you can create; you can do whatever you need.

Often times you might ask yourself, "Well I'm right here, I'm in the zone, I prophesying, I'm believing, I'm creating, I see it, but it doesn't seem to happen." Well there are two answers for that: First of all, what we create is being created both in the spirit, and the natural. The problem is that sometimes we do not at first see it manifest on the natural plane. Was it created? Yes, but on the spirit plane. As we walk in this violence of focus, then we will see it manifested on this level as well. This violence of focus has a great deal to do with everything that God is bringing the sons into.

So, lets go back to England for a moment... depending upon where I directed my focus, I found that could keep my consciousness there; whether it was in England, or back here. The aggressive focus was the steering wheel; the method through which you could control where you chose to manifest. We need to work with this issue of a violent focus, because it is more important that we understand. And even if we just set our intent to do this, God can meet us half way and help bring us through this.

In many ways we have experienced the flip side of this where the negative problems and assaults and illusions and battery of things that come against you can create such a negative focus, that the negative focus becomes very intense, very aggressive. So much so that what was a mouse, has grown into a roaring lion, because of your focus on it, when all it was ... was an illusion. You could even say, "Yes, but there was so much power behind this illusion." It's just power. It's just illusion. Satan can manipulate all of that. And as long as he can get you to respond with a focus on it, then he has achieved his goal.

On the flip side, a violent focus set upon the word, and set upon manifesting what you know He has directed you to do, is extremely powerful. But it is nothing that can happen overnight, however, it is something that God has been working within the sons for a very long time.

I would recommend that you work with this as you are going to bed and resting; as you begin to drift off into that theta state, before sleep, or when you wait before Him, quieting yourself. Quiet all of the external confusion and all of the internal fears and come to a place of silence. This is very, very powerful. The power of silence is something that we will also experience more and more. It is in this state of quiet that you can summon up a violent, intense, aggressive focus that can literally blow through the damns and the barriers. Work on it. Visualize it. See it.

This is one of the channels that God is using to bring the sons into a transformation. And there will be a point where you won't need to work on it, because it will be so solidified within you, that in a moment of time, you can summon what you need and you will be right there. But we are in this transition, as we have said, and this is something we should work on.

We have brought words over the years on visualizing and the power of visualizing. We are talking about something very similar here, between the aggressive, violent, fixed focus, and entering into an atmosphere of absolute silence. As you visualize and see your focus come into play, the atmosphere of absolute quiet, or silence, is where you can begin to take that which seems like an imagination, and bring it into a reality. You can project yourself to wherever it is you see yourself. And even though you have done that in the past, and experienced measures of release, it was only the partial[9]. Everything we have walked in has been the partial, until now.

The day of fullness has come. I know that the more we can give ourself to this, the quicker this will happen. Start with these three things:

First of all quiet yourself, externally, internally, stop the chatter. Stop all of the noise, and come into a state of silence.

Second, enter into a visualization.

Third, reach into that intense, aggressive, and violent focus. You will know you are there, when you feel that "particle of union" extend from you.

These are the keys to the power to create and manifest beyond what we have known, and this is where we are headed.

At this point in time, before we move into the breakthroughs that will come with the change physically to us, there remains a need for the ministry of the sons to move to another level. And that will greatly be achieved through what we have been talking about. There are places, people, dimensions, and worlds that need to be visited; that need to be released, even prior to the release that we are to enter into.

At one point a young man appeared to me. He was from a different world and he was very excited to have come and met with me. He came to say that all of them on their world had been in preparation and training for what was coming. That they would also partake of the end time judgements and warfare because it was going to affect his level as well. And so he was excited to have made the contact and they were waiting. Like this young man, there are others where there is still a need for them to be touched, for the preparation to be made complete in them, for what they are to perform during this time.

God's creation is magnificent and so beyond[10] what we understand. God has been preparing all of creation for this time. And we have a ministry to help in assisting their completion or readiness. To a large degree we are doing this ... we have had glimpses of it from time to time of what our spirits are doing. But more and more, we are going to enter into a real-time experience on every level.

Don't forget we are talking about an extended consciousness. We are talking about God extending the tent pegs of your dwelling. Someone could say, "Well, that sounds kind of like you are out in space." But we are not talking about that. I know in the new age movement they talk about being "grounded" and we have looked at that over the years. But what we are talking about here, is that we only have one tether and that is in His presence. We have no tether to this natural plane. Nothing else holds us back, and the Lord can take us where He would. He is our anchor.

You recall during the time that Paul was imprisoned in the cell, that he walked in this. Many times he said, "*When you gather together there I am with you.*[11]" If there was a problem in the churches, he would send spirit to bring judgement upon that one.

Paul moved with a very unique grasp of this extended consciousness. He was able to move and function throughout the churches even though in body he was limited to the cell. And so, even though we may feel limited to this body, or limited to what we feel are circumstances, the truth is that we are not limited whatsoever. God is pulling you up, higher and higher, that you might be free to really move and function in the administration[12] prior to the transition.

Many years ago when we used to pastor churches, we would minister to people who were, what we would call, free spirits. We would have to help them reign in their spirits, and for the young ladies, we had to help them often times to keep their spirits in their shoes, so to speak. Sounds funny, but a free spirit can go off and flirt, in the case of many of these young girls, and they would not understand why all these young men were being drawn to them.

For the sons at this time, your spirits have been freed. This is the starting point to enter into the extended consciousness that God is bringing the sons into. It may feel like you don't even know where you are half the time, but that is because your spirit is free and it is moving.

I know how often I have spoken to Anne and said, "Well, I know we are in the midst of something, because I'm not here." And she would say, "Well, I'm not here either." And I said, "Well, we just need to figure out where we went." And we would laugh. Sometimes it is just hilarious.

God is not holding back. He is not waiting for us to catch up. He is pulling us into the ministry of sonship[13] and the administration of the kingdom. We are just playing a little bit of catch up here as we come into that extended consciousness ... that awareness of what we are doing.

God has spoken to us a number of times about resurrection life, and about the close proximity of resurrection life right now. In one very profound statement He said, "Visualize it. See yourself on the other side of this transition."

We have worked with this, off and on. But it is easier said than done. But we will just keep working on it. It could be as simple as the scripture, "As a man[14] thinks in his heart, so is he." We need to see ourselves in resurrection life. We need to see ourselves on the other side of this transition. That is one of the things that He has required. Don't see yourself as limited. Don't see yourself up against a wall. Don't see yourself in battles without answers, or situations that you have no idea what to do. See yourself on the other side of this transition.

We recently spoke in one of the other chapters about breaking the bonds with yourself. That God is not only breaking the bonds within you to humanity, to mankind, to your DNA, to your genealogy but He is bringing a deliverance within the spirit of your mind so that you would stop identifying with yourself as how the carnal mind has seen you and known you. This has been a type of visualizing. On the negative side, we have seen ourselves as this body with limitations and hindrances and impasses; and we haven't realized that we were visualizing that. So we must be careful with our thoughts.... The sons have lived with limitations so long that the mind just defaults to that. But this is over.

The Lord is saying, "That is all a lie and that is all an illusion." This is another level that we are letting go of, that we might see ourselves in resurrection life, and not with the limitations of the past.

This can be called, spiritual isometrics. You are exercising your spiritual muscles. Not everyone loves to go to the gym and work out for an hour. There are those that enjoy working out, but the vast majority don't. And this is spiritual workout 101, but it has to be done diligently. We could probably put three or four different titles to this word, and "Spiritual Workout 101" would be another title. What we are doing is rehearsing the truth in obedience.

Since we are going down this path of talking about extended consciousness, let's talk about something else as well. We have spoken about all of creation being comprised of frequency, vibration, and energy. Each of the sons, themselves, vibrate at a unique frequency. In many ways you are like a song[15] to the Lord. Your frequency, your vibration, your energy is like a song. It is more than just what you are, as far as a physical manifestation.

Reach with me here for a minute. What you are is a song. You are worship. I believe it is in Romans that it talks about the acceptable service of worship[16] has to do with what we are, not what we do mechanically as far as lifting hands and singing songs. That is all fine and that is part of everything; but take it on a deeper level. You are worship. You are a song before the Lord. And you could probably research that throughout the Psalms and find some very interesting scriptures. And the more you change, the more your frequency and vibration changes, and the more your song changes as you begin to emanate worship to the Lord.

For you to live at this point is for you to be a living worship to the Lord. Whether you have had a bad day or a good day; whether you waited on Him or not, what you are in your essence is an energy, is a vibration, is a frequency, is a song back to Him.

A few years back I was shown another level of creativity that is happening with the sons. I saw threads of gold. The threads were sound, and we were weaving "reality" from these threads. We were like a seamstress, taking these golden threads and weaving them. And these sounds, these golden threads, were coming out of the sons. Both the sounds that you make, when you open your mouth, and the sound of what you are as a son, is creating threads. And we took these threads and began to weave them together to create the reality of what God is speaking that needed to be done.

Very mystical, but it goes back to the fact that what you are is so much more than just a finite person. As I said earlier ... you are judgement; not the spirit of judgment. You are the word, not limited to just what you speak audibly. And you are worship, and you are the light. It is very, very, mystical what the sons are entering into and what they are beginning to realize. This is just another aspect of what the sons are, and have always been.

There is always a flip side and we have spoken of this before as well. The flip side are the dark sounds that are emanating in the earth right now. And if you tune into it, you can hear the frequency and the sounds of chaos and judgment. The sounds of war, and anger and hatred. All of that is emanating through the consciousness of the people on this planet. And they are simply a megaphone, if you will, for the satanic spirit world behind it.

These sounds of darkness are going into the earth. They have been going into the earth for some time, with the intent to create illusion, deception, despair, war; you name it. The counter action of that are the sons. They are the sounds of light; the sounds of righteousness. The sounds that are creating dominion and authority. The sounds that are weaving the releases of what God has for this time.

It is very interesting what is happening. The sounds have been increasing both negatively in the earth plane, but as well, as the sons begin to manifest what they are is beginning to resonate through the heavens.

In the book of Psalms there is a great passage I always like and it says, "with each new day a new song[17] is sung". And as you arise each day, you realize you are different. You are not the same person you were the prior day. We are in a time of accelerated change, and the sons are changing daily. You may not be able to quantify it. You may not be able to discern it, but it is happening. And every day that you rise, a new song is sung by virtue of what you are, and are becoming, to the Lord.

We have covered a lot of ground with this word and it is only the tip of the iceberg, because the extended consciousness that is happening to you is only going to increase. It is part of sonship, and there are so many aspects to it. What you are doing is affecting every level of life, and it is far more than we understand. God is wanting you to come into a deeper level of understanding, that you might be able to work this and begin to move more fluidly into the administration of sonship during this time.

You are not limited. God has freed you. It is just your mind and the rest of you that need to catch up and realize what He has already done. So we let go. We let go and let the deepening experience of consciousness happen to us. In many ways, it is like the omnipresence of God, who can be everywhere simultaneously. We may not walk exactly in that, but God is expanding our consciousness to where we can be many places at the same time ... we just need to learn how to process the information as it comes to us from different realms and different levels.

It may seem like I am speaking ahead of myself, like we are not quite here, but I can tell you that this is not only coming and to be expecting, but to a large degree, it is here. We just need to recognize what is happening and give ourself to it.

Scriptures (NASB)

[1] Ephesians 5:26
so that He might sanctify her, having cleansed her by the washing of water with the word,

[2] Isaiah 61:10
I will rejoice greatly in the LORD, My soul will exult in my God; For He

has clothed me with garments of salvation, He has wrapped me with a robe of righteousness, As a bridegroom decks himself with a garland, And as a bride adorns herself with her jewels.

[3] Revelations 12:5
And she gave birth to a son, a male child, who is to rule all the nations with a rod of iron; and her child was caught up to God and to His throne.

[4] 1 Thessalonians 5:23
Now may the God of peace Himself sanctify you entirely; and may your spirit and soul and body be preserved complete, without blame at the coming of our Lord Jesus Christ.

[5] Isaiah 54:2
"Enlarge the place of your tent; Stretch out the curtains of your dwellings, spare not; Lengthen your cords And strengthen your pegs.

[6] Ephesians 3:19
and to know the love of Christ which surpasses knowledge, that you may be filled up to all the fullness of God.

[7] Acts 3:4
But Peter, along with John, fixed his gaze on him and said, "Look at us!"

[8] Mathew 11:12
"From the days of John the Baptist until now the kingdom of heaven suffers violence, and violent men take it by force.

[9] 1 Corinthians 13:9-10
For we know in part and we prophesy in part, 10but when the perfect comes, the partial passes away.

[10] Psalms 147:5
Great is our Lord and abundant in strength; His understanding is infinite.

[11] 1 Corinthians 5:4
In the name of our Lord Jesus, when you are assembled, and I with you in spirit, with the power of our Lord Jesus,

[12] Ephesians 3:9
and to bring to light what is the administration of the mystery which for ages has been hidden in God who created all things;

[13] Ephesians 1:4-6
For He chose us in Him before the foundation of the world to be holy and blameless in His presence. In love 5He predestined us for adoption as His sons through Jesus Christ, according to the good pleasure of His will, 6to the praise of His glorious grace, which He has freely given us in the Beloved One

[14] Proverbs 23:7
For as he thinks within himself, so he is. He says to you, "Eat and drink!" But his heart is not with you.

[15] Ephesians 2:10
For we are His workmanship, created in Christ Jesus for good works, which God prepared beforehand so that we would walk in them.

[16] Romans 12:1
Therefore I urge you, brethren, by the mercies of God, to present your bodies a living and holy sacrifice, acceptable to God, which is your spiritual service of worship.

[17] Psalm 96:2
Sing to the LORD, bless His name; Proclaim good tidings of His salvation from day to day.

Notes

Chapter 25

Communication in the Kingdom

To understand the seducing spirit that exists in the earth today, you need to understand communication and what happens between spirit and soul. Behind the darkness, that is so prevalent in this age, is the seducing[1] spirit. And it is something that we need to understand more carefully. When you think of this age, and time that we live in, you realize that all of the people of this world lie under the power of the wicked one, for we have come to a time of gross[2] darkness.

Millions of people walk the face of the earth, and everything can appear just fine and normal. But they don't know that they don't have eyes[3] to see, nor ears to hear. Even in the Christian household, the darkness is astounding. Very few truly have the light and the ability to hear the Lord and understand what is happening during this time.

At the forefront of this darkness is what we would call the seducing spirit. You might say, "What causes a person to be blind? Why do not they see? Why do not they hear?" Within the circles of Christianity are those who have been called or anointed at one point or another in their life to walk with God. The darkness enters because of the choices that are made.

The word talks about how people chose[4] the darkness verses the light. It is in the New Testament. We don't understand that every day we live we are constantly making choices ... even if your choice is to get up and have breakfast, something as simple as that. Your life evolves around a constant flow of making choices. And that is on a very simplistic level.

But in your walk with God, the warring[5] of the soul and the spirit needs to be understood much more. We do not realize how hostile the soul of the man is to the spirit of the man. We do not get that. If we did, we would be much more aggressive and violent in our heart. That is the enemy within you. It is the soul that is set against the spirit. And that is one of the greatest problems that any man of God or woman of God faces.

As you walk in your daily sojourn, you are making choices. If you have chosen to walk with God, then what does Hebrews say that He does? He scourges[6] every son whom He receives. This scourging, also known as the work of the cross[7], is where the soul progressively dies out. Generally not by choice; the soul tends to go down fighting and scratching.

Nevertheless, people face choices on a daily basis. The darkness enters into people's heart because of choices. The process of purification is a choice that you make; God will not force you. If you choose to step back, then that is when the darkness begins to enter in. A lot of people do not realize what happens to them in the act of this. They don't realize that they are making choices. They may realize that they have stepped back maybe from His demands. But they don't realize the consequences of it. They don't realize that they begin to lose the ability to hear and see because they have begun to reject the word and to reject the Lord.

This is how the darkness enters into the heart of the Christian that has been called to walk with God. In the world, the darkness is much easier to transfer, because it is tied into the illusion that is propagated constantly through the media and the channels of communication, and people's acceptance of those lies and darkness. Even as the word points out, the default of the human nature is to choose darkness. When it comes down to it, the soul of man does not want the light. It does not want the truth. It wants the darkness. And that can be hard to really understand.

So we are talking about the darkness that is upon this age. We are talking about the seducing spirit and how it moves and manipulates through mankind, and through the thinking of people. But, we are also talking about communication.

When we think of communication, we generally think in terms of what we speak to one another, and what we therefore convey as concepts or theories or ideas or belief systems. But that is really not true communication. Because what happens when you communicate to one another in that fashion is the filter and belief system of the individual you are speaking with will filter what you are saying. It doesn't even happen within the scope of their awareness. It is just a natural mode of how people function when you speak a word to another, whatever it might be. That word will be filtered. And the person will hear it based upon their personal paradigm, or their view of reality; what they believe is possible or not possible born out of their experiences and exposure through their sojourn.

So communication is a tricky thing. And it is within the canopy of communication that deception works. If you walk on the plane of the soul, then it is relatively easy to be deceived. But if you walk in the spirit or you are careful to hold everything that comes to you before the Lord, then the likelihood of being deceived is much, much less.

There is a tendency in this day and age of email and texting and everything else, that people will just shoot a twitter, shoot an email out and expect that immediately you are going to respond. This type of communication did not exist a decade, two decades, or three decades ago. But now everything is instant. And so, rather than having the opportunity to hold it, people tend to respond or react based on this constant input and projection that is coming to them. And that is something that we have to be very careful of. We would have to give the Lord enough room to respond and to give you proper input on how to think about what is coming towards you, lest you would be easily deceived.

We think in terms of communication as a conveyance of thoughts and words and principles. But in truth, communication is spirit. I am not really interested in communicating to your soul, or to your mind, because that is only the partial[8]. You will hear me, but it will be filtered through your soul/mind, and you are not even aware of it.

But, if I am speaking to your spirit, then there can be a step where you by-pass the mind and all of its filtering processes. More and more we are going to become great communicators. The sons of God will be great communicators, because they will understand the whole realm of communication, seduction, and darkness; how all of this is so intertwined together.

I recall years ago when our young daughter was with us and we were speaking with a man of God at his home. She was only three or four, and it was a very special time and we wanted her to be awake, but she fell asleep. We tried to wake her and the man of God said, "No. Let her sleep. She will receive more if she is sleeping than if she is awake." Here again bypassing the mind.

How often have you heard in New Age circles - and perhaps you have tried this - that to take a tape or a CD and play it over and over again as you are drifting off to sleep will allow the teaching to go deep, bypassing the mind and entering the subconscious. The New Age is focused on your subconscious, but to go down to the super conscious, or the spirit, is really what you want.

People are trying to change their lives and they realize that they are dealing with aspects of their incarnation that they don't understand. They are dealing with a subconscious that really controls so much of how they think and how they move. It is the old principle of Pavlov's dogs. You probably remember the story. The scientist would ring the bell and feed the dog. And so he did that for a number of times until every time the bell rang the dog knew that he was going to be feed and he began to salivate. So ring the bell, feed the dog, ring the bell, feed the dog. Then he stopped. He just rung the bell, didn't feed the dog. What happened? The dog began to salivate. There was a subconscious pattern that had been created. And it is very similar to what we have within our existence.

The realm of darkness understands the principle of the subconscious and that is why the media, on every level, whether it is TV, books, or the internet, are mediums they use to send subliminal messages to the subconscious to control you. It is not so much what is being portrayed initially in the communication, but their outreach to the subconscious, that is dangerous.

You may read a story and it may be put out across the globe. A story of some event happening, even though it is false information, completely false. But millions of people are exposed to it. So you would say, "Well, then as they read that, as they absorb it, they are creating a global consciousness at that point." And we have talked about this. But it doesn't happen quite at that point. What happens is that eventually that article or broadcast, as it is broadcast over and over, goes down into the subconscious until it becomes part of a way of thinking that people themselves are not even aware of.

I have mentioned to you before that mankind is being herded like sheep, by the spirit world, into a predetermined outcome. That is happening because of the manipulation of the subconscious of the population of the world. Not the manipulation of the conscious mind but the subconscious mind.

So - going back to what we were saying. The sons of God are going to be the greatest communicators that there have ever been, because they are going to understand that communication is a spirit realm reality. And, because they understand how it works, it will then work for them.

Let me be more specific. If you understand that a certain principle exists, in this case communication of spirit and soul, then as you consciously begin to communicate with people **you can, by your intent and by your awareness, direct your communication on a spirit level to reach the spirit of the individual.** All of the evangelism coming, and all of the outreach coming, is not going to be done on a natural plane or even on the plane of the mind and the soul. That will all abort.

It has to be on a plane of spirit. And that will only happen because you are aware of how it works. Do you follow me? **If it is in your awareness; if it is in your consciousness, then you will be able to project what you are speaking to the spirit of the individual. And that is where the change will happen.** That is where the understanding will happen, even if the person consciously says "Oh, yes. Oh, yes I understand." It doesn't matter. We are not interested in their mind. We are not interested if they understand the concept or not. We are interested in plumbing the depth of communication to their spirit, because that is where change happens.

It may take weeks. It could take a month. It could take days, hours. It is hard to say. But the impartation of communication that went to the spirit will manifest a change on a natural plane, and they will change. But it starts from the top down, not from the bottom up.

Change does not happen because you communicate a concept to the soul, and the soul understands it and says "I got it. I am changing." A change happens because the spirit communication coming out of you, (God), touches the individual on the plane of spirit, brings the change, and then it filters down to the natural plane and the plane of the mind. That is how change comes.

It is important to understand this, as you approach everything that you do - even in your day to day work. Whatever is set before you, where you have to communicate with people; whether it is a spiritual thing or an issue of the natural; understand that communication is a principle of spirit.

How many times do you talk to someone until you are blue in the face, and they just don't seem to get it? And you repeat, and you repeat, and you repeat. So what will make the difference? Only one thing will make the difference (assuming they have ears to hear in the first place) and that is the fact that this principle has come alive within you. You are the actuator of this principle to work. When it is real to you, when you have come alive and you have changed and you understand what spirit communication is, then you can begin to function on that plane. And it will work for you.

You cannot take this teaching and say, "Okay, I get it. Whatever I do is a spiritual thing. I've got to project it out." It has to go deeper than that. This has to become an experience within you that changes something within your make up and then you begin to understand, "Okay, this is how it works." And every time you talk to someone, you know consciously what you are doing. You are communicating by spirit and you are bypassing their mind, even though their mind is right there, filtering and working away and coming up with an analysis and understanding. That communication is going to go from your spirit to their spirit, bypassing the soul.

This is more important than we understand. We have spoken about the scripture that says, "If it were possible even the very elect[9] would be deceived." How is it that the very elect of God, those sent, could be deceived? Well there is really only one way and that is if they are still dwelling on the realm of the soul. Because it is in the plane of the soul, or the mind of the soul, that the deception works.

Here again you must understand that all communication is spirit. The spirit world knows what they are doing as they move through human channels, even if the channel may not be aware. The spirit world is very much aware. And so deception to an individual who is on the plane of the soul, can be conveyed very easily. It is both spirit, but it is also concepts like we spoke of that go through and touch the subconscious. So we are talking many planes here of existence.

I remember one time several years ago we were speaking with a couple. It really had nothing to do with spiritual things. It was more, I think, of housing or rental. And as I spoke to them we felt an anointing but we didn't really pursue any type of spiritual dialog.

But as I spoke to them about things that were rather unimportant Anne saw a green mist begin to flow out of my mouth and flow to them. It was the first time I believe that she may have visually seen the living word as it came out of my mouth. But it was substance. It was not concept. It was spirit, as it flowed.

Visualize with me for a second. Just imagine what happens when you speak to someone. You are speaking from the plane of spirit. There are more than just concepts and words coming out of your mouth. Spirit is coming out of your mouth[10].... because you are the word. You may not see it, but it does not mean that it doesn't exist. But as you speak[11], more than just concepts or words are conveyed. Their mind may be responding to the concepts or words, filtering them into their own paradigms, trying to understand what you are saying; but when you are speaking from the spirit, the spirit is what flows to them. What happens when the word of God flows out? That spiritual essence merges with them, and a positive transference happens.

It is both very interesting, and very mystical. But when we talk about all of these aspects: communication, seduction, and darkness, it is a lot more than just concepts. It is even a lot more than just dealing with the subconscious of man, or dealing with the fake news that might be perpetrated. We are dealing with a realm of spirit. And we have said this before, "God is bringing you into functional reality in the realm of spirit."

Everything in the realm of spirit has a basis of consciousness; has a life to it. It is not inanimate. And so the Word is spirit, and the word that comes out of the dragon[12] to deceive the whole world, has spirit behind it. That is why it can be so powerful, because it is more than concepts, more than words, more than theory. It is actually essence, spiritual essence of darkness, that penetrates the masses and begins to merge with their consciousness.

We have seen that. We have gone to churches, sitting in the back, and you can see the speaker bringing his word yet all that was coming out of his mouth was darkness. It was like black ink coming out of his mouth and just enveloping the congregation as they thought; "Oh, what marvelous teaching. What a marvelous word and they were absorbing the darkness and they had no understanding of what they were doing. Most likely the preacher was not that aware of what he was doing. He had been down that path long enough, and in his choices and rejection of the dealings of God in his life, he probably didn't even realize what he had become.

Most of the church world does not realize what they have become. They think they have got it together. How does it go in the book of Revelation? "I have need of nothing[13]..." and they don't realize that they are blind, that they are destitute, wretched, and filthy.

I know that is a strong statement, and I am not talking about the world. I am talking about the Christian movement. I'm not even talking about the Muslims and all of the other religions of darkness that exist, and there are many. But within Christianity, they don't realize what they have become by virtue of their choices and the darkness that they have assimilated and in turn become the mouth piece of Satan. They have become "megaphones" as they re-speak the same darkness that they had received.

The only way out of being affected by a seducing[1] spirit is to walk in the plane of spirit, and to be careful not to respond or to react, but to hold everything before the Lord that He can show you exactly how to think. That is the only way to navigate through this darkness right now.

But I want you to understand that we are dealing with a realm of spirit. The sons are dealing with a realm of spirit. They are being brought into a functional life in the spirit realm. And as such, everything in the spirit realm has consciousness; has life. What we are looking for is another level of awareness, because with a higher level of awareness you can move with an authority[14] and dominion to truly communicate, as well as to understand, what is happening - even when people communicate with you.

I've seen it - even with emails or texts - they all carry cords. Cords of light, cords of darkness, cords of confusion, and so on. No communication is void of spirit. You might say, "Well that was just a little communication from someone that you know." All of it carries something with it. Maybe not a spirit, but certainly soul, and you need to be aware of it. In your awareness you can move with the ability to have authority. Without that awareness, you are susceptible to being controlled and manipulated. People don't realize it. Cords are attached to everything. Cords to your emails, cords to your texts, cords to even your thought processes.

We are entering into a world that is not limited. In this world of the natural, everything is limited ... everything is defined by what can be done, and what cannot be done. Very structured. But in the realm of spirit, everything is unlimited. You are dealing with something that bypasses the mind, and bypasses the consciousness. To have ascendency over deception, one must understand how deception works, and how it is sown within the hearts and minds of people.

To move as a great communicator in God, one must understand how communication truly works in the realm of spirit and in the realm of the natural and soul. More and more, the sons are going to begin to release the captives[15]. They will begin to bring people into releases and changes that God has for them, but it won't happen because they are communicating thoughts and concepts, theories and mental projections that people can then go and accept or reject. It is going to happen because the sons of God are great communicators of spirit and they know what they are doing.

They may speak to someone and bring a great word and talk about concepts and teaching. Absolutely, and the mind will work with it. But they also know consciously, as they are speaking, that they are projecting a communication from spirit to spirit, **but it has to happen with an awareness on the part of the sons that they know what they are doing and as such it will be done. That is the key.**

That is what unlocks the magic of communication. It is not that it is just going to happen, in spite of yourself. It is going to happen because you know what you are doing. You understand the spirit realm. You understand the soul. You understand how the mind works and filters. You understand that what exudes from your mouth[16] is spirit and it will be even more powerful the more you understand it. And you will project it so that it will reach the individual and assuming the individual is open in their spirit, they will be able to receive the teaching, and it will become part of them, and they will change and it will all catch up with the rest of their mind.

It is interesting when you think about the word and you think about the changes that we are experiencing as the sons go from glory[17] to glory, for God is revealing more and more of Himself to you. In a very scientific way, God is communicating Himself, spirit to your spirit. More than just a general - ethereal presence of God - we are talking about substance. As you are open and reaching in to God, God is conveyed to your spirit and merges with you until you have these two substantive things; your spirit in its state of fluidity, and the Spirit of God as its being conveyed to you, and they merge together.

It is almost like mixing liquids together; once they are mixed you cannot separate them. And so the Spirit of God comes and merges with your spirit and you become that deeper extension of God; because of the transformation that happened on a plane of spirit.

I want this word to reach you deeply, because this is changing the playing field for His sons - from this point on. The promise has always come in the spirit that God is training His people, "I will show you[18] how to do it and you will know when it is done". It is like Moses and the children of Israel, if you remember the scripture? Moses knew[19] the ways of God, but the children only saw the acts. Moses knew the ways of God. And so the sons are to know the ways of spirit. They are to understand how the spirit works. As such, they can begin to use that in getting done what God has sent them to do.

This should change your awareness of how you communicate and of what happens every time you open your mouth. And communication can even transcend that; communication can be conveyed even when all that you do is to think on someone. Your thoughts, and your words, have spiritual essence. Remember that. You can create or you can destroy, just by your thoughts or words.

We are cautioned to guard[20] our hearts and minds, because even in the scope of how you think[21], without putting words to it, it can be very creative or destructive. And this is all within the realm of communication. God is continuing to teach the sons about the realm and world of spirit. And you are being loosed into being the greatest communicators the earth has ever known, because you understand the realm of spirit and you understand what you are doing and you will know when it is done.

Scriptures (NASB)

[1] Timothy 4:1
But the Spirit explicitly says that in later times some will fall away from the faith, paying attention to deceitful spirits and doctrines of demons,

[2] Isaiah 60:2
"For behold, darkness will cover the earth And deep darkness the peoples; But the LORD will rise upon you And His glory will appear upon you.

Or [2] Joel 2:2
A day of darkness and gloom, A day of clouds and thick darkness. As the dawn is spread over the mountains, So there is a great and mighty people; There has never been anything like it, Nor will there be again after it To the years of many generations.

[3] Ezekiel 12:2
"Son of man, you live in the midst of the rebellious house, who have eyes to see but do not see, ears to hear but do not hear; for they are a rebellious house.

[4] John 3:19
"This is the judgment, that the Light has come into the world, and men loved the darkness rather than the Light, for their deeds were evil.

[5] Galatians 5:17
For the flesh sets its desire against the Spirit, and the Spirit against the flesh; for these are in opposition to one another, so that you may not do the things that you please.

[6] Hebrews 12:6
FOR THOSE WHOM THE LORD LOVES HE DISCIPLINES, AND HE SCOURGES EVERY SON WHOM HE RECEIVES."

[7] Galatians 6:14
Being found in appearance as a man, He humbled Himself by becoming obedient to the point of death, even death on a cross.

[8] 1 Corinthians 13:10
but when the perfect comes, the partial will be done away.

[9] Mark 13:22
for false Christs and false prophets will arise, and will show signs and wonders, in order to lead astray, if possible, the elect.

[10] 2 Samuel 23:2
"The Spirit of the LORD spoke by me, And His word was on my tongue.

[11] Ephesians 6:17
"And now, Lord, take note of their threats, and grant that Your bond-servants may speak Your word with all confidence,

[12] Revelation 16:13
And I saw coming out of the mouth of the dragon and out of the mouth of the beast and out of the mouth of the false prophet, three unclean spirits like frogs;

[13] Revelation 3:17
'Because you say, "I am rich, and have become wealthy, and have need of nothing," and you do not know that you are wretched and miserable and poor and blind and naked,

[14] Ephesians 1:21
far above all rule and authority and power and dominion, and every name that is named, not only in this age but also in the one to come.

[15] Luke 4:18
"THE SPIRIT OF THE LORD IS UPON ME, BECAUSE HE ANOINTED ME TO PREACH THE GOSPEL TO THE POOR. HE HAS SENT ME TO PROCLAIM RELEASE TO THE CAPTIVES, AND RECOVERY OF SIGHT TO THE BLIND, TO SET FREE THOSE WHO ARE OPPRESSED,

[16] Luke 21:15
for I will give you utterance and wisdom which none of your opponents will be able to resist or refute.

[17] 2 Corinthians 3:18
But we all, with unveiled face, beholding as in a mirror the glory of the Lord, are being transformed into the same image from glory to glory, just as from the Lord, the Spirit.

[18] 1 Samuel 16:3
"You shall invite Jesse to the sacrifice, and I will show you what you shall do; and you shall anoint for Me the one whom I designate to you."

[19] Psalms 103:7
He made known His ways to Moses, His acts to the sons of Israel.

[20] Proverbs 4:23
Watch over your heart with all diligence, For from it flow the springs of life.

[21] Proverbs 23:7
For as he thinks within himself, so he is. He says to you, "Eat and drink!" But his heart is not with you.

Section 7

The Seal of Sonship

Chapter 26

A New DNA is in the Earth

I'm going to give you a quick overview of what we are going to cover, because this is going to give us a greater insight into what is happening right now in the earth, and what we should be expecting. We're going to talk about global consciousness, bloodlines of the fallen angels[1], the blood of Christ, flesh and blood not inheriting the kingdom[2], a new creation[3], the genetic DNA and chromosome makeup of the human species, the Nephilim[4], a new genetic code, the issue of Abraham and Ishmael[5], and the issue of the Israelites and their disobedience[6] when they went in to possess the land. There is quite a bit of material here we want to cover, as well we're going to review a vision that came last October 2015, during the blood moon.

Isaiah 43:19, ***"Behold I will do something new.[7] Will you be aware?"*** We are dealing with issues of awareness as we move more deeply into this timeline. This issue of awareness has been at the forefront of what the sons have had to deal with because they're coming out of a state of unawareness, and into a state of clarity ... *the sons are coming alive.*

The more you ascend in the Father's house, the more you are caught up, and the greater your awareness is of what is truly happening and unfolding in the realm of spirit. The Lord asks, "Will you be aware?" That all depends upon whether you are a wise or foolish virgin[8], for only the wise will have eyes to see during this time.

Lord, we ask Your blessing as You pull back the shrouds of deceit and illusion, and our misunderstanding of what exactly is happening and how You have positioned us.

Several weeks ago we began to look into issues concerning the bloodlines and ancestry of civilizations. It has always been very interesting to me to go into the Gospels, as well as some of the early books of the Old Testament ... Genesis, Exodus, and Leviticus. The Lord was so precise in laying down the genealogy of those that walked the earth, and I always wondered why. Why does this really matter?

In the Gospels it traces back the lineage of Christ. And I always wondered what that was really all about. You can say, "Well, Christ came from the lineage of David. And David was a man of God." The anointing can be traced back generation to generation. And you can go back to Jacob[9] and the passing down of the blessing. And you can say, "Well, what was that all about?" But I began to understand that it wasn't necessarily about any of that.

In the circles of darkness of the Nephilim, the sons of Satan, and even those that are very active in the governing and administration of the current state of affairs right now in the earth—the pecking order is largely influenced by their ability to trace their lineage back to the original fallen angels. Odd but interesting. It has only been in the last generation or two that the public has become aware of some of this.

The satanic web that has been sewn so intricately throughout all mankind, has gone on for thousands of years. The presence of Satan is so broad and expansive, that it can really stagger the mind to grasp just how much infiltration the satanic spirit realm has had into mankind.

Our focus has been, and will continue to be, breaking through into sonship; breaking through into the deep transformation that God has set as part of our destiny .... and you don't do this by backing into it with a burgeoning awareness of all the evil. That is not going to create faith. That is not going to do anything. If anything, it would create more of a fear in the un-regenerated soul-mind of man, which of course is what they intend.

A few years back I was led into a meeting, in the spirit, where I observed the satanic hosts. I saw in the spirit what was happening as Satan began to give out his orders for the day, and I saw, at that point, that God was beginning to bring a deep confusion in the camp of the enemy - an inability to communicate. It was already beginning at that time, and I know that we are further into this as God begins to bring a confusion in the camp of the enemy and an inability for them to move in any type of oneness or agreement.

You remember what happened in the Old Testament in the time of the Tower of Babel[10]. That basically was the gathering of the Nephilim seed in the earth at that time. Those weren't just ordinary people. That was the seed of the Nephilim that had spawned throughout man. And as they met together they knew that if they were of one mind and one accord that they could do anything.

The building of the tower of Babel was a foreshadowing of what could be achieved through a level of agreement and oneness, which was being tapped into by the children of wrath, at that time.

The flip side, of course, is the oneness that the sons of God are moving into. Nevertheless, what did God do as this began to unfold? He didn't allow it. He brought confusion and literally an inability to communicate. And the Nephilim seed was dispersed throughout the earth.

This is something that we need to understand a little bit more, so we are going to talk about bloodlines. When those of the upper echelon of the satanic circles meet, the position that they have is based upon their direct lineage to the fallen angels[1], to the first that came and dwelt with the women and begat the Nephilim and the Rephaim and the various satanic seeds that began to unfold in the earth. That really began the whole story. Now, in this time line, the position of the satanic seed and their input into this generation is tied to the hierarchy of their direct ancestry.

There is a lot to be said about bloodlines. What we are talking about here is a very vast subject, and there is a lot we are trying to cover here. One of the words which came in the first book ,*The Manifestation of the Sons of God,* was breaking the bonds with your past, breaking the bonds with your genealogy.

The Lord began to speak that we are in this process of breaking bonds; bonds with ourself, bonds with how we relate to people; bonds on every level. However, the greatest bond that we need to break, is the bond with humanity, for God is creating something new within the sons. The sons are not even to be bonded to the Adamic[11] nature ... and this is a big one.

Like many words that come from the Lord, this can be difficult to walk in. And often times you really don't know. Often times you have to take it like Mary and ponder[12] it in your heart and say, "Okay, Lord, I accept this. I am determined to break this last bond, therefore I speak it and I prophesy it and I give myself to whatever the process might be."

In the word says, *"Be ye not a part of this age[13] but be transformed by the renewing of your mind."* We are definitely being pulled out of the last attachment to this age[13]. This is happening in direct correlation to the renewing of the mind that the sons are experiencing. The only way you can step outside of this age and no longer be a part of it, is through the deep renewing[14] of the mind. It is not a product of your decision or determination or dedication.

As you enter into the mind of Christ, the ties you had to this age are severed progressively deeper and deeper. It can be a challenge because relationships you have had will potentially cease to exist on the levels that they were. People will not understand that God is pulling you out of this age. And when the renewing of the mind happens, it is something so complete that you cannot go back and say, "Well, I've decided to walk the fine line between the two.

No. When God delivers you out of this age, He delivers you. It's a lot more than just saying, "Well, I'm not a part of this age. I am born again." We know that this is only the beginning of the process.

God is extracting the sons out of a paradigm that has been limited and dictated by virtue of their involvement in this age. The sons have not really understood how much they have been effected by the governing spirit world that they have lived under, which has been a canopy over the face of the earth. We have spoken about this before, a number of times; that all of the world lies under the power of the evil one and the vast darkness that pervades the earth during this time.

God is pulling the sons out of a paradigm, out of an identity to the human race, to mankind, to this age, and the sons are literally beginning to manifest the commandment where it is said, "Be ye not a part of her[15]." The deliverance out of this age is a deliverance from the whore, as it speaks of in the book of Revelation, that has fed off the blood of the martyrs.

Everyone may think that walking with God is a decision. But walking with God is a transformation. It's a life of transformation. In the word it talks about how the blood of Christ cleanses us from all sin[16]. And yet the word says flesh and blood will not inherit the kingdom[2], but a new creation[3]. Let's stop for a minute and go back to the days of Genesis. Imagine as we review this. Visualize with me what is happening.

So the fallen angels[1] become very interested and decide they are going to come and lay with women and beget giants. What was that really all about? Was that really just an act of lust and rebellion? Or was there something else that was happening?

What we are talking about is literally the corruption of mankind that happened at the time of Genesis 6. What was Satan looking to achieve? He was actually looking to literally corrupt the DNA of mankind. He already knew the prophecies of what was going to come, that the seed of the woman was going to bruise the serpent[17] and that Christ was going to come out of a pure lineage. A pure lineage. So what happens back in the time of Genesis?

Well, we have a DNA adjustment that happened with mankind. Mankind was corrupted from what God had originally created them to be.

People during this time think they can change their DNA. That all they have to do is deep breathe and visualize, or go online and do a few steps to change their DNA. But you can't change your DNA. You can control aspects of your DNA - or genes - that may determine how you are to be or how you are to act or what your illnesses might be, for this carries down from your ancestry. So you can do that. You can control ... but you can't change, your DNA. So it's very interesting.

How do you change DNA? There has to be something that is grafted in that brings about a change. What happened when the fallen angels[1] came into mankind? They brought about a DNA change. And you saw it manifest as they begat giants in the land that were born of the seed of man and the seed of the fallen angels. Presto! You have a new DNA in the earth, and it's not pure, by any means.

The purity of mankind now becomes an issue and a concern regarding the prophecies of what was to come. Maybe you have not thought about it like this, but it continues to get worse and worse. I can't say to what degree, but I would say by far and large the majority of mankind within generations of the initial act, had a DNA that was compromised ... that was not pure.

It became so compromised that God had to bring an act of literally wiping out the human race. And so He brought the flood. It was a lot more than Satan coming in and manipulating people and people being turned over to their own lusts[18]—a lot more than that had happened. Mankind had evolved into a different DNA. You no longer had the purity of what God the Father first introduced in Adam and Eve. So what was the answer? The answer was to wipe them all out.

If you go back and read about the accounts of Noah; Noah and his three sons —and their wives— were brought on the ark[19]. Noah and his sons were of a pure DNA. And it makes you wonder, after the flood, what happened? Over a course of time, once again the Nephilim were in the earth. You have the Canaanites, the Amorites, the Hittites, all of those clans had the Nephilim DNA, the seed of the Nephilim. The seed of the fallen angels once again arose out of the flood. How did that happen?

There are no accounts of the fallen angels coming back and repeating what they did, but one of the wives, did not have a pure DNA. I believe reference has been made to Ham's wife. That something in her was not pure. Even if it was so minute - it was not pure. It was something of a hybrid.

Somehow the Nephilim made it through the flood. Somehow a small genetic aberration came through the flood. And we saw what happened through the act of Ham in the days that followed. So as time unfolds, you see the rise of the Canaanites, the Midianites, the Philistines, all of them. These were the giants in the land. These were the children with the Nephilim DNA code. Some say they were huge. Twenty feet tall. Thrity feet tall.

These were the ones that the children of Israel faced when they went to spy out the land[20]. They were so intimidated by what they saw that they came back with great fear. And yet Joshua and Caleb saw the truth, that God had removed the shadow[21] off of these giants. There was no longer a satanic protection on them. At that time the children of Israel could have gone in and just cleaned house completely. But we know what happened in that story.

So it's interesting that at the end of the forty years, the children of Israel are brought back to the river and they are commanded to go in and take the land. One of the commandments that was given to the children of Israel was that everyone must die[22], every father, son, baby, child, even the animals slaughtered and wiped off the face of the earth. And people can look at that and say, "Well, how can that be God? Why would God kill innocent children? What is this really all about? This can't be of God."

But you must realize that what was at stake here was the genetic code of the Nephilim, the seed of the Nephilim. This seed was growing and multiplying in the earth, once again. And if it was not completely annihilated, it would carry forward into the future. This was not God's plan, nor intention; so you had the commandment, "kill them all."

Well, unfortunately, the Israelites did not walk in that word. They did not kill them all. And the prophecy that came to the children of

Israel: if you don't do what I have commanded you to do today, they will be as a prick in your eye[6] and a thorn in your side. And to this day those signs come up in the spiritual warfare that we live under, because they have to do with the infiltration of the satanic seed that is still in the earth that comes against the sons of God to undermine, to blind, to block, and to abort the progress of the manifestation of the sons of God.

So here we are once again in the earth, at the end of days. And so the prophecy is ... *as it was in the days of Noah[23] so shall it be in the days of the Son of man.* We're dealing with a wide-spread input of the Nephilim seed as they go about to control mankind and to drive them into a very specific, and very planned, end result. That end result primarily has to do with the wiping out of humanity. That has always been their plan. A lot more is happening during this time, yet so much of this would have been removed had the children of Israel been obedient to what was commanded of them.

Let's talk a little bit about what God is doing. What happens when Christ is brought forth? Once again we have the pure lineage. We know that there has always been a remnant[24] throughout time, and that remnant has been the pure seed. They have always been in the earth.

But what did the Father do that was a little bit different with Christ? Well, we saw what Satan did when he brought the fallen angels. He chose to change the DNA genetic code. So when the Father overshadowed[25] Mary with the birthing of Christ we literally have a new genetic code that was created. A pure genetic code.

And Christ was - and is - the first-born[26] of many sons to come to birth now. The first of many that will be of this new DNA, this new gene, this new chromosome structure that's happening even if we don't really quite understand it yet.

The word says that flesh and blood would not inherit[1] the kingdom. Why is that? Well, it has to do with the blood, and it has to do with the genealogy. To some extent, and I don't know how wide spread the genetic makeup in mankind has been tainted by the Nephilim influence at this point, but the word to the sons is "Behold I will do something new[7]." The prophecy is that God will bring about a new creation[3], not following the order of Adam or mankind as we know it, but patterned after Christ.

We don't realize how pervasive the satanic input has been in this generation by virtue of the DNA within mankind. It could be millions that walk the face of the earth that have been tainted with this impure lineage.

There is something happening here in the change of our DNA and chromosome structure that we haven't understood yet. It is hard to understand what is happening with this change, yet the prophecy is "in the moment, in the twinkling[27] of an eye, you will all be changed at the last trump".

We know that a change is happening. We know that God is bringing forth something new in the earth. We know that the sons of God are being changed from a worm to a butterfly. We realize that the sons have been in like a cocoon, while in their present sojourn, waiting for the time that they would emerge as a whole new creation.

To me that speaks of a whole different DNA. Something that has nothing to do with the earth, with mankind, with what we've known. And that has always been the word, "Behold I will do something new[7]." ... as God begins to bring forth a whole new creation.

I know you can look at the people that walk the face of the earth, and they may not be completely the seed of Satan—they may not be a Nephilim—but there is something not right about them. Something in their genetic makeup that just is not correct. If you look you'll see that. More and more it's become evident that you have various levels of creation or humanity walking on the face of the earth that you really can't quite explain, but you know something is different.

Some people may say, "Well, there are aliens walking amongst us." And that may or may not be true, but definitely there is something happening within mankind that is not good. You have the flip side that God is bringing something new, a totally new creation. But on the other side of that, in the vast darkness that encompasses the earth at this time, we have seen how mankind, how the evil in mankind, has been driven to manipulate the DNA; has been driven to create hybrid humans; hybrid animals. We only see the tip of the surface, the tip of the iceberg of what is being done by mankind at this time in manipulating the DNA structure of human beings. We have no idea how vast and extensive this goes, but it's a lot deeper than what we have known.

A vision came about a year ago during the blood moon and it has to do with what is unfolding right now, during this time. The word was that the lining up of the various celestial bodies will cause a release of a negative satanic energy that was going to affect all of mankind. Unless you were really walking with God, everyone on the face of the earth would be touched by this energy that was being injected into the earth plane.

Let me be more specific. A teaching that came maybe twenty years ago had to do with celestial bodies lining up, whether it be conjunctions or various other celestial manifestations. And, every time something like this happens, there was going to be a release into the natural plane of spiritual energy. And generally it was a release of a negative level of spiritual energy.

We began to watch this over the last twenty years and began to document that. When this vision came, we understood that this last major conjunction of the blood moon in October of 2015, was indeed going to see a major, major release of a vibration and energy that was going to touch everyone in mankind unless they were on the path to sonship, on the path to really walking with God.

The specific word was that we were going to begin to see a greater manifestation of violent outbursts, a lot more shootings. A lot more violence on the earth plane. It would be within people, families, and relationships; you name it, but on every level. And over the past year we have seen this increasing. A great deal more volatility, hostility, and anger. A lot more of that has been escalating and we are only at the beginning of what is going to really possess the earth ... for there is no doubt that a "violence" is beginning to possess the earth.

The scripture talks about how people will think that they are doing God a favor[28] by killing the sons. This is in the book of John. I believe that only comes about because something of a pervasive spirit like this, so possesses people, that they are driven with this violent spirit to react and literally become a channel for what Satan is wanting to do.

Had the children of Israel been obedient and wiped out the Nephilim input and the Nephilim seed, I am confident that many of the cultures and races that we have today, whose genetic code can be sourced back to these various races, would not even exist on the face of the earth.

Go back to the time of Abraham and Ishmael. Abrahams' prayer was; "*Oh that Ishmael may live in thy sight*[29]." And Ishmael became the father of so much of the evil that has been handed down from generation to generation. What would have happened if Ishmael did not live and was taken out? A great deal of change in history that we know of, and a great deal of change in what we are presently dealing with in the earth. So many things are a product of choices and decisions made by the children of Israel and by individuals in the early days of the human race that would have changed the future, as we know it, considerably.

However, we do know the promise is that God is doing something new[7]. The manifesting of the sons of God is not going to be a people who have just been redeemed mentally with the mind of Christ , who have just come alive and walked more and more in the realm of spirit, ***but literally they will be a new creation.***

You are in the process right now of walking this out. And it can be very hard to quantify. You know you live with yourself every day. How do you look at yourself and say, "Well, I feel different. Something has changed. Something in my DNA just shifted. It's very hard to quantify what's happening."

But I know that the sons are going through these changes. And even if we don't understand it, the end product is that God is creating something new, an entirely new race of people called the sons of God. That is who you are. That is what you are. And this is the transformation that you have been destined to experience.

Scriptures (NASB)

[1] 2 Peter 2:4
For if God did not spare angels when they sinned, but cast them into hell and committed them to pits of darkness, reserved for judgment;

[2] 1 Corinthians 15:50
Now I say this, brethren, that flesh and blood cannot inherit the kingdom of God; nor does the perishable inherit the imperishable.

[3] 2 Corinthians 5:17
Therefore if anyone is in Christ, he is a new creature; the old things passed away; behold, new things have come.

[4] Genesis 6:4
The Nephilim were on the earth in those days, and also afterward, when the sons of God came in to the daughters of men, and they bore children to them. Those were the mighty men who were of old, men of renown.

[5] Genesis 25:12
Now these are the records of the generations of Ishmael, Abraham's son, whom Hagar the Egyptian, Sarah's maid, bore to Abraham;

[6] Numbers 33:55
But if you do not drive out the inhabitants of the land from before you, then it shall come about that those whom you let remain of them will become as pricks in your eyes and as thorns in your sides, and they will trouble you in the land in which you live.

[7] Isaiah 43:19
"Behold, I will do something new, Now it will spring forth; Will you not be aware of it? I will even make a roadway in the wilderness, Rivers in the desert.

[8] Matthew 25:1-2
1At that time the kingdom of heaven will be like ten virgins who took their lamps and went out to meet the bridegroom. 2Five of them were foolish, and five were wise....

[9] Genesis 27:27-29
27So he went to him and kissed him. When Isaac caught the smell of his clothes, he blessed him and said, "Ah, the smell of my son is like the smell of a field that the Lord has blessed. **28**May God give you heaven's dew and earth's richness—an abundance of grain and new wine. **29**May nations serve you and peoples bow down to you. Be lord over your brothers, and may the sons of your mother bow down to you. May those who curse you be cursed and those who bless you be blessed."

[10] Genesis 11:19
Therefore its name was called Babel, because there the LORD confused the language of the whole earth; and from there the LORD scattered them abroad over the face of the whole earth.

[11] 1 Corinthians 15:21-22
[21]For since by a man came death, by a man also came the resurrection of the dead. [22]For as in Adam all die, so also in Christ all will be made alive.

[12] Luke 2:19
But Mary treasured all these things, pondering them in her heart.

[13] Romans 12:2
And do not be conformed to this world, but be transformed by the renewing of your mind, so that you may prove what the will of God is, that which is good and acceptable and perfect.

[14] Romans 12:2
And do not be conformed to this world, but be transformed by the renewing of your mind, so that you may prove what the will of God is, that which is good and acceptable and perfect.

[15] Revelation 18:4
I heard another voice from heaven, saying, "Come out of her, my people, so that you will not participate in her sins and receive of her plagues;

[16] 1 John 1:7
but if we walk in the Light as He Himself is in the Light, we have fellowship with one another, and the blood of Jesus His Son cleanses us from all sin.

[17] Genesis 3:15
And I will put enmity Between you and the woman, And between your seed and her seed; He shall bruise you on the head, And you shall bruise him on the heel."

[18] 2 Peter 3:3
Know this first of all, that in the last days mockers will come with their mocking, following after their own lusts,

19 Genesis 7:13
On the very same day Noah and Shem and Ham and Japheth, the sons of Noah, and Noah's wife and the three wives of his sons with them, entered the ark,

[20] Numbers 13:33
"There also we saw the Nephilim (the sons of Anak are part of the Nephilim); and we became like grasshoppers in our own sight, and so we were in their sight."

[21] Numbers 14:19
"Only do not rebel against the LORD; and do not fear the people of the land, for they will be our prey. Their protection has been removed from them, and the LORD is with us; do not fear them."

[22] Deuteronomy 20:17
"But you shall utterly destroy them, the Hittite and the Amorite, the Canaanite and the Perizzite, the Hivite and the Jebusite, as the LORD your God has commanded you,

[23] Luke 17:26
"And just as it happened in the days of Noah, so it will be also in the days of the Son of Man:

[24] Isiah 10:21
A remnant will return, the remnant of Jacob, to the mighty God.

[25] Matthew 1:18
Now the birth of Jesus Christ was as follows: when His mother Mary had been betrothed to Joseph, before they came together she was found to be with child by the Holy Spirit.

[26] Romans 8:29
For those whom He foreknew, He also predestined to become conformed to the image of His Son, so that He would be the firstborn among many brethren;

[27] 1 Corinthians 15:52
in a moment, in the twinkling of an eye, at the last trumpet; for the trumpet will sound, and the dead will be raised imperishable, and we will be changed.

[28] John 16:2
"They will make you outcasts from the synagogue, but an hour is coming for everyone who kills you to think that he is offering service to God.

[29] Genesis 17:18
And Abraham said to God, "Oh that Ishmael might live before You!"

Notes

Chapter 27

The Mystery of God

In the book of Romans is one of the most hidden verses that is still waiting for us to experience; Romans 8:15. *For you have not received a spirit of slavery leading to fear again, but you received a spirit of the adoption of sons by which we cry out, "Abba! Father!"* (Romans 8:15) We are only now beginning to understand that this is all about the Father's family, and it is about entering into a relationship whereby we cry out, "Abba, Father."

There has been a great deal of emphasis on the manifestation of the sons of God, and rightfully so. This is the time that God is bringing forth the sons, but we need to understand equally, that this is the time of the manifestation of our heavenly Father. You must realize that there are no sons without which you have a Father. It is all about the Father's family, and if we don't get this revelation, then we're going to miss it.

Christ said; *"The Father and I will come and we will take our abode*[1] *in you."* He was saying that it was not going to stop with the Holy Spirit, but He said, *"If you love me and keep My commandment My Father will love you and My Father and I will come and take our abode within you."*

Right here is the greatest mystery of all. This is the mystery Ephesians speaks of - Christ in you - the hope of glory[2]. This is a mystery that is still veiled to the sons - themselves. There is a reality unfolding about the indwelling of the godhead within the sons that is coming to a completion. It is the reality of the Father and the Son and the Holy Spirit, within the sons. We are at the time of the culmination of the ages. God is wrapping up the dealings with the sons, and we are at the time of fulfillment; the time of completion.

This is a different time than it was two hundred or three hundred years ago. Was this promise in the book of Romans a reality for them as it is for us now? Well, it was a reality, yes. According to their faith, the indwelling of the Father and the Son was there for them to enter into and experience. But we know that even at that time, so little had been restored in the restoration of the kingdom.

As we have come closer to these days of culmination, God has been restoring truth after truth within the sons—not an external restoration of a truth and a concept—but the restoration of a truth that is already dwelling within the sons.

Two or three hundred years ago this level of restoration had not yet happened. Even though Romans 8 existed as a truth, it was more of a potential than a kinetic, realized energy. It was a potential, but the restoration of God's moving in the earth had not gone deep enough yet. And the sons, or those walking with God at that time in the earth, had not broken into that depth of reality. Now we are at the time of the wrap-up, and this has become the mystery that God is restoring, that even the sons have yet to really grasp.

Imagine with me, for a moment, the indwelling of the Father, the indwelling of the Son, and the indwelling of the Holy Spirit. It has been done. It is within you. They are within you. But the sons have not realized that level of indwelling. It has not yet been real enough for them. There has still been a veil over their mind, where they have not yet seen what God has already done. In some ways the sons have walked in poverty, because they have not yet seen themselves as abundance. The truth is that the sons are abundance, not poverty. You are; "My cup runneth[3] over," not, "My cup is half full."

The indwelling of the Father, and the indwelling of the Son, is here. The groaning and travail that is happening, along with the deep work of the cross, has one end point: to remove the veil[4] over your heart where you really see the indwelling that has happened within you. When the sons realize this, then truly nothing will be impossible to them. Nothing will be impossible to them. They will have realized that they are at one with the Father and the Son ... and whatever they ask or think will be done for them. All they must do is speak it, visualize it, see it, and embrace it, for it is done.

What has kept this at arm's distance has been the veil, the veil within their mind. The sons have need of nothing ... they have everything, yet the enemy has tried to convince them that oneness with the Father is something yet to be obtained. The enemy has tried to convince them that Christ Jesus, the Lord, must be put on a pedestal and idolized rather than being embraced in a relationship. And therefore, the Father and Son have been held at arm's distance in a relationship that seems unattainable.

The word which came at the beginning has been about the Father's family. "I will be a Father to you and you will be sons and daughters to Me[5]," says the Lord. That is the promise. That is the reality. That is the intent of the Father. And we're still running to catch up with that understanding.

Often times we think, "I just need some time to go in the closet, close the door, wait upon the Lord." That's what they did in decades and eons past. But it's different now. The only closet you need is your inner closet, where you quiet the commotion, and silence your mind. You bring yourself into abject submission before Him, and listen to that still small[6] voice within you, speaking. He is here. He is present. You just haven't been aware of it on a deep enough level.

I am not saying that we have not been aware of it—to some extent, yes—but not on the level that we need to. More and more we will go to the inner closet within. We quiet the mind, the fears, the commotion, the screaming, the groaning, and we silence everything. How does the word go? ***Be silent[7] and know that I am God!*** Psalms 46:10

Interesting. Quiet your mind. Quiet everything that is coming at you externally, and internally. Paul spoke of his own fears within, and his fears without, but he did not let that overshadow his drive to be in His presence. Quiet your fears. Quiet the commotion, and come before Him and know that He is God. And that which we seek - a oneness with the Father - is here, and is within us.

I am bold enough to say that we have this. We have this. You have not walked on the path of the cross for so many years for it to yield nothing. The deep work of the cross[8] has done many great things within you. As Paul said - *I die daily*. You have put off the mind of the soul, and you have put on the mind of the spirit. The more that God has crucified the soul and taken it out, literally extracted it surgically from you, the more room you have for the indwelling of God.

It is the principle of displacement. He can't come before the Lord and be filled, if you are full already. So He pours you out, as a drink offering, even as Christ was poured[9] out as a drink offering. So the sons are poured out as a drink offering unto Him, to make room for the deep indwelling of the Father and the Son and the Holy Spirit. That is what you have been going through for so many years, and they have taken up their abode within you ... in great power and majesty and glory.

And yet the sons have not yet realized how much they have become in God. Not by their personal attainment, but by virtue of His presence totally possessing them. How else can you manifest the radiant light that you are, but that it is just a reflection of the deep indwelling that is happening within you.

This is the time that God is going to finish ripping off the veil and the limitations within our thinking, and we will realize what He has become within us. We are going to lay aside the fears, the weights, and the sins, which have so easily beset[10] us, and just know that He is here and that we have become.

I cannot convince you of what He has done, but there is an inner knowing that's happening. You are coming to a place where there is a deep knowing within you of who and what you are and, what you've become by virtue of the indwelling that is here. You are the temple[11] of God, but you have not seen yourself as that - *not enough*. You are the temple of the Father and of the Son and the Holy Spirit; and as you walk throughout the day, you are the living temple; the indwelling of the Godhead.

A living temple, as the word says, made without hands. This is what you are. You are a living temple right now, we have just not realized this on a deep enough plane - but that is changing now. It has nothing to do with our personality or our attainment or our capabilities, or how much we can discern, or any of that; but, it has everything to do with the fullness of Christ and the Father indwelling us[12]. And what comes of that will be the unique expression of God and Christ in you, that you are to be.

Each son is a unique expression of God, and that expression is not dictated by your personality, your abilities, or your achievement. It is dictated by the unique expression that the Father and Christ have determined to be through you. And this is waiting to be discovered by the sons, as God finishes this.

We lay aside the fears. We throw off the unbelief, we throw off the illusion and we come to a place of rest and peace. We reach in to embrace an awareness of what He has already done.

How can you look in the rear view mirror and gauge your progress? You can do so by virtue of the fact that you know that He chastens[13] every son whom He receives. We have been in a long process of being received by the Father. One of the many experiences happening to the sons is this indwelling. What a mystery it is.

You have been living in the book of Malachi. As the word says, *when He comes who can stand*[14] *when He appears for He is like a refiners fire and He sits and purges and purifies the sons of Levi.* This has been happening and as the purging and purifying has gone on, less and less of you has remained, and more and more of Him has taken over. The Father and the Son are receiving you unto themselves, and we have yet to realize the deep impact of the oneness that we have with them, right now.

This is not a word for the future. This is a word to those who have been in the race, for we are at the closure of this time of God's dealing with the sons. We know there is only one place that we die, and that is in His presence. Even as the Psalmist spoke: *Precious*[15] *in the sight of the Lord is the death of His godly ones.* This has been your address for a very long time. But now, the next thing on the docket, is that whatever has held the veil in place - that has not allowed you to see what you've become and what He has become within you - is to be removed.

Wherever the sole[16] of your foot doth trod there He is. Whomever you touch, is touched by the Lord. Whomever you speak to, the Father speaks to. This oneness is a present reality, and now is the time that it all comes together for the sons.

Scriptures (NASB)

[1] John 14:23
Jesus answered and said to him, "If anyone loves Me, he will keep My word; and My Father will love him, and We will come to him and make Our abode with him.

[2] Colossians 1:27
to whom God willed to make known what is the riches of the glory of this mystery among the Gentiles, which is Christ in you, the hope of glory.

[3] Psalm 23:5
You prepare a table before me in the presence of my enemies; You have anointed my head with oil; My cup overflows.

[4] Isaiah 44:18
They do not know, nor do they understand, for He has smeared over their eyes so that they cannot see and their hearts so that they cannot comprehend.

[5] 2 Corinthians 6:18
"And I will be a father to you, And you shall be sons and daughters to Me," Says the Lord Almighty.

[6] 1 Kings 19:12
After the earthquake a fire, but the LORD was not in the fire; and after the fire a sound of a gentle blowing.

[7] Psalm 46:10
"Cease striving and know that I am God; I will be exalted among the nations, I will be exalted in the earth."

[8] Philippians 2:8
Being found in appearance as a man, He humbled Himself by becoming obedient to the point of death, even death on a cross.

[9] Philippians 2:17
But even if I am being poured out as a drink offering upon the sacrifice and service of your faith, I rejoice and share my joy with you all.

[10] Hebrews 12:1
Therefore, since we have so great a cloud of witnesses surrounding us, let us also lay aside every encumbrance and the sin which so easily entangles us, and let us run with endurance the race that is set before us,

[11] 1 Corinthians 3:16
Do you not know that you are a temple of God and that the Spirit of God dwells in you?

[12] Ephesians 3:16
that He would grant you, according to the riches of His glory, to be strengthened with power through His Spirit in the inner man,

[13] Hebrews 12:6
FOR THOSE WHOM THE LORD LOVES HE DISCIPLINES, AND HE SCOURGES EVERY SON WHOM HE RECEIVES."

[14] Malachi 3:2
"But who can endure the day of His coming? And who can stand when He appears? For He is like a refiner's fire and like fullers' soap.

[15] Psalm 116:15
Precious in the sight of the LORD Is the death of His godly ones.

[16] Deuteronomy 11:24
"Every place on which the sole of your foot treads shall be yours; your border will be from the wilderness to Lebanon, and from the river, the river Euphrates, as far as the western sea.

Notes

Chapter 28

The Ascension of the Sons

There are times in our day-to-day routine that we can get so caught up with our temporal affairs, that we lose our awareness of the spirit realm, and what is truly unfolding. Now I will admit in the past year or two that this is becoming less and less of a concern, because our spirits are being constantly drawn into the dynamics of the conflict that is unfolding during this time. However, it is still an issue we face, until we come into complete, and open vision.

The signs, which have been coming over the last several months, have been signs of submission. If you wonder what I am speaking of; I am just referencing the unique signs that come in your body. We have taught for years about the reality that your body is coming alive to the realm of the spirit, and as such, your body is functioning more and more like a switchboard to the spirit. Your body is responding to what you are walking in, and the spirit of the Lord is giving you insight into the realm of spirit through the signs that come to you in your physical body.

If you have read any of our books, you will recall that the signs of submission are in the knees. And before the sons begin to subject every kingdom back to the Lord, they must fully bow and submit themselves to His lordship over their lives.

> **For it is written, "AS I LIVE, SAYS THE LORD, EVERY KNEE SHALL BOW TO ME, AND EVERY TONGUE SHALL GIVE PRAISE TO GOD." Romans 14:11**

In the past the Lord has been, shall we say, looking the other way, at times. As we have been maturing in Christ, He has allowed areas of immaturity to remain; areas of rebellion, areas of resistance, areas of independence. It is not so much that He has allowed, but that He has been patient for the precious fruit of the earth, for the Lord knows that as you mature, these last vestiges will be removed. As we come closer to the fulfillment of all things, without question, a deep submission is being completed and worked within the sons. Before you go out and subject every kingdom, God must first complete the work of submission in your own heart. He has been doing this.

It may sound wonderful; "I am going to take the rod of iron and I am just going to run out there and just start beating the heads of the spirit realm that have so strongly resisted the Lord and His holy ones." I mean, you feel that way at times, I know I do!

However, you realize the first thing that has to be done, is that He must complete that deep submission to His lordship, within you. Then, He directs you and empowers you to move forward.

Another way to look at this, as we have taught before, is that the authority of the Lord Jesus Christ is as effective and powerful, as the work of your submission to His lordship is within you. They go hand in hand.

Authority just doesn't come to any Christian that says, "Okay, I'm just going to take the authority of Jesus name. I'm going to go out and do this." Authority comes to one in whom a deep submission to His lordship has been worked.

Perhaps we should redefine "lordship", because the Christian world does not know what that word is. They can profess that Jesus is Lord, but they have no idea what they are talking about, unless they have gone the way of the deep work of the cross in their life. It is the religious spirit that goes out and says, "Jesus is Lord! Jesus is Lord!" until they throw it in everyone's face. What a mockery of God.

What we are talking about is the real lordship of Jesus Christ, and that is something that must be deeply wrought within the sons. Before His sons begin to move in the incredible power and authority and dominion of Christ - that will subject every kingdom back unto the Lord - this work of submission must be completed.

At times we can deceive ourselves to think, "Oh yes, Jesus is my Lord. I pray every day and I'm looking to Him." But you don't realize how active the antichrist[5] still is within your heart, as it rises up to buck what God is speaking, or the demands that He puts upon you. The religious spirit has a very unique way of sugar-coating everything, of just believing that they're doing what they are supposed to do and it is all just a façade. It's not real.

You have a lot of that in the world. The religious leaders who say, "Oh yes, Jesus is Lord. He's my Lord." Right. Until He gets in their face. And that is their problem. The Christian world is on the fast track going the wrong way, and I wouldn't want to be on that train, because that train is going nowhere.

So where are we going with this word? Well, let's go back to the title: "The Ascension of the Sons". There is a pull happening. And that pull is strengthening. And like so much of the word, you read the word and it just gives you that idea that it's out there in the future. You know, some day you're going to be caught up. But it's always someday. It's never right now. It's never right here, right now - this very moment.

What is the teaching out there in the New Age circles? It is always about living in the now. The power of now ... all of that. It is pretty wild what the atheistic and unbelieving and unclean can do when they tap into a basic spiritual truth. The sons must live in the present; not in the future, and not in the past ... **"nowtime"**

What the Lord is doing is here, right now. It's not "what is going to be" or "what was". So many people are still living in the "what was" and they haven't gotten over it and they haven't moved on. But it's the present.

Go to 1 Thessalonians 4:17. Classic scripture. One that the Christian world has bantered about and put so many different slants on. We will read from verse 15.

For this we say to you by the word of the Lord, that we who are alive... (1 Thessalonians 4:15) Now that is interesting. What does that mean to you.... "we who are alive"?

You're probably saying, "Well, everyone that is alive, which means they're breathing, right? They're seeing. They can walk. They're alive at the time of the Lord's coming." No..... Read on ..

And remain until the coming of the Lord, will not precede those who have fallen asleep. For the Lord Himself will descend from heaven with a shout, with the voice of an archangel and with the trumpet of God, the dead in Christ will rise first. Then we who are alive and remain will be caught up together with them in the clouds to meet the Lord in the air. And so we shall always be with the Lord. **1 Thessalonians 4:15-17**

Interesting scripture, because this is not talking about being "physically" alive. **But .... spiritually alive and awake!** So much of Christianity is looking to be caught up, taken out of all of this that is going on—removed from it until it's gone its course. What great deception has been sown ever since the day that Charles Scofield brought the teaching of the rapture to the forefront.

What about "caught up"? Even more important is this scripture ***they who are alive***. I will tell you this; there are not very many living right now that are alive. There are a lot of corpses. Corpses everywhere —the walking dead, if you will. How many people are really alive?

We are not just talking about just breathing. We're talking about spiritually being alive where the senses have been quickened, and you are tracking and hearing in the realm of spirit. Not many are alive. The Lord has made it known that what needs to be done would be done by a remnant; Gideon's 300[7]. It's going to be a remnant - of a remnant - of a remnant. It was never going to be by thousands, but God is going to do this by the few[8]. The kingdom is being brought to birth by ... few.

Understand that this is the qualification for sonship. You must be alive, and so many are dead. They who are "alive" are being caught up. Not those who are dead, which encompasses most of Christianity.

I don't know if we realize what this means. If you are hearing this - truly hearing this - then you realize that you are a part of a very few. Few are called. Few[8] are chosen. Few are they that have been raised up during this time that can really bring in the kingdom. Very, very few. *Very few.*

What is this scripture really talking about? It's talking about what is happening right now. No, not tomorrow. Right now. What's happening? *They who are alive at the time of His coming* (1 Thessalonians 4:15) and we have said this over and over ... we are in the time of His coming. We are in the time of the presence of the Lord. And what is happening? They who are alive are being caught up right now. **Do you feel the pull? If you're alive, then you're feeling the pull.**

Let's go to Revelation 12 verse 5. *And she gave birth to a son, a male child who is to rule the nations with a rod of iron; and her child was caught up to God and to the throne (Revelation 12:5).* And the woman went and fled into the wilderness[9]. *Another sign appeared in heaven: and behold, a great red dragon having seven heads and ten horns, and on his heads were seven diadems* (Revelation 12:3).

Verse 4. *And his tail swept away a third of the stars of heaven and threw them to the earth. And the dragon stood before the woman who was about to give birth, so that when she gave birth he might devour her child* (Revelation 12:4). We've read that a number of times. I'm sure you have.

What's happening? What's happening to God's sons? They have been birthed. They are not being birthed; they have been birthed. Maybe we haven't put the pieces together in our thinking and we're still thinking, "I'm being birthed. I'm being birthed." At some point you have to stop and say, "I may not be aware of this, but I have been birthed." You have been birthed.

What happens immediately after that? They are caught up into the presence of the Father[10]. You're being caught up. It's happening now. Are you feeling the pull?

The sons are being caught up[1]. They have been transformed and are being transformed. We need to understand where we are in this timeline. You're not going through the birthing process; you have been birthed. And the draw in the spirit is strengthening. And you're walking with one foot on each level and it's being hard to cope from day to day because your awareness, your sensitivity, and your consciousness is shifting.

Your body is going through contortions, trying to stay up with the changes happening, because our body has not been designed to be a spiritual body to walk and live in the spirit. This body is for the flesh; physical. The body that is coming to us is going to mirror our spirit. It will be a body designed for the spirit, and it is time for it ... *we cannot go much further without it.*

So how do you explain the transition from this body of death[13] into a new body of life? I can only tell you that it's happening right now. You just need to believe it. You need to realize it. You need to look in the mirror and say, "This is happening right now. Absolutely refuse to put it in the future, or to put it on the shelf. It is time to deal with the reality of resurrection life. You have been birthed. You are in a transition. You are being caught up, and the pull is only going to strengthen.

Imagine a mini-vortex above your head and it's growing in size. You are being sucked up into the presence of God. It's becoming a bit more difficult to function on a natural plane Things don't make sense, and you can't explain the energetic things that are happening within you.

You can't explain how you feel off balance because a shift is happening within you. Understand, you have been birthed.

Now there is nothing in the scriptures about the timeline of being birthed and being caught up. Well it's only one sentence, you say. That must mean something. Well, between sentence one and sentence two could be a thousand years, or it could be a moment. I'm not going to define it, but the purpose is to say, "You have been birthed." Don't look at it any other way. Understand you are now being caught up[1] and it's going to strengthen and it's going to intensify. And the more you identify with the truth, the more it's going to work in you.

You say, "What can I do? How can I facilitate the process?" By recognizing it and going with the flow. And saying, "I understand this is what's happening. And I yield myself and I let it happen. I let it happen and I let go. And oh, by the way, if there's something that is still not done within me concerning the submission to the lordship of Jesus Christ, then just finish it Lord."

God is not going to have a bunch of rebellious sons being caught up - with their own opinion, their own agenda, and their own insecurities. He is going to have a people that are so completely submissive to Him that they literally lay down their lives[14] for one another - they lay down their lives for the Lord. There is no "My ministry. Oh, well, recognize me." There is none of that. There is none of that left. You understand?

There's nothing left. There are no points to prove. "Oh, I have to be recognized." No, you have to be crucified. God is doing this simultaneously, as we bow the knee. And daily we bow the knee, deeper and deeper, and deeper. And this is our cry; "Oh, God that I might be completely 100% submissive to You."

There is no way that you can do that as long as the soul is sitting on the throne, on any level. The soul is dying out, a little bit more quickly now, and the submission is being completed in the sons so that the authority can be fully released. **Fully released.**

Talk about a word that is going to shake the heavens and the earth ... it is here now, and it is resident within the sons, but there just might be a few finishing touches which need to be done within them to see that word fully released.

History talks about the sound that was heard around the world at the time of the American Revolution. Well, I tell you this, the sound that is coming out of the sons, is a sound that is going to be heard around every level of creation. Every universe. Every world. A sound so strong that says the king of kings has arrived, and every knee shall bow and every tongue shall confess His lordship, because it has been fully wrought within the sons.

You don't have the right to react any longer. You don't have the right to get emotional. You don't have the right to get hit. Do you realize that? You don't have the right to react. Here's a good gauge for your progress; if you find yourself in that position, then you know you have not had the submission to His lordship fully worked within you, because there's still that self that says, "Ah, I'm having a hard day. Oh, woe is me. Oh, I'm not feeling recognized. Oh, whatever." That's just strictly the soul.

You do not have the right to react. You do not have the right to be discouraged, encouraged, whatever. You're a zero with the rim rubbed out. "Lord, I'm nothing." You are nothing, but He is everything through you. That is our cry. That is our position. This is what is happening, we just need to realize it.

We are not waiting to be birthed. We are not waiting to come into the fulfillment. It is here upon us. And we say, "Lord, we submit. Every ounce within me submits to Your lordship and Your demands." You are being caught up[1].

You are being caught up[1]. ***Are you feeling the pull?*** Think about that for a second. As you go through the day, think about that, and you will feel that tug growing. It is a tug that is coming in the spirit. You can hear that distant word; *"come up higher, come up higher."* You are being caught up.

You are being caught up into His presence; the presence of the Father, and the presence of the Cloud of Witnesses. You will experience them more and more, because we're being caught up as one church before Him. And there is going to be more and more interaction, because an overflow is happening between the veils.

It's happening now. They're here. I mean they are so on the edge of their seat reaching for what we're reaching for. Waiting for the word. Lord, bring us the word. Every word that is spoken they are tracking on it with us. Just because they're not physically here, it's a small detail. We're being caught up[1]. We're feeling the tug. And I know they're feeling the tug.

We have this thing in our thinking that because they're on the other side of the veil that they're millions of miles away, or wherever they are. And they've got a leg up on us. They really don't. And I know it's hard for us to understand. The only thing is their vibration is higher. The body is gone. It's you know, dust to dust[15]. But there is only just a little bit of a frequency between us. I don't know if I can explain that to you, but we are all frequency. And we have been coming up higher and higher and higher in our vibration and frequency over the last five years.

The distance between us and the cloud is so thin. Imagine something paper thin. We're here. They're there. What remains of the veil is paper thin. And that is going to give way.

So here we are. Whether visible, or invisible, it makes no difference, we are contending for the same thing. Even the deep work of submission is being completed in them, as it is being completed in us.

They're right here. They're listening to every word that we speak. They're tracking on every word that comes from the mouth of God, just as we are. We are so close. We are so close.

Are you feeling the pull? Because you're experiencing it. You may not have recognized it. You may not have isolated it and said, "Oh that is what this is." Now maybe you'll see it differently. The pull is on and the pull is going to get stronger and stronger, because we're coming into a very quick wrap up of what God is doing in the earth.

Scriptures (NASB)

[1] 1 Thessalonians 4:17
Then we who are alive and remain will be caught up together with them in the clouds to meet the Lord in the air, and so we shall always be with the Lord.

Or [1] Revelation 12:5
And she gave birth to a son, a male child, who is to rule all the nations with a rod of iron; and her child was caught up to God and to His throne.

[2] 1 Corinthians 15:28
When all things are subjected to Him, then the Son Himself also will be subjected to the One who subjected all things to Him, so that God may be all in all.

[3] Romans 14:11
For it is written, "AS I LIVE, SAYS THE LORD, EVERY KNEE SHALL BOW TO ME, AND EVERY TONGUE SHALL GIVE PRAISE TO GOD."

Or [3] Isaiah 45:23
"I have sworn by Myself, The word has gone forth from My mouth in righteousness And will not turn back, That to Me every knee will bow, every tongue will swear allegiance.

[4] Psalm 2:9
'You shall break them with a rod of iron, You shall shatter them like earthenware.'"

Or [4] Revelation 2:27
AND HE SHALL RULE THEM WITH A ROD OF IRON, AS THE VESSELS OF THE POTTER ARE BROKEN TO PIECES, as I also have received authority from My Father;

[5] 1 John 2:22
Who is the liar but the one who denies that Jesus is the Christ? This is the antichrist, the one who denies the Father and the Son.

[6] Revelation 19:16
And on His robe and on His thigh He has a name written, "KING OF KINGS, AND LORD OF LORDS."

[7] Judges 7:7
The LORD said to Gideon, "I will deliver you with the 300 men who lapped and will give the Midianites into your hands; so let all the other people go, each man to his home."

[8] Matthew 22:14
"For many are called, but few are chosen."

[9] Revelation 12:6
Then the woman fled into the wilderness where she had a place prepared by God, so that there she would be nourished for one thousand two hundred and sixty days.

[10] Revelation 12:5
And she gave birth to a son, a male child, who is to rule all the nations with a rod of iron; and her child was caught up to God and to His throne.

[11] John 3:19
"This is the judgment, that the Light has come into the world, and men loved the darkness rather than the Light, for their deeds were evil.

[12] Romans 12:2
And do not be conformed to this world, but be transformed by the renewing of your mind, so that you may prove what the will of God is, that which is good and acceptable and perfect.

[13] Romans 7:24
Wretched man that I am! Who will set me free from the body of this death?

[14] 1 John 3:16
We know love by this, that He laid down His life for us; and we ought to lay down our lives for the brethren.

[15] Ecclesiastes 3:20
All go to the same place. All came from the dust and all return to the dust.

Chapter 29

The Resurrected Body

Let's start this word by defining what resurrection life is to be:

Resurrection life will be an existence in a world that is invisible, yet very much maneuvering and living in a world that is visible; but not vulnerable in it.

We are in a window of time that will be marked by a breakthrough into resurrection life. This is the door that we stand before. The word has been coming: "Keep speaking the word, keep prophesying, keep speaking the judgment", because it is flowing and we are seeing the world progressively implode.

Day-to-day developments are happening in countries far and near. We have never seen such an implosion of the world system as we are seeing happen now. All of this is because of one paramount truth: God is bringing the sons to birth and the sons are in the process of birthing the kingdom. All along the word has been that the judgment will precede the release that God has for the sons.

The limitations and the roadblocks are being removed. The sons have been faithful to give themselves to the work of the cross[1] and to the deep purging fires of His presence. As the road blocks are removed, the breakthroughs will follow. It is time that we will see the work completed now, within the sons.

What is completion? In Romans it speaks about the seal[2] of sonship. You could say, "Well, what is the seal of our sonship?" The seal of sonship is your breakthrough into resurrection life, the resurrected body. And this is where we are right now. This is the final seal of your sonship.

Changes are happening within the sons on a daily basis. We are so close to the changes happening that it can be very difficult to discern it within yourself. Over time you will look back and bear witness, but when you are in the middle of these changes, it can often be very difficult to see.

The word has come that *you will barely be able to remember what it was like to have known life under the restraints and limitations that you have existed in - once resurrection life fully completes.* That is the word which came a few years back.

We knew all along that it was coming ... that resurrection life[3] was going to happen at some point. Perhaps we did not realize that we were the ones that God sent, on point, to bring this release that has been destined for so very long. We have known all along that the ascension[4] of the sons goes hand in hand with the redemption of physical body; and with this comes a release of judgment so catastrophic on the face of the earth, and in the realm of spirit, that it is very difficult to even fathom.

However, the word has always been that the judgment against the spirit realm, the hordes of evil, and that which has fed off the life of the sons, will happen in concert, or in a similar timeline, to the breakthrough of resurrection life. With judgment comes resurrection. With resurrection comes judgment[5].

Now, more than ever, this is what we need to be focusing on – resurrection life. This is what needs to be in the back of your thinking. This is what you need to be meditating on. This is what you have been sent here to embrace and to manifest. This is your destiny. And this is the window and the time for it to happen.

Over the last several years the word has come in the spirit that we are so close. We are so close to this breakthrough ... that it is right here, right here in front of you. And yet we can feel, "Lord I accept that. I believe that," yet in some ways it can feel like a million miles away, *but that is only an illusion.*

The time is here for change, a change that literally brings forth a new creation. We're not looking for an extended life or a long life. We're not looking for the ability to live nine hundred years, but we are looking for a change within our physical body that will bring forth resurrection life. We don't know exactly the full experience of what this is to be, but we know that changes are happening within us, even now, day by day.

It would be interesting to be living in the time of the disciples and to experience what they went through when they waited before the Lord in the upper room[6]. They had been told to wait there for the promise. They did not know what the promise was going to be; they did not know what was going to happen to them, but faithfully they waited before the Lord.

In a similar fashion, the overshadowing[7] of the Father is beginning to unfold within the sons, and it's only going to increase. The promise has always been that the very power that was exuded toward Christ in the change of His physical body, is the very same power that will be focused toward the sons. The awareness of the Father has been increasing during this time ... you can feel it. It is like an overshadowing, and we are on the Mount of Transfiguration[7].

The disciples did not know what to do when that experience happened. They were ready to build three tabernacles and yet the Father spoke and said, "Silence, this is My Son in whom I am well pleased[8]". And the transfiguration of Christ happened at that point. A glory that radiated even beyond what we can even imagine in the scriptures.

That same hovering over the sons is beginning to happen now. But how do you explain it? It's a hovering of the Spirit of the Father over the sons. The sons have been in an incubator, of sorts, waiting for this time of final change, the confirmation of their calling and the confirmation of their sonship, to which they have been sent into the earth to manifest[9]. This is where we are right now.

Regardless of what appears, or the illusion that may scream at you about your physical body, or the things that you are going through, the fact remains that we are here, positioned at the time that resurrection life is going to break forth upon a people. It will begin with perhaps a handful, but that's only the beginning.

We are not looking for a rapture. We are not sitting back waiting for God to resurrect this body, as if everything is just on hold. No, we're not doing that. We are pressing in, we are pushing hard; we are bringing in the kingdom. This is the time of our change, and we embrace that, we anticipate it, we visualize it, and we see it happening.

Paul spoke about living on tip-toe[10] in the book of Philippians, that he might attain the out-resurrection from the dead. He had not possessed it, but he saw it. The eyes of his spirit saw the provision, saw the reality, saw the close proximity or availability of the provision. And Paul lived on tip-toe to attain it.

In a very similar way, the sons are living on tip-toe, reaching to attain this level of life that will change everything on the face of the earth. Right now the breakthroughs are happening, a little here, a little there. Right now judgments are happening, a little here, a little there. Right now things seem to be moving a little bit in slow motion. However, with the breakthrough of resurrection life, the world will never be the same. The world, as we have known it, will truly be turned upside down.

We know that the balance of authority and power in the spirit has shifted. Perhaps the sons have not realized that it has shifted, but it has. The balance of power, so to speak, has changed.

God has been changing our thinking and changing our lives. He has been changing our paradigm which we have spoken of so many times. We know that a paradigm is a way of thinking; how you view reality, literally how you view everything around you. The paradigm that people live under can be both freeing, or limiting. If your paradigm still does not see certain levels of reality that God has decreed to be, then your paradigm is limiting. And the power the mind has to control your realm of reality is still unacceptable. And so, the paradigm within our minds is changing and must change for resurrection life to come forth, for we know the truth of the matter is that resurrection life is already here.

In the book of Thomas, Thomas says that the kingdom[11] of God, or the kingdom of the Father, is spread out upon the earth and men see it not. What he was saying is that the provision and the reality was present, but the eyes to see it were not. That has been one of the greatest challenges that those who have been called to sonship during this time have faced ... the ability to see.

It is one thing for God to give a dream, a vision, or a word and declare what is. And we know that as He speaks, it is done in the spirit. But if the eyes of your spirit have not been enlightened and you are still limited by the paradigm of yesterday, then you are greatly impaired in being able to bring that truth and reality into this level of existence. And that has been the challenge.

A number of times God has said, "Resurrection life is here. It's just beneath your skin. It is that close." So why have we not manifested it? Is it something that we're still waiting for the Father to do? In part I would say that's a perhaps, "Yes." However there is a big part of that equation that has to do with how we see reality, and how we view the word that God has spoken. Do we still see it as a promise in the future, or have we been able to make the shift and see it as a truth that is here now and it's just waiting for us to embrace?

I believe that we have the ability to do so much more than we presently do. And I think that if you ponder on that, that this will bear witness to you as well. And yet what we are manifesting is far short of what we know in our heart to be available. This comes back to the shifting of how we think, how we perceive, or how have been conditioned. And God is tearing that off as quickly as He can.

One thing we do - we set ourselves to let go of anything that would still be a limitation to us. Lord, we're ready to go and to be taken wherever You would move us to. It's time that we move into resurrection life. It's time that our existence in this world changes.

God is bringing us into a change that is beyond what we have known. Up until now resurrection life has been a prophecy. It's been on the periphery; but no longer. Perhaps in past years we have not focused on resurrection life because it has seemed so far outside the box and unattainable. And yet all of that has changed because we're at the time of completion. The most important thing that we can do is to keep it in our thoughts.

That was a key of Joshua. A key to his success was that he meditated[12] on the word of the Lord day and night. And a key to the shift that is going to happen now, for us, is that we start rehearsing, meditating, dwelling, and visualizing, resurrection life. Even if we don't know exactly what form it will first take, or how it will first begin to manifest. The word from the spirit of the Lord has been: embrace it, visualize it, imagine it, reach in. And that's all we have to do. It's really pretty simple. We just keep it in our visor, right in front of us.

If you stop and think about it a little bit, resurrection life is also the reality of the full indwelling of Christ Jesus, for it says Christ is the resurrection[13]. A lot of the truths in the Bible are very mystical and very deep and hard to understand from the plane of our natural mind. Although we can read them, we can look at them, but it's not easy to have it all make sense.

But we're talking about the full indwelling of Christ which cannot be separated from resurrection life; or the indwelling[14] of the godhead, within the sons. How it's all going to happen is hard to say. We know that the Cloud of Witnesses, (the prophecy in Hebrews is that they[15] without us will not be made perfect) are poised at the door, waiting for us to kick that door down. So there is something that is going on hand-in-hand right now with the Cloud of Witnesses, as God brings us forth.

We need to begin to see ourselves in an entirely different light. The interpenetration of God and man is not a future event. It's an event happening right now - to the sons - on a daily basis. It is the takeover of the Father within the hearts of His sons. And the more that takeover happens, the cause and effect will be resurrection life, the renewed body - the renewed mind[16].

There cannot be the full possessing of the Father within the sons without the manifesting of resurrection life. It would be impossible to say you have the full indwelling of the Father and yet don't walk in resurrection life. They come together. It is the indwelling of God and the indwelling of the Father and Christ, that is happening within us right now.

We need to see it. We need to have eyes to really grasp what is truly happening. We are no longer praying to a God outside, but to He who dwells deeply within us. And with this deep indwelling of the godhead comes the redemption of this physical body. It is here and it is time. Resurrection life and the indwelling of the godhead is happening simultaneously.

As Isaiah the prophet spoke, "Behold I will do something new[17]. Will you be aware?" And Isaiah 52; the prophecy .... Come Alive! That is the challenge. The challenge is to become aware of what is happening, right now.

Father, You are doing something new, something so entirely new that has not existed on the face of the earth before this time. The world is deeply asleep and in slumber, but the sons are arising and seeing. And we declare, "Lord, yes. You are doing something new and we are aware. We are embracing the change." We don't know how it's going to manifest. We know it is unfolding, day by day, and we know that there is a quantum step forward that is slated to happen.

I believe that time is before us, where the body that we've had, changes like the scriptures say - from a worm[18] to a butterfly. It's hard to imagine that the physical body that you've lived in all of your life has been but a cocoon, waiting for the time that you burst out into resurrection life and manifest the butterfly.

You've been living in a cocoon, a cocoon of the physical body. And now it's time that the cocoon is shed and the wonder of sonship and the new creation of God in resurrection life becomes manifest.

Scriptures (NASB)

[1] Galatians 6:14
But may it never be that I would boast, except in the cross of our Lord Jesus Christ, through which the world has been crucified to me, and I to the world.

[2] Romans 8:15-17
...15For you did not receive a spirit of slavery that returns you to fear,
but you received the Spirit of sonship, by whom we cry, “Abba! Father!”
16The Spirit Himself testifies with our spirit that we are God’s children.
17And if we are children, then we are heirs: heirs of God and co-heirs
with Christ—if indeed we suffer with Him, so that we may also be
glorified with Him....

[3] John 5:29
and will come forth; those who did the good deeds to a resurrection of life, those who committed the evil deeds to a resurrection of judgment.

[4] Revelation 12:5
And she gave birth to a son, a male child, who is to rule all the nations with a rod of iron; and her child was caught up to God and to His throne.

[5] Isaiah 26:9
At night my soul longs for You, Indeed, my spirit within me seeks You diligently; For when the earth experiences Your judgments The inhabitants of the world learn righteousness.

[6] Acts 1:3-5
3After His suffering, He presented Himself to them with many convincing
proofs that He was alive. He appeared to them over a span of forty days
and spoke about the kingdom of God. 4And when they were gathered
together, He commanded them: “Do not leave Jerusalem, but wait for the
gift the Father promised, which you have heard Me discuss. 5For John
baptized with water, but in a few days you will be baptized with the Holy
Spirit.”...

[7] Luke 9:34
While he was saying this, a cloud formed and began to overshadow them; and they were afraid as they entered the cloud.

[8] 2 Peter 1:17
For when He received honor and glory from God the Father, such an utterance as this was made to Him by the Majestic Glory, "This is My beloved Son with whom I am well-pleased "--

[9] Romans 8:19
For the anxious longing of the creation waits eagerly for the revealing of the sons of God.

[10] Philippians 1:21
For to me, to live is Christ and to die is gain.

[11] Book of Thomas saying
(113) His disciples said to him: On what day will the kingdom come? <Jesus said:> It will not come while people watch for it; they will not say: Look, here it is, or: Look, there it is; but the kingdom of the father is spread out over the earth, and men do not see it.

[12] Joshua 1:8
"This book of the law shall not depart from your mouth, but you shall meditate on it day and night, so that you may be careful to do according to all that is written in it; for then you will make your way prosperous, and then you will have success.

[13] John 11:25
Jesus said to her, "I am the resurrection and the life; he who believes in Me will live even if he dies,

[14] Colossians 2:9
For in Him all the fullness of Deity dwells in bodily form,

[15] Hebrews 11:40
because God had provided something better for us, so that apart from us they would not be made perfect.

[16] Ephesians 4:23
and that you be renewed in the spirit of your mind,

[17] Isaiah 43:19
"Behold, I will do something new, Now it will spring forth; Will you not be aware of it? I will even make a roadway in the wilderness, Rivers in the desert.

[18] Philippians 3:21
who will transform the body of our humble state into conformity with the body of His glory, by the exertion of the power that He has even to subject all things to Himself.

Notes

Chapter 30

In Conclusion

It Must Be Real To You

We have given a great deal of thought as to the last word in this book. We considered talking more about the elemental world, as fascinating as it is; or the path to seer vision, which I know that we all seek. I believe, however, the most important topic to be addressed in this last chapter is that this word must be real to you.

We have touched on this throughout the entire book, from different perspectives. But the problem that everyone faces in the scope of maturing in Christ, is in being able to change and being able to hear the word on the level that will change you. I have found the common mindset out there is to listen or hear a word, only to find that your mind makes an assumption that you got it; that you have received what was being said, and so therefore you go on to the next star, so to speak. And that is a problem that we face, because of the subtlety of the Adamic nature that we still have.

Once again realize the greatest warfare we face is not with the satanic hosts, but with the Adamic nature within each of us. The antichrist[1] that we all face is the soul nature. We know the scripture references the warring of the soul[2] against the spirit, for the soul is enmity[3] to Christ.

A revelation of the soul and spirit needs to go much deeper so that we understand truly, what we are dealing with, within our own hearts. The spirit that God has put within you, that He earnestly[4] desires, is reaching on tip-toe[5], seeking for that embodiment, and that union and oneness, with Christ and the Father.

The soul on the flip side tends to want to hide[6] ... look for a rock and hide behind a rock, side-step the dealings[7] of God, side-step the fire[8] of God. The soul tends to want to put on a parade and show as though it has changed, when it really has not. It is just parading itself saying, "Look at me, see how much I have changed", when it really has not changed.

This is a problem that we have seen on a very large scale, throughout Christianity. The inability to hear comes from sidestepping the cross. This sidestepping, in turn, causes a darkness to rest upon people, born out of their conscious, or subconscious, choice to draw back. Even though people may love God, there truly is no capacity to see or hear and there really is no hunger. They have bought a bill of goods. They believe they are doing God's will and they are walking with God, and they don't realize that they have fallen short. As it references in the book of Revelation - they have become blind[9] and naked and do not realize their state. They feel as though they have need[9] of nothing ... that is the prevailing spirit, if you will, within Christianity, as a whole.

Within the sons that God has called and raised up, there exists a great jeopardy. And that jeopardy is that the soul, until it has fully has gone to the cross[10], will try to side-step the dealings[7] and the fire[8] of God. A word will come and it may quicken to you—you might find a delight in it and a joy, but unless you embrace the process for that word to come forth within you, it will all be for naught. As it speaks in the book of Revelation; the word[11] came and I ate it and it was a delight to my mouth and to my senses, but it became bitter to the stomach. That is the process of ingesting the word. And there are very, very, few who want to walk that path.

And so the soul within man will say, "I've got it. I have heard that word. It has come alive to me. I love it. I bear witness to it. I am excited. I've got it." And yet that is only the first step. Because the Lord has to plumb that word deep within you, until you are changed by the word, and you have become that word. That is what is at stake.

Everything that we talk about in all of the books must be real. So many people come and they are out there seeking truth, they are looking for the next word, the next revelation, the next dream or vision, but they are not prepared to pay the price. And so we have had many come and buy our books. "Oh, this is wonderful. I love it. Thank you." And now they are on to find another book, another dream, another vision. And the word never became part of them. It never really became real. It may be real to their mind and they may understand the concept, but not real enough to bring the change in their spirit.

There is such a tendency in the spirit of man, to always want to look for the next star, and the next star, and the next star. The word talks about having one's ears tickled[12]. And I know that it is hard to imagine that we could be that way. We would say, "Well, I don't want my ears tickled. I just want the truth, Lord. And that is all I want." But we don't realize how much that is still a prevalent thing within the soul. Have something tickle your ears until it sounds great. "I like that. I like the concept. Now go ahead and give me another revelation. And okay, now I want another revelation. Give me another dream." And nothing ever really took root.

That is why the work[13] of the cross has been in your direct path every step you have taken, so that the word might bear fruit. I do not believe that the sons of God have been raised up to yield 30 fold or 60 fold. They have only been raised up to bear 100 fold[14]. What does that mean? Well if you are only bearing 30 or 60 fold, then it means the word did not penetrate deep enough … it did not bring enough of a change, because the fruit of what you are, is what comes forth.

You do not bear 100 fold by running around with tracks on a corner. It is born out of what you become. In the New Testament it talks about faith[15]. Is faith a concept or is faith an action? Is sonship[16] a concept or is sonship an action? People can say, "I love to hear about your faith, it is wonderful. Now show me. Do you walk your talk? Or is it just another concept?"

We have a lot of people in the Christian world that walk in very little of what they talk about. Great theories, great revelations, but they don't really walk what they speak of. God has set a plumb line[17] in the earth. That plumb line is the sons of God. And that plumb line is only viable because the sons themselves have become the word - which is the plumb line through which God will judge and move accordingly; but He must have a plumb line.

It is so important that the word become real. In a very mystical sense, it is no different than the Lord and the Father becoming real to you. That is really what we are talking about. Forget about the word for a minute.

They must be real to you. The Father must be real. The Lord must be real. And I know you say, "Well, they are real to me. I walk with them and I know the Lord and I know the Father." Yes, you do. But are you satisfied? Paul was not. Paul lived on tip-toe[5] which would be the

Greek interpretation of Philippians 3. He lived on tip-toe. And the word said he hadn't attained it, but he was reaching to attain the out-resurrection[18] of the dead.

Paul had a relationship with the Lord. He had a relationship with the Father. But he didn't settle there. He didn't settle and build three tabernacles and say, "Okay. This is it." He saw what was available in a relationship with the Father and with the Lord, and he desired that with all of his heart. He continued to strive, reaching in, because to truly embrace that level of relationship would be to attain the out-resurrection from the dead. And Paul knew that.

Christ is the resurrection[19]. He is not a concept. He is an individual. He's our Lord. He is the resurrection. And so as we reach in for the word to become real, we are looking for more than just a concept or theory, but we are looking for Christ to become real on that depth of your heart that changes you. Right?

How does change happen? Change happens because you are exposed to the Lord and you are changed from glory[20] to glory. So what happens when the word is exposed to you? You reach in and it becomes you, because you have gone through the work[13] of the cross and that word then gets written on your heart[21]. You don't have to go around and recite it. You are that word.

So in a mystical sense, what has happened? You have taken in the Lord on a level far beyond what you had. The penetration of God in man took a much deeper level within you. You may be the word made flesh[22] but you have also entered into a oneness[23] with the Father and a oneness with the Son that you did not have. That's really where we are headed, and this is what we are talking about when we say that the word must be real to you.

The word comes and presents keys of functioning and principles that will change your paradigm and your outlook of reality. When ingested, that word will change everything about you. But that only comes because it touches your spirit and changes you. And that usually comes because of the work of the cross. Read Malachi 3.

What we desire, with all of our heart, is that the Lord Jesus Christ becomes real on a deeper plane. Maybe becoming real is not the right term - call it an awakening, a quickening, a realization - of your connection with Him. The grasp of who He is, and what He is in you, comes alive like an epiphany within you and changes you forever. You are at a new plateau in God and you keep moving up in His presence because He has come alive to you.

Your ears are being quickened[24] and you have been brought alive within every facet of your being. As you hear Him afresh, you move from level to level. That is what we seek. And if that is not in your heart, if that is not your drive, then you really need to seek the Lord, because we are not looking for our ears to be tickled. We are not looking to do things, manifest certain gifts or receive pats on the back or whatever. It's really about one thing: to know[25] Him and the power of His resurrection, as the word goes.

You cannot separate the word coming alive within you, from your relationship to the Lord going deeper and deeper. And as you attain new levels in God, they belong to you. As you reach in, God comes alive to you on a new level and His word comes alive to you on a new level and you are changed. You own that. And that is a whole new relationship to the Lord from which you will springboard onto the next level of exposure and quickening.

The end result; the manifestation of resurrection life[26], which as I have said, is closer than we understand. How many times the word has come: we are so close. Just reach a little bit higher. It is here. It is within your grasp. You don't see it, but it is here. All you have to do is reach up just a little bit higher, and you will have it all.

This word has come a few times, conveyed in different ways, but the essence of it has always been the same - *what we seek is here.* It is already here. The Father has released it. Resurrection life is already here. Why aren't we in it yet? That is a good question, because it is right here; the change and transformation of sonship. It is right here.

We are in a short season of the final preparation of the kings and priests of God. God is equipping[27] the kings and priests, His sons, with an understanding of the spirit world, and an ability to move and function in the spirit. He is bringing them into a relationship with Him and a oneness with Him, that they have not had heretofore. He is deepening the final work of the cross, until the last remains of the soul is gone and all that is left is the purity of the Father and the Son within[28] you.

This is the final preparation. This would be the parable of the wise and foolish[29] virgins. The foolish virgins do not have oil in their cup. They have gone down another road and been distracted or made various choices. But those whose hearts have been prepared are right here. And the Lord comes and says, "*Enter in. The door is open. Come and enter in.*" That is what we have waited for.

Because there is a door opening in the spirit, there is a beckoning of the Lord that says, "*Good and faithful servant*[30]*, you have born the heat of the day, you have given all. You have submitted yourself. You love Me with all of your heart. The door is open. Come and enter in*[31]*.*"

We bless this book to yield a hundred fold[14&32]. We bless every word in this book to come alive; to change and transform, to empower the sons, and to finish the equipping needed at this time.

Edward & Anne
January 2017

Scriptures (NASB)

[1] 1 John 2:22
Who is the liar but the one who denies that Jesus is the Christ? This is the antichrist, the one who denies the Father and the Son.

[2] Galatians 5:17
For the flesh sets its desire against the Spirit, and the Spirit against the flesh; for these are in opposition to one another, so that you may not do the things that you please.

[3] Romans 8:7
because the mind set on the flesh is hostile toward God; for it does not subject itself to the law of God, for it is not even able to do so,

[4] James 4:5
Or do you think that the Scripture speaks to no purpose: "He jealously desires the Spirit which He has made to dwell in us"?

[5] Philippians 3:13
Brethren, I do not regard myself as having laid hold of it yet; but one thing I do: forgetting what lies behind and reaching forward to what lies ahead,

[6] Revelation 6:16
and they said to the mountains and to the rocks, "Fall on us and hide us from the presence of Him who sits on the throne, and from the wrath of the Lamb;

[7] Job 33:29-30
29"Behold, God does all these oftentimes with men, 30To bring back his soul from the pit, That he may be enlightened with the light of life....

[8] Hebrews 10:27
but a terrifying expectation of judgment and THE FURY OF A FIRE WHICH WILL CONSUME THE ADVERSARIES.

[9] Revelation 3:17
'Because you say, "I am rich, and have become wealthy, and have need of nothing," and you do not know that you are wretched and miserable and poor and blind and naked,

[10] Matthew 16:24
Then Jesus said to His disciples, "If anyone wishes to come after Me, he must deny himself, and take up his cross and follow Me.

[11] Revelation10:10
I took the little book out of the angel's hand and ate it, and in my mouth it was sweet as honey; and when I had eaten it, my stomach was made bitter.

[12] 2 Timothy 4:3
For the time will come when they will not endure sound doctrine; but wanting to have their ears tickled, they will accumulate for themselves teachers in accordance to their own desires,

[13] Philippians 2:8
Being found in appearance as a man, He humbled Himself by becoming obedient to the point of death, even death on a cross.

[14] Matthew 13:8
"And others fell on the good soil and yielded a crop, some a hundredfold, some sixty, and some thirty.

[15] James 2:22
You see that faith was working with his works, and as a result of the works, faith was perfected;

[16] Ephesians 1:5
He predestined us to adoption as sons through Jesus Christ to Himself, according to the kind intention of His will,

[17] Amos 7:8
The LORD said to me, "What do you see, Amos?" And I said, "A plumb line." Then the Lord said, "Behold I am about to put a plumb line In the midst of My people Israel. I will spare them no longer.

[18] Philippians 3:11
If by any means I might attain unto the resurrection of the dead.

[19] John 11:25
Jesus said to her, "I am the resurrection and the life; he who believes in Me will live even if he dies,

[20] 2 Corinthians 3:18
But we all, with unveiled face, beholding as in a mirror the glory of the Lord, are being transformed into the same image from glory to glory, just as from the Lord, the Spirit.

[21] Romans 2:15
in that they show the work of the Law written in their hearts, their conscience bearing witness and their thoughts alternately accusing or else defending them,

[22] John 1:14
And the Word became flesh, and dwelt among us, and we saw His glory, glory as of the only begotten from the Father, full of grace and truth.

[23] John 17:21
that they may all be one; even as You, Father, are in Me and I in You, that they also may be in Us, so that the world may believe that You sent Me.

[24] Matthew 11:15
"He who has ears to hear, let him hear.

[25] Philippians 3:10
that I may know Him and the power of His resurrection and the fellowship of His sufferings, being conformed to His death;

[26] John 5:29
and will come forth; those who did the good deeds to a resurrection of life, those who committed the evil deeds to a resurrection of judgment.

[27] Ephesians 4:12
for the equipping of the saints for the work of service, to the building up of the body of Christ;

[28] John 14:23
Jesus answered and said to him, "If anyone loves Me, he will keep My word; and My Father will love him, and We will come to him and make Our abode with him.

[29] Matthew 25:2-3
2"Five of them were foolish, and five were prudent. 3"For when the foolish took their lamps, they took no oil with them,

[30] Matthew 25:23
"His master said to him, 'Well done, good and faithful slave. You were faithful with a few things, I will put you in charge of many things; enter into the joy of your master.'

[31]Luke 13:24
"Strive to enter through the narrow door; for many, I tell you, will seek to enter and will not be able.

[32]Matthew 19:29
"And everyone who has left houses or brothers or sisters or father or mother or children or farms for My name's sake, will receive many times as much, and will inherit eternal life.

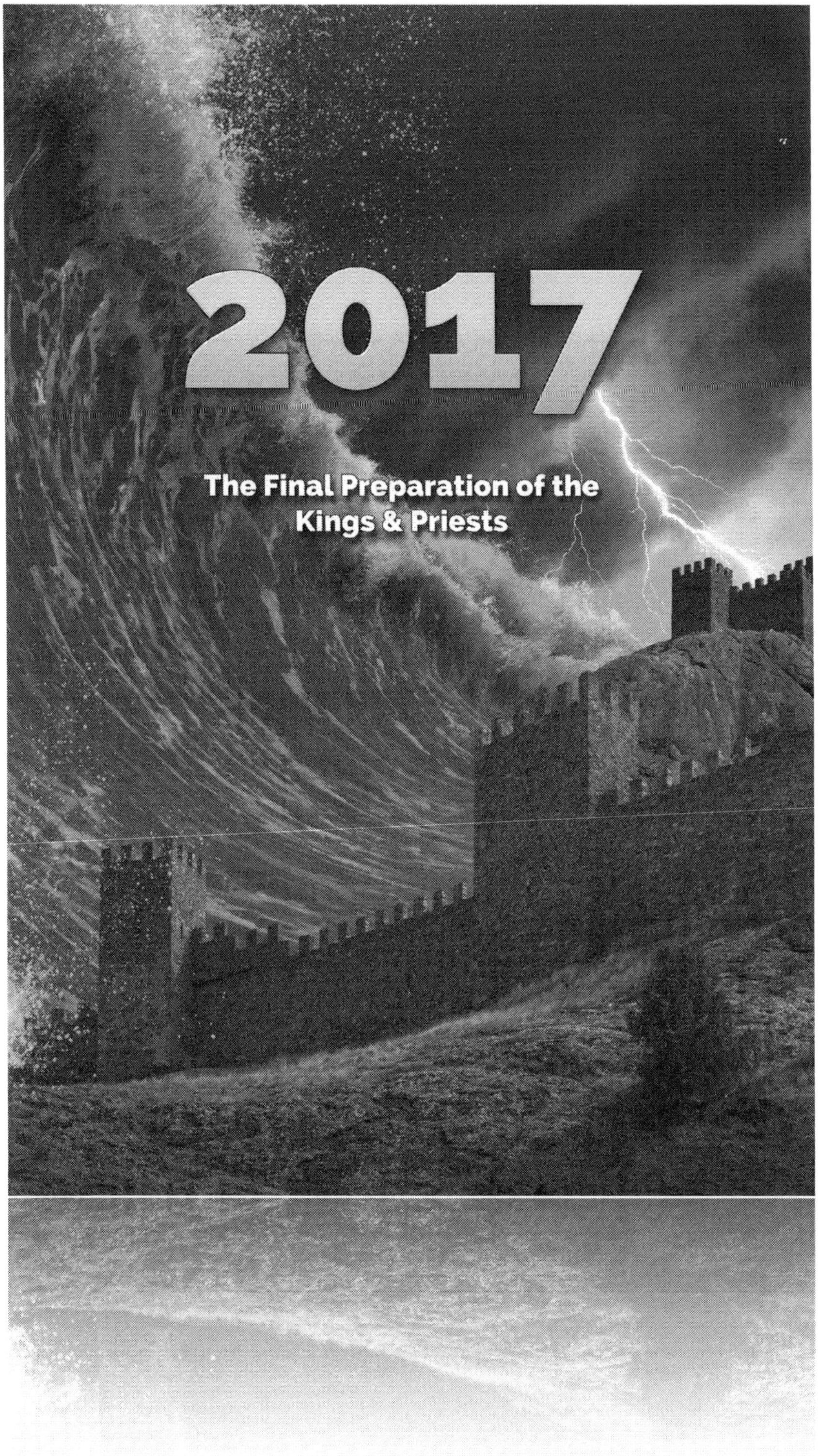
2017
The Final Preparation of the
Kings & Priests

40643341R00180

Made in the USA
Middletown, DE
19 February 2017